Beckett's Laboratory

Related Titles

Beckett's Creatures: Art of Failure after the Holocaust
Joseph Anderton
978-1-4742-3453-5

Postdramatic Theatre and Form
Edited by Michael Shane Boyle, Matt Cornish and Brandon Woolf
978-1-3500-4316-9

The Sixth Sense of the Avant-Garde: Dance, Kinaesthesia and the Arts in Revolutionary Russia
Irina Sirotkina and Roger Smith
978-1-3500-1431-2

The Plays of Samuel Beckett
Katherine Weiss
978-1-4081-5730-5

Beckett's Laboratory

Experiments in the Theatre Enclosure

Corey Wakeling

methuen | drama
LONDON • NEW YORK • OXFORD • NEW DELHI • SYDNEY

METHUEN DRAMA
Bloomsbury Publishing Plc
50 Bedford Square, London, WC1B 3DP, UK
1385 Broadway, New York, NY 10018, USA
29 Earlsfort Terrace, Dublin 2, Ireland

BLOOMSBURY, METHUEN DRAMA and the Methuen Drama logo are trademarks of Bloomsbury Publishing Plc

First published in Great Britain 2021
This paperback edition published 2022

Copyright © Corey Wakeling, 2021

Corey Wakeling has asserted his right under the Copyright, Designs and Patents Act, 1988, to be identified as author of this work.

For legal purposes the Acknowledgements on pp. viii–ix constitute an extension of this copyright page.

Cover design by Charlotte Daniels
Photography: Billie Whitelaw in rehearsal, *Not I* (© Zöe Dominic)

All rights reserved. No part of this publication may be reproduced or transmitted in any form or by any means, electronic or mechanical, including photocopying, recording, or any information storage or retrieval system, without prior permission in writing from the publishers.

Bloomsbury Publishing Plc does not have any control over, or responsibility for, any third-party websites referred to or in this book. All internet addresses given in this book were correct at the time of going to press. The author and publisher regret any inconvenience caused if addresses have changed or sites have ceased to exist, but can accept no responsibility for any such changes.

A catalogue record for this book is available from the British Library.

A catalog record for this book is available from the Library of Congress.

ISBN: HB: 978-1-3501-5312-7
PB: 978-1-3502-3877-0
ePDF: 978-1-3501-5314-1
eBook: 978-1-3501-5313-4

Typeset by Newgen KnowledgeWorks Pvt. Ltd., Chennai, India

To find out more about our authors and books visit www.bloomsbury.com and sign up for our newsletters.

For Nina and George

Contents

Acknowledgements	viii
List of abbreviations	x
Introduction	1
1 Laboratory acts without words	23
2 Sensory deprivation	49
3 Impediment and the symbolist dramaturgical inheritance	73
4 Dream space, the other laboratory	97
5 Catastrophe and the politics of spectacle	109
6 Hypnosis: A theory of Beckett spectatorship	125
7 *Adaphatrôce*, or the contentious fringes of Beckett's dramaturgy	147
Notes	169
Bibliography	193
Index	205

Acknowledgements

In 2010, the University of Melbourne School of Culture and Communication assigned me Peter Eckersall, as the primary supervisor, and Clara Tuite, the secondary supervisor, upon my acceptance as a PhD candidate for a research project on Beckett and experimentation. Ten years later, writing the acknowledgements to this book from Takarazuka in Japan, I am struck by how indebted this work is to my life in Melbourne at that time and to the people at Melbourne University. Although the book retains barely a single word of the thesis awarded a PhD in late 2013, that doctoral experience remains for me the crucible of this book. I find myself ever more grateful for the inspirations and interventions experienced in those years, for these two supervisors, and for the many other mentors and associates I was lucky to interact with at the university, and outside of it. Peter's help with my research in theatre and performance in general continues to this day and has been of incalculable importance to me. Thank you.

Joshua Comyn and Sarah Comyn not only provided me with the introduction to a scholarly community as fellow postgraduates at Melbourne, but were there inspiring me even before we all came to live there. Of those whose ears I most abused with hypotheses, I thank Sarah Balkin, Elena Benthaus, Javant Biarujia, Bonny Cassidy, Justin Clemens, Sandra D'urso, Ken Gelder, Tim Grey, Michael Farrell, Fiona Hile, Joe Hughes, Peter Otto, Eddie Paterson, Antonia Pont, Lara Stevens, Ann Vickery and Tim Wright for listening. I'm sorry. The formulation of this argument was at one point a conversational cloister. Office raven, Duncan Hose, your influence is especially threaded throughout. Sydney friends, whose time I also recall stealing to discuss matters pertaining to this book, include Andy Carruthers, Toby Fitch, Tom Lee, Kate Lilley, Astrid Lorange, Peter Minter and Mark Steven. Other Beckett scholars in Australia, Mark Byron and Russell Smith, have offered encouragement at intersections. Helen Bailey and Iain Bailey – both met in separate moments of happenstance, the former at the University of Reading Beckett archive, the latter in Melbourne – I am grateful to you for offering those chances to discuss in Beckett scholar-to-Beckett scholar fashion my ideas with you at critical moments of generating this book's research. Melissa Hardie, for suggesting in early 2019 that I never give up, I am enormously grateful.

I extend special gratitude to Anna McMullan and Anthony Uhlmann, examiners of my PhD thesis, whose commendations inspired the will to continue with the unruly medley of ideas that drove the thesis towards the very different book you hold before you. Influential suggestions for publication in that examination commentary provided directions for this monograph. Anthony has allowed the robbery of his time on many occasions since the PhD; distance and time never once appeared to have tempered his willingness and generosity whenever I have called upon him at Western Sydney University.

For the administrative and collegial support that sustains my research day to day, enabling me to devote much time and resources to this book, and providing the ensconcement needed to realize it, I thank my colleagues at Kobe College.

Finally, for the constant support and patience all these years, I reserve my final acknowledgement for Kimi. This expression of gratitude is a feeble acknowledgement of the true scale of my debt to you.

Chapter 2 revises and develops work first published as ' "Only Her Mouth Could Move": Sensory Deprivation and the Billie Whitelaw Plays', *TDR: The Drama Review* 59, no. 3 (2015): 91–107.

Chapter 4 in an earlier version was published as 'Sleeplessness in Sleep: Beckett's Gestures of Dream', *Performance Research* 21, no. 1 (2016): 42–8.

Chapter 6 revises and develops work first published as 'Samuel Beckett's Hypnotic Theatre', *Modern Drama* 60, no. 3 (2017): 342–63.

Abbreviations

AWW I	*Act Without Words I*
AWW II	*Act Without Words II*
CDW	Samuel Beckett, *The Complete Dramatic Works* (London: Faber, 1990)
DF	James Knowlson, *Damned to Fame: The Life of Samuel Beckett* (London: Bloomsbury, 1996)

Introduction

Performativities of the laboratory

Beckett's writing for theatre treats the theatre as a laboratory of performance. By design, this laboratory realizes new configurations of attention for encounters with performance that test the spectator's capacity to interpret, feel or recognize them. In Beckett's laboratory, the protagonist is absent (*Waiting for Godot*, *Breath*) or a (seemingly) silent human puppet (*Catastrophe*); the antagonist is the stage spotlight (*Play*) or a changing figural relation to a hierarchy of address (*Footfalls, Come and Go, What Where*); duration is unhinged from time, and threaded through enigmatic, self-resonating narrative fragments (*Waiting for Godot, Happy Days, Rockaby, Ohio Impromptu, A Piece of Monologue*). Cherished definitions of what constitute the human, subjectivity and affect in theatre simulation are transfigured, or even erased, by experimental calculations of performance which miniaturize, spectralize and occlude the mechanics of spectatorship and observability that conventionally govern them. Acts without words, monologues without 'I', catastrophes without tragedy – Beckett's revision of the theatre as a laboratory for experiments in simulation has come to incite a total reconfiguration of the conventional focal points of theatrical spectacle on behalf of the contemporary theatre and performance landscape. Beckett's theatrical work continues to be the subject of debate in theatre and performance circles for good reason. These theatrical works are calculated with underlying experimental effects in design that challenge audiences every time that these works are adopted for performance.

The word 'laboratory' has commonly been used synonymously with that more popular designation, 'workshop', in the experimental context of modern theatre. While new, complementary approaches to performing and composing the body in experimental performance were avowedly underway in the workshops of San Francisco, New York, Tokyo and Kraków, for example, it is otherwise rare in the 1950s and 1960s to discover such a comparable experimentation in a *writer's* approach to theatre as Beckett develops with the acts without words in the same decade. Laboratories have tended to be the prerogative of ensembles, not writers. Yet, Beckett becomes an inadvertent prophet of what becomes of the fraught category of writer in an interdependent and cross-germinating world of performance art to come, a sphere in which texts and conceptual graphics are entangled with circumstances in which the conceptualization of new medial relations will govern the future of experimental art. Contradiction prevails. We know at once how odd but also how necessary it is to include Beckett, the grand late modernist in literary history, among the artists that would come to define the performative turn away from literary text. Beckett's own remarks have sometimes obstructed this interpretation.

Beckett once infamously remarked to Deirdre Bair of some of the most influential figures and practices in experimental theatre at the time, for example, 'Not for me these Grotowskis and Methods … the best possible play is one in which there are no actors, only the text. I'm trying to find a way to write one.'[1] And then, to Colin Duckworth, also quoted in Bair:

> When Duckworth asked, 'What do you think the theatre is for?' Beckett replied, '*I'm not interested in the theatre* … I very rarely go to see other people's plays – only to see friends acting, in fact.' Duckworth points out that Beckett likes to see his own plays, but only in the semi-private situation of rehearsal, not in public performance. 'I'm not interested in the effect my plays have on the audience. I simply produce an object. What people think of it is not my concern.'[2]

I am concerned about the continued influence of such anecdotes over interpretations of Beckett's attitude towards the theatre. For one thing, such remarks do not seem to be the words of an experimentalist. Nor do such remarks suggest those of a leader of a particular theatre laboratory, working in the lively decades following the Second World War, who espoused the agency of performance in its unrestrained liberty to realize unanticipated horizons of the human body, performativity and the spectatorial gaze. I do not believe that such remarks can be taken as definitive assertions about dramaturgy, for a number of reasons. Chief among the reasons that I chronicle in this book is that Beckett espoused very little in terms of coherent dramaturgical theory. Instead, Beckett formulated a profoundly influential dramaturgical experiment in world theatre. Beckett's dramaturgy features in as many debates about post-war theatre as do Bertolt Brecht, Jerzy Grotowski or any other of the most paradigmatic figures.

Unlike other vanguard figures in the history of theatre and performance, Beckett never asserted a manifesto or practice. However, Beckett's evident preference for capturing indeterminacy in his performance compositions endows his experimentalism with a special value of autonomy from authorial intent. The disruptions to accepted ideas of theatricality and performativity in Beckett's dramaturgy inspired a wide range of experimental artists to assimilate Beckettian compositions into their own practices in ways that are far more desultory than those of professed leaders of methods or discrete workshops whose own disciples were sometimes obliged to follow like scripture. As Herbert Blau remarks,

> The performances of Beckett at the [San Francisco Actor's] Workshop not only attracted artists – the painters, sculptors, filmmakers, the new developing hybrid types – who had no previous interest in the theatre but also served as models for the alternative modes of theatricality eventually known, through the era of happenings and multimedia events, as performance art. Along with these developments we were doing productions that involved direct collaboration in the American theater and not much like it even today. Beckett was also determinative in some of this, not only in an altered sense of dramaturgy but visual style as well.[3]

A fine example of this kind of American mid-century experimentalism that took Beckett for inspiration would be the ground breaking video and performance art of Bruce Nauman. A brief mention of that artist's assimilation of Beckettian attitudes to performance here may illuminate the profound implications of understanding Beckettian compositions for performance as being inherently experimental.

The example of Nauman's work shows that the Beckett laboratory comprises a way of conceptualizing Beckett's work for performance in a manner that exceeds the view of it as the writer's sole imaginative domain. Indeed, it was such a movement beyond solo authorship which originally prompted Beckett himself to enter into the theatrical sphere. Multimedia performance artist Nauman forged his practice early on in the pursuit of encounters aided by intermedial reflexivity between video recording and performance – that is to say, new modes of intermedial representation, here involving durational performance occasioning a video event and video framing a performance event – such as his long duration physical pieces recorded on tape. His best known of the video choreographies is likely to be *Slow Angle Walk (Beckett Walk)* (1968), a piece that inadvertently presages the direction of Beckett's own dramaturgy arrived at in its late stage in video dance work, *Quad* (1982). *Beckett Walk* creates a fixed-frame record of a performance of one repeated movement in a long duration work intended for installation in a gallery.[4] Nauman's use of film to preserve choreography suggests a complementary concern with performativity and the compositional diagram to Beckett's, as Beckett too would makes more use of screen recording and presentation to realize performance works later on in his career. Blau:

> The recursiveness of the language and the extremes of human behaviour … excited the video artist Bruce Nauman in the work of Beckett. What attracted him first of all, like others to this day, were the clownish types or gestures, from the Chaplinesque of the tramps to Buster Keaton in *Film*, along with the incapacity in the ashcans or the urns or up to its neck in the sand. Thus, in *Clown Torture* (1987), there's a figure stressed out on one leg, and then – as if with the carafe and cubes in *Act Without Words* – forced to balance two fish bowls and a bucket of water, while shouting 'No, no, no' and 'I'm sorry' to the nobody listening there. Even before that, in *Slow Angle Walk*, which was subtitled *Beckett Walk*, Nauman himself performed a series of impaired or spastic Clov-like movements, including a stiff leg up in the air, with his body swivelling around to get the leg back on the floor.[5]

Kathryn Chiong and Derval Tubridy, in separate instances, indicate that the manoeuvre was taken from Beckett's novel *Watt*.[6] But Clov's exhaustively delineated opening mime in *Endgame*, achieved in a 'stiff, staggering walk', is Beckett's closest theatrical echo to this manoeuvre.[7] The most obvious parallel dramaturgical conjunction, aside from Clov's body, is the physical tracing of an enclosure in both instances. It is as if the activities happening were some kind of obscure laboratory experiment, rendering a choreography that many of Beckett's plays will bear a resemblance to. Importantly, the image is achieved by a choreographic test. Nauman's tracing of the space of play creates a sort of cartography of possible moves limited by the Beckett-inspired 'walk' manoeuvre within a particular space. Repeatability of a form, not virtuosity of a discipline, guides the principle of Nauman's, and Beckett's, choreography. Experimentation, not expertise.

I present the example of Nauman here, in the introduction, to show that experimentalism, while expanded by multimedia artists of this ilk, captures a pioneering spirit lying within Beckett's own adventure into spectacle. Studies of experimentalism in Beckett's drama have gained interest in recent years. Yet, the proposition that theatre was Beckett's laboratory for experimenting with hypotheses of composition has somehow been a neglected part of this effort. A growing and compelling body of research flourishes around the performance studies of Beckett, aspects of which I refer to in this monograph.[8] A theory of Beckett's own performance practice as an experimental dramaturgy has proven to be a key neglected component of this field nonetheless. It is not so much that assertions to this effect have not been made in the scholarship of Beckettian dramaturgy – I will be utilizing many. Rather, various influential remarks have not been consolidated into a coherent argument about Beckettian experimental performance. I want to examine how the adoption of Beckettian work for performance involves making use of works whose inherently contingent elements enclose uncertainties as part of their compositional fabric. This view of Beckett's theatre of laboratory thus disputes the still-influential characterization of Beckett's dramaturgy as an inflexible art.

In adopting the laboratory path for examining Beckett's theatre, I discover a dramaturgy involving experiments in diminution, self-reflexivity, fugue, diagram and transfiguration among the effects. Crucially, many of these experiments build upon the results of earlier experiments. Notable productions, collaborators and situations in the performance histories of Beckett that contribute to this changing trajectory of dramaturgical modification sometimes represent new paradigms in Beckett's compositional direction. Not all playwrights, and rarely Nobel laureates, are necessarily so influenced by the real activities and events of the living theatre; I argue that Beckett was so influenced. As I show in this book, collaborations for Beckett came to spur new works and modifications to his dramaturgy; perceived failures induced new horizons; actors, scholars and designers inspired entirely new works. Then there are the implications of self-experimentation. Self-experimentation and play, I argue, prompt Beckett's early forays into live spectacle. The desire for editing, refinement and reimagination stimulate some of Beckett's later frustrations with his own writing. Beckett's experimental diagrams, deprivations of presence and the theatrical sensorium, self-imposed impediments and challenges, spectral and mechanical stage paradoxes, new arrangements of the spectatorial gaze, and revisions of the division of labour in the making of spectacle all feature in Beckett's laboratory practice of performance.

The journey into writing for performance as expressly performative can best be located in two minor acts written by Beckett at a critical moment in this writer's career. *Actes sans paroles I* (*Act Without Words I*) (1957) and *Actes sans paroles II* (*Act Without Words II*) (1959) look like performances mounted to observe human performance itself. These two plays were written between 1955 and 1956 in the early days of Beckett's still-tentative contemplation of writing for live spectacle, a time that nonetheless Theodor Adorno views as the creative moment for the defining work of post-war theatre, *Fin de partie* (*Endgame*). Looking at the experimental dramaturgical attitude adopted in these two acts reveals the ways in which the wider theatrical oeuvre of Beckett later engages in ongoing self-experimentation. In the first act without words, a man is thrust from the wings into a desert setting. There, the man is interrupted by props dropped from the flies. The player is literally being tested. This relation between *AWW I* and ethology, the study of animal behaviour, is in fact not merely a resemblance. As James Knowlson writes of the first act:

> The mime also reflects Beckett's readings in behavioural psychology as a young man in the 1930s, when he looked at Wolfgang Köhler's book, *The Mentality of Apes*, about the colony of apes in Tenerife, where experiments were conducted in which the apes also placed cubes one on top of another in order to reach a banana.[9]

The analogous dimensions of Köhler's ethological laboratory work from 1914 to 1916 with the laboratories of the acts without words show how curiously explicit Beckett's interest in the laboratory as a space akin to the theatre was.

Köhler's and Beckett's spectacles both present the observation of repetitive behaviour in premeditated circumstances. Both portray behaviour goaded by a supposedly objective, impersonal power – the scientist governing the ethological lab in Köhler's case, and the invisible hand of the theatrical sphere in Beckett's. Further, the laboratory logic under critical examination in Beckett's case conveys the fact that the purpose of the examination of performance is not disclosed to the actors enclosed in the performance space. The purpose of the man's futile performance in *AWW I* is certainly not presented to the audience in Beckett's case. Both Köhler and Beckett's laboratories involve spectacles that appear to operate following the assumption that performance within their enclosures is mounted arbitrarily for the sake of observation. The unawareness of the suffering this artificiality and distancing entails for the performer that occasions the spectacle – the ape in Köhler's case, the human performer in Beckett's – reveals a critical power imbalance. While Köhler's case of power imbalance follows scientific conventions of the time, Beckett's dramaturgical interest makes a metatheatrical subject of the assumptions underlying the observation and spectatorship of human life.

The resemblance is so strong that some of Köhler's experiments seem almost like isomorphic reproductions of the situations in *AWW I*, even when we know that the chain of influence is the reverse – as Knowlson showed, Beckett was influenced by Köhler. Consider, for example, when 'Sultan' fails to utilize two boxes to reach an 'objective', that is, an assigned food objective encumbered or put out of reach to test the chimpanzee's intelligence.[10] With two boxes alone, Sultan fails. He succeeds in the subsequent experiment when provided with a ladder. Sultan's situation mirrors the scenario in the first act without words when the man receives from the flies three cubes, one by one, each following a failure to reach a carafe of water dangled to tantalize him in this deserted no-place. Notably, the man learns: first, the carafe cannot be reached with one cube. Another, small cube comes down from the flies. He fails to stack them properly by size, then succeeds. Upon mounting the two cubes, the carafe returns to the flies. The next event of learning is crucial: a third cube is offered which, after landing, the man 'looks at [], reflects, turns aside, reflects'. As a result: 'The third cube is pulled up and disappears in flies' – the man has learnt the futility of life in the laboratory.[11]

Bruno Latour and Steve Woolgar propose that we describe the human space of the laboratory as 'an enclosure where previous work is gathered'.[12] Similarly, a theatre laboratory tends to stand for theatre in a state of progress – a space yet to be defined. Beckett shows that logic and utility prove to be limited categories by which to understand the enigma of self-awareness when frustrations and acting out against incarceration may in fact better define what sentience means for cognitive modelling of human norms in their supposed difference from that of primates. When Sultan fails, his emotional descent into an array of seemingly nonsensical and purposeless actions unforeseeable to the experiment's plainly laid solutions reflect real sentience, a property ungoverned by the logic of observability imagined in the experiments, and sometimes displaying outright rejection of the gaze that encloses him in his cage. Sultan

> seized the intractable box and rushed up and down the room, bumping the box behind him and dashing it with his whole strength against the wall. When his rage had spent itself, he gave a calm, quiet look at the scene before him and made a long step in advance by *lifting* the first box, which was still directly beneath the objective, and placing it upright on end with a powerful and dexterous movement. … After his second disappointment, he again gazed round helplessly and finally noticed the table. He seized it by one leg and dragged it towards his goal, but turned it over through his hasty, jerky movements.[13]

The narration of events shows that the scientist's priorities are different to a more generally focused reader; where the scientist later makes a matter-of-fact observation about how the problem should have been solved, readers are more likely to wonder about the apparently despondent conclusion of this particular experiment where Sultan seems to express angry resignation.

Indeed, elsewhere in this diary of chimpanzee behaviour of varying success and failure, the obvious opacities in the observational gaze often raise the most evocative moments of the account. Man or ape, the knowledge of incapacity and the limits of a world illuminate more profoundly the depth of sentient life than assertions about its essential form.

Beckett's transposition of the Köhler primate spectacle to the scene of theatricality recalls a very different thinker of the interwar years, and one more proximal to the author's philosophical tendencies but also belonging to the writer's library: Ludwig Wittgenstein and his *Tractatus Logico-Philosophicus*. As Tim Lawrence writes: 'For Wittgenstein, the subject exists at a kind of limit point that bounds the world as it appears, a boundary which is also marked out by the limits of language'.[14] Lawrence makes a compelling argument about Beckett's sense of the limit via Wittgenstein and as the category and dilemma of the self-perceiving subject engendered through language. In his 'Lecture on Ethics' of 1929, the philosopher even evokes a scenario like *AWW I* as an analogy for the subject's enclosure in language: 'I believe the tendency of all men who ever tried to write or talk Ethics or Religion was to run against the boundaries of language. This running *against the walls of our cage* is perfectly, absolutely hopeless'.[15] As Lawrence explains, in this language-inflected ontology

> the subject may speak, but subjectivity in itself remains unspeakable, just as the perceiving subject, *as* subject, remains unperceivable. For the subject to speak upon his life as a whole would necessitate a self-negation – he would have to be simultaneously subject and object to himself. The impossibility of this act inscribes those limits on being that are expressed in silence and by the mystical.[16]

Köhler's book represents an early resource in Beckett's long career in studying spectacle through experiment, or, in other words, studying the subject 'running against the walls of their cage'.

An underrecognized essay by Bert O. States, one of the major theorists in theatre studies of the late twentieth century, provides a key inspiration for the critical approach to Beckett's theatre adopted in this book. Beckett's self-critical examination of theatrical spectacle in the late play *Catastrophe* (1982) receives the characterization in States's essay as presenting a 'metaphor of theatre-as-laboratory'.[17] States conducts an analysis of the cruelty that spectacle-making represents in this late play. He then speculates about whether this representation of spectacle-making emblematizes Beckett's view of theatricality in general. States suggests that the short play presents a methodical distillation and reconstruction of classical tragedy's dramaturgy. Tragedy, for States, exemplifies the earliest recorded spectacle of human suffering in Western theatre history. *Catastrophe* is seen as an experimental inquiry into the fraught and contradictory spectacle of tragedy and its presumed empathic consequences: '[*Catastrophe*] has a double implication: it is at once generic and horrific, beautiful and ghastly, and somewhere in the oscillation of the two meanings, the play asks – where, and what, is the catastrophe? What is this empathy with the victim, this pleasure in pain?'[18] For States, Beckett provides a way for spectators to view the mechanics – the *anatomy* – of tragedy, deconstructing the conventions shaping the spectatorial gaze that validate human suffering for spectacular ends. Deconstruction of tragedy's dramaturgy has an ironic as well as ambivalent effect. The irony of making a spectacle about the very cruelty of spectacle escalates in recursiveness when we consider what the setting and scenario of the play is: four characters in rehearsal *preparing to make a theatrical spectacle*. The denouement of the play deepens the uncertainty of what the true status of Protagonist, and of this cruel experiment, amounts to. Rather than finally speak, Protagonist simply raises his head and faces us. Simulated applause follows after a pause. The effect is to preclude or cast doubt upon the convention of applause, estranging the audience from their once-unconscious and conventionalized activity. If we are applauding something in this play, 'What is it that we are celebrating?' Keir Elam cannily asks.[19] The debatability and uncertainty of the outcome, of this most conventional of responses to spectacle, becomes the real denouement of the play. The unsettled spectatorial experience of this play's conclusion constitutes a rare Brechtian moment in the Beckett dramatic corpus.

Laboratories are inflected by the disciplines and actors that institute them. As Latour and Woolgar argue:

> Each text, laboratory, author and discipline strives to establish a world in which its own interpretation is made more likely by virtue of the increasing number of people from whom it extracts compliance. In other words, interpretations do not so much *in*form as *per*form.[20]

Laboratories perform experiments, more so than informing their audience and auditors about them. Experiments are an activity of persuasion and inquiry, rather than neutral transmissions of fact. Laboratories belong to sociocultural contexts following historical trajectories that at once substantiate and audit the activities that take place within them. Spectacle according to naturalism, following Émile Zola, trusts in the verifiability of an informative reality when properly rendered by a dramaturgy that sensitively utilizes real space and real time, 'in the end we will see that everything meets in the real'.[21] By contrast,

Beckett's non-naturalistic, deconstructed, experimental theatre continually exposes this performance of reality according to the foundations of theatrical simulation, even down to the ways in which light is controlled to illuminate cardinal points in a drama's dramaturgical and figural construction, such as the head of the human figure. Laboratories have existed at each stage of theatre history, including in Zola's naturalism. Beckett's more self-conscious use of theatre as a laboratory for examining theatrical representation actually strengthens our ability to study his theatrical work within theatre history, rather than making it some exception to that history.

Additionally, States shows that the reconfiguration of the theatre as a laboratory can intensify stage presence:

> Imagine the possibility that characters in a play did not entirely condense themselves into the actors playing them, that somehow, in an additional sensory dimension, the ghost of the *real* Lear – the Lear idea, the Lear fact – hovered in the vicinity of the catastrophic last scene of *King Lear*. Further imagine that during the agony of Lear portrayed so movingly by the actor – during, say, 'Thou'lt come no more, / Never, never, never, never, never!' – that this ghost, or idea, or fact, should suddenly crystallize into a face and 'fix' us [as Protagonist does in Beckett's play, fixing his eyes upon the audience], in effect asking in a look of deep admonishment why we were there, we 'men of stones', painlessly feeling his pain, how we could sit still during *that*, and why if we had tongues and eyes we did not use them to crack open heaven's vault. This is what I think the fixing means – mischievously, for there is a glint in Beckett's eye, not a sermon. And the shame felt by the first audience as its applause falters and dies is the double shame of being caught mistaking someone else's pain for your pleasure ... But in the Theatre of the Real, or the Now, where the Lears are still alive and unwell, agony doesn't settle into images very comfortably, and theatre comes face to face with its double, *the thing* it can never be.[22]

States here imagines a new relation between actual performers and stage virtuality to emerge out of a focalization upon new relations between the real and the virtual. Here, the Lear *idea* captivates the Lear *role*, a speculative manner of accounting for an early modern forebear to a post-classical quality of the deconstruction of testimonial spectacle that concerns both Beckett and the theatre of the real. In this way, States affirms a matter that Carol Martin urges regarding the value of self-critical theatre. Martin argues that the theatre of the real mounts a challenge to the norms of testimonial simulation: 'Theatre of the real is not a tragic form. ... Through the citation and reconstruction on stage of what audiences understand as real events, theatre of the real begs spectators to cultivate and use their moral imaginations'.²³ While examples of verbatim theatre might rely upon the validity of the represented words in a given work to justify its spectacle, other forms of theatre of the real are engaged with deconstructing received notions of how the real should or can be simulated in live performance.

Experimentalism can be understood in various ways depending upon the discipline. Experimentalism's place in defining modernism in aesthetic theory is somewhat fraught. Given Beckett's work's prominence in modernism studies, a field concerned with the category of experimentation in some part, I must attend to this particular relation before more confidently applying to my notion of Beckett as an experimentalist. The relationship between experimentalism and modernism often depends upon the legacy of particular philosophical views of art's autonomy within corresponding frameworks of representation. Experimentation for some represents the apex of aesthetic autonomy, while for others experimentation explicitly undermines aesthetic autonomy. For those thinkers that view modernism as the assertion of an emergent tradition that alights from the past to define the future, the embrace of contingency in experimental practices becomes the problematic or ungovernable dimension that resists historical periodization and interpretation. For those thinkers that take experimentalism as an essential confrontation between art practice and a contingent world, experimentalism can be understood in more utilitarian, purposive, or periodic senses, dependent upon a historical review of the directions undertaken through procedures with a variety of actual experiments in art. I want to look at one notable discussion that has emerged in recent years about autonomy and modernism that circulates around the figure of Clement Greenberg.

Robert Mitchell, in a recent disquisition on the trajectory of Romantic experimentalism, *Experimental Life: Vitalism in Romantic Science and Literature*, draws attention to the shortcomings of Greenberg's concept of medium refinement as the central motivation of modernism emerging out of Romantic practices that lead into a multimedia modernist framework.²⁴ Mitchell suggests that experimentalism was in Romanticism and in its aftermath a more contingent practice of aesthetic discovery than has often been understood following the influential Greenbergian notion that modernist art tends towards abstraction. Mitchell uses his concept of

'Art-network' to confront Greenberg's aesthetic theory to formulate a caveat about the relations that can exist between works of art in different media and their sociocultural reception, especially the interactions forged with scientific premises and practices:

> Even ... Greenberg's powerful interpretation of modern art as a collective attempt by artists to locate the pure form of each medium by means of abstraction – to reduce painting, for example, to the bare minimum of conditions necessary for an object still to count as a 'painting' – is fundamentally a narrative of the diaspora of the separate arts (and is, in any case, a narrative that has been undone by the rise of multimedia art). In place of the serial 'progress' that occurs in the sciences, the artistic experiment instead facilitates the emergence of new nodes and links within the Art-network.[25]

Greenberg's view of modernism, in other words, lies at odds with the material imbrication of modes of representation with other forms of extension innovated by modernists. For an approach to the vexed question of what media and medium mean in modernism after Greenberg, Emmett Stinson proposes that the lauded autonomy of modernist art cherished by the New Critics complementary with Greenberg's theory might be better understood not as a devoted sublimation of form, as it was for New Criticism, but as a provisional strategy within a wider aesthetic economy. Stinson: 'Rather than serving as a coherent philosophical position or a model for utopia, modernist autonomy [can] be viewed as a *rhetorical strategy or gambit* that posits the work of art's separation from political or social forces from which it can never truly be free'.[26] Stinson's position, inflected by Jacques Rancière and Pierre Bourdieu, determines that experimentation need not be reduced to an authoritative practice; experimentation can rather be understood as a counterpart to modernist pioneering of uncharted domains in art. Experimentation can retain the integral contingency that attends pioneering activities without meaning predetermined formations with a certain destination or intentionality in view. Stinson's account of modernist autonomy smooths out the hard distinctions between modernist and postmodernist practices in this regard. Such a revision of the fraught modernist concept of autonomy allows for the desultory and unpredictably achieved aesthetic strategies that do often escape satisfactory isolation within one or the other camp to be reconsidered in a less predetermined fashion. Following Stinson's understanding of a *conditional* modernist autonomy, if you like, we might say that Beckett's laboratory enterprise seems to incorporate the negative, obverse side of the concept of autonomy:

As ... Bourdieu has argued, autonomous forms of art tend to result in a 'reflective and critical turn by the producers upon their own production' that causes such works to self-consciously wrestle with their own conditions of possibility. The irony here is clear: claims of autonomy are never completely autonomous because they can only derive their meaning from the disavowal of an external tradition, institution, or discourse. Autonomy is thus always defined by this negative relationship to a disavowed externality, and autonomy has no content aside from not possessing the very content that it seeks to differentiate itself from (attempts to define modernist autonomy as an emphasis on 'form' over content are also misleading, since form – which by its nature is protean – does not possess an essential character for the reason that, by relational definition, it is not content, and thus has no content, as such). In this sense, claims of autonomy are always shadowed by the externalities they seek to escape.[27]

In theatre and performance studies, these tensions within modernism orient around one cardinal principle of modern performance practice: the freedom to experiment. This assumption of freedom to experiment has been extraordinarily important for the progressions in modern theatre in transforming the once-restrictive conventions of conventional drama, even going beyond what was once called 'drama'. However, the assumption that modern theatre's autonomy is defined by the freedom to experiment encounters problems of interpretation due to an inherent indeterminacy. The most radical experiments can often be self-directed and such experimentation has an ironic reliance upon restricting the autonomy of the artwork from the intentionality of the artist. Self-experimentation means tampering with that autonomy. Tadeusz Kantor sits in a chair on the fringes of the stage in *The Dead Class*, visibly supervising and reflecting upon the performance of a memory play he has devised, directed and written. Spalding Gray performs himself as character, witness, narrator and actor in The Wooster Group's *Rumstick Road* and every utterance therefore comments upon at the same time as performs the narrative frame of the work. In a Greenbergian sense, such visual and medial interference limits the freedom experimental modernist work might enjoy from its creators; such works are not as medially refined realizations of abstract or conceptual vision as they might be without this metatheatrical, recursive, or material interference. On the other hand, such theatrical innovations have established Kantor and Wooster as historically significant experimentalists; the interference these artists explore introduces or explores new contingencies in dramaturgy. Kantor's theatre renounces supposed creative neutrality and personalizes in new testimonial ways the memory play. Gray and Wooster experimentally renovate the very premises of what audiences deem fact, reference, testimony and dramatization to be.

With regard to Beckett, I do not propose to have answered how he stands in relation to the essential paradoxes of modernist experimentalism. Instead, I elect to embrace the paradoxical, undecidable ends of experimentation that the unresolved question of modernist autonomy raises. The reason for this is that Beckett's practice seems clearest when his work presents the two apparently incommensurable principles of experimentation together. We shall see how the notion that a performance piece should follow creative design, and the contrary notion that works for theatre should be defined by the contingencies of live performance, often present together in a paradoxical interrelation in many of Beckett's works for performance.

Adorno represents the most visible figure in the history of Beckett studies to tender the view that Beckett experimented with a view of a more refined theatrical medium more deeply concerned with abstraction than materiality. This view of modernist aesthetics and Beckett's contribution to it shares much with Greenberg's theory of aesthetics. For Adorno, Beckett's art represents the zeitgeist of post-catastrophic ontology. A play such as *Endgame* represents modernist stagecraft left experimenting with itself in culture's post-apocalyptic wake, progressing towards a comprehension of the terms of absolute negation: '[The play] draws back from the nadir through no other means than by calling to itself like a sleepwalker: negation of negativity'.[28] Such a view maintains that Beckett is the master of the theatrical domain, and sustains, in Mitchell's terms, a 'diaspora' of the arts in which theatre is decoupled from the wider arts and practices that it relies upon, not to mention the social and material field of the moment in which the play is performed. In Chapter 1, I consider pantomime's place in Beckett's laboratory and contrast this view with Adorno's excision of pantomime from modernist theatre history. To this end, Elin Diamond's view of the role of medium in experimental theatre proves more amenable to accounting for Beckett's experimentation, in my view. Diamond isolates a new point of focus for the media of live performance: the performing body:

> Twentieth-century performance dreams of the body that will gesture and present, not imitate and represent, a body of 'subjugated knowledges' (Foucault) that resists social discipline. Meyerhold's biomechanical exercises (1920s), Brecht's epic theatre training (1920s–1950s), Artaud's 'affective athleticism' (1930s) with all their differences, seek to destroy the body/mind split that authorizes the bourgeois cogito and its regime of power/knowledge. … In the environment of political experimentation in the 1960s and 1970s, the Living Theater, the Open Theater, the

Performance Group, the Omaha Magic Theater, and many others, developed their own versions of 'psycho-physical exercises' to release the body's unauthorized truths.[29]

The Adorno-derived view of Beckett's theatre tends to delink it from the experimental practices catalogued here, whereas I hope to understand this dramaturgical practice entangled with elements of this version of 'twentieth-century performance'. Mitchell shows how a materialist account of context can be critical for understanding artistic experiment. Similarly concerned with networks of practice as Diamond is, Mitchell's account of the scientific practices of experiment that fed into Romanticist literary experiment shows that intersections between science, culture and art practice often proved to be desultory rather than epochal. To this end, Mitchell treats the multimedia compositional practice of John Cage, the defining experimentalist in art following the Second World War, as a horizon of the real intersections of science and art experiment that shape the Romanticist–modernist connection. The experimental performance practices Erika Fischer-Lichte chronicles in her book also have their strongest conjunction in the work of Cage. For Fischer-Lichte, Cage the multimedia artist and composer revolutionizes what the term 'theatricality' comes to refer to in the second half of the twentieth century:

> Cage explicitly referred to [the] experience [of the dissolution of space through sound] as a theatrical experience: 'I think the thing that distinguished my work from the others ... was that it was more theatrical. My experience is theatrical'. Cage's notion of theatre is defined by this very lack of intentionality and planning; openness for what could occur; the impossibility of control; coincidence, transience, and perpetual transformation without any outside intervention. For Cage, the performance of 4'33" epitomized theatricality: 'What could be more theatrical than the silent pieces – somebody comes on the stage and does absolutely nothing'. He merely lets something happen which occurs without his interference.[30]

This experimental view of theatricality concerns 'the sphere of events rather than works of art' – that is, rather than works of art in isolation.[31] In Fischer-Lichte's reckoning, any binary of intentionally staged versus intentionally unstaged spectacle no longer proves sustainable after Cage.

Cage develops an experimental compositional mode that refers to what cannot be disclosed in a composition. Beckett, to a similarly unprecedented degree of inventiveness, develops an experimental compositional mode that refers to what *remains* to be disclosed in a composition. Stinson, Mitchell, Diamond and Fischer-Lichte all suggest in varied ways that experimental modernism cannot be understood unidirectionally with regard to medium. By extension, the kinds of decreative and subtractional approaches that are the signature of Beckett's spectacle may similarly concern contingent ends for art, rather than predetermined ones. I mean 'decreative' in the sense Simone Weil does: 'to make something created pass into the uncreated'.[32] Only the starkest conception of potentiality such as Weil's accords with Beckett's remarkable, expansive negativity. In my view, a negative process, rather than a negative vision, underpins the Beckett laboratory's activities.

Part of the project to resist the reading of Beckett as wholly predetermined in his aesthetic orientation to spectacle is to revise the concept of authority that we bring to understand this writer. Indeed, according to Anna McMullan in 'Beckett as Director: The Art of Mastering Failure', Beckett's act of externalization that writing for the stage meant enabled the writer to engage in a resistance to the assumption that writers enjoy authority over their creations. There can be many artistic reasons for this apparently self-undermining manoeuvre. Following a general trend in experimental art practice of deposing authorial control, Beckett's practice problematizes the widely accepted assumption of singular authority underlying authorship since the Enlightenment:

> Beckett's aesthetic ... exposes and parodies the continuing conceptual constraints of the dualisms which the Enlightenment relied upon: the opposition between power and powerlessness, and between form and chaos. According to this epistemology, truth, knowledge and personhood are dependent upon a will to discipline, abstraction and authority. All areas of mystery and the unknown are relegated to areas beyond laws and codes of dominant models of knowledge and representation, and can only be referred to in terms of absence and lack. In order to present powerlessness, and indeed to give it a shape, Beckett recreates a framework of entrapment or authority, however much he proceeds to parody or erode it.[33]

McMullan's notion of giving 'shape' to 'powerlessness' is critical to understanding the practice of experimentation that would orient much of the writer's work for the stage and the ceding of performative power that Beckett attempted to realize for his theatrical creatures. Following McMullan, theatre provides Beckett with an external realm through which to examine how his creatures relate to the world and its auditors. The self-examining element of Beckett's work is at once a call to the work's autonomy as it is a critique of

Introduction   17

its premise. The shape autonomy takes following this conception concerns, most of all, autonomy from the page, the writer's domain. Paradox ensures that these stage creatures emerge into the restrictions of live appearance in the domain of spectacle in such a provisional and doubtful autonomy from the written word.

Beckett's innovativeness tends to involve such tensions of creative representation as tensions that begin with the genesis point of writing. This externalization of writing's ends also corresponds to the revised view of theatre's relationality to the world in which it appears that emerges with avant-garde theatre's explorations of forms of living theatre. Samuel Weber describes the making of spectacle at base as an 'expropriation' of living space and time. Theatre is a requisitioning of the moment and scene for event that is at once embedded and temporary in the real.[34] Such expropriation is marked by an ephemerality and interstitial relation to the world at large while nevertheless irrevocably taking place within it. Jacques Derrida describes a similarly Antonin Artaud-inspired principle of performative transformation as 'an experience which produces its own space'; 'it must permeate me'.[35] Theatre following this intensified understanding can be understood as an irruptive coordination of live materials for performance – a definition amenable to a laboratory view of theatre. Theatre mounts a provisional, ephemeral, dynamic installation; of course, installation is the conception that Weber also attributes avant-garde theatre figure Artaud with revolutionizing as the thrust of live art's appearance in real time.[36] The apparatus, records, commentaries, and procedures of self-auditing, inquiry, and modification come to figure as components of a collaborative enterprise like theatre as they do a laboratory.

A directorial assistant to Beckett, Michael Haerdter, kept a rehearsal diary for the 1967 Schiller-Theater Werkstatt production of *Endspiel* (*Endgame*) in Berlin directed by the writer; this diary features important supporting evidence for the laboratory view of Beckett dramaturgy in its entry of 9 September. We might consider the critical affirmation of this principle of experimentation that we endorse by reviewing Beckettian dramaturgy entangled with these drafts, marginal anecdotes, diary entries and production notes:[37]

> Beckett's drama focuses on the sense of a universe controlled by mechanistic laws, imposed by the author–direction: '... one must make a

world of one's own in order to satisfy one's need to know, to understand, one's need for order ... There for me, lies the value of the theatre. One turns out a small world with its own laws, conducts the action as if upon a chessboard ... Yes even the game of chess is still too complex'. On the other hand, his drama also evokes the undefined spaces which escape or are excluded from the laws of the dramatic world – the area beyond the shelter in *Endgame*, for example. In all of the later plays, the illuminated acting area, where every movement of the actor is choreographed with the text, is juxtaposed with an area of darkness impossible to comprehend intellectually or perceptually. Beckett therefore establishes a central tension between the need to control through knowledge and perception, *and the foregrounding of the limits of that control.*[38]

In this characterization, we read that Beckett's theatre involves the imposition of a provisional, fallible order that the medium cannot fully govern due to the disorder in which it is contained; disorder is also what remains 'excluded' from or 'undefined' within the spectacle, in accordance with McMullan's view related earlier. As Latour and Woolgar argue, a laboratory also is a limited domain of order installed within a milieu of disorder.[39] Disorder is what haunts every experiment, then, and also what drives the experiment to reimagine what it cannot govern.

A theory of Beckettian dramaturgy that integrates the mechanisms of this laboratory put into motion by the collaborative partners, media and adaptors involved draws attention to the contingencies that play out before audiences in the real circumstances of immersion and interaction. Chapter 1 considers this question by examining the beginnings of a diagrammatic urge in Beckett's writing that starts in his acts without words, two plays that were also integral experiments in physical theatre that would lead to Clov's opening mime in *Fin de partie* (*Endgame*). Diagrams suggest an effort to calculate experiment with the choreographic implication for the dancers, physical performers and other producers that would be solicited by Beckett's compositions.

Chapter 2 assigns new value to the sensorium that emerges from Beckettian compositional experiment. The plays that Beckett imagined for actor Billie Whitelaw, *Not I* (1972), *Footfalls* (1976) and *Rockaby* (1981) have sensation-depriving agency. We can observe this phenomenon by examining Whitelaw's eventful collapse in rehearsals of the first of the three plays, and to what extent the architectural model imagined in the work contributed to a revision of the influence that the play text can have over the construction of a performance sensorium. This capacity for sensory deprivation becomes a compositional interest of the Beckett theatre, in my view, and comes to concern more and more the spectatorial field instantiated in part by the renovated stage role conceived in the writer's performance works. Beckett's textual constraint, an element of avant-garde theatre that has long been the subject of resistance in the name of the freedom to experiment, becomes the counter-intuitive practice of experiment for the late Beckett theatre as a result.

Chapter 3 visits the aesthetic and philosophical attitude to simulation that long concerned itself with sensory experiment on the stage: symbolism. Beckett's earliest full-length work for the stage *Eleuthéria*, never officially produced after being written in 1947, and the defining work of modern theatre, *En attendant Godot* (*Waiting for Godot*), completed by the end of that decade, indicate the writer's closest affinities with the movement's visions. The argument posed in this introduction suggests that such visionary conceptions of spectacle diverge from Beckett's own more indeterminate, experimental ones. Therefore, Chapter 3 explores Beckett's deauthorization of symbolist stage conventions in his use of metatheatricality, negativity and miniaturization to redirect the efforts of the avant-garde stage which in Beckett's first efforts grappled with the still palpable ghost of Artaud in the Parisian scene in which Beckett started his career.

Chapter 4 extends the discussion of laboratory to the context of consciousness. Dream features in a number of Beckett's stage works as the promise of an external field invisible to simulation that nonetheless engages in its own; such a paradox of conscious and unconscious life features also in screen works such as *Nacht und Träume* (*Night and Dreams*) (1983). The subject of dream becomes another means, like physical theatre, for examining mute gestures. The muteness of gesture is a matter that philosopher Giorgio Agamben has theorized as 'the other side of language' undergirding expression.[40]

A play such as *That Time* (1976) embeds its experiment in imagining this unspoken domain in testing how close sleeplessness can come to the brink of sleep. Chapter 5 further enquires after that most sleep-disturbing of dimensions which life inhabits – light. We have seen in this introduction how Protagonist's catastrophe is not some singular event, but rather a fundamental condition that applies to all simulated life – the catastrophe of being seen. Chapter 5 observes the political valencies of this critical late play in light of historical parallels the work bears with theories presented by Herbert Marcuse and Agamben. The *political* stage becomes the subject of Beckett's experiment here; *Catastrophe* employs a deconstruction of spectacle, I argue, in an effort to discover infant hauntings of the 'spectre of dissent' that once occupied this play's dedicatee, Václav Havel.

The experiments that compel the Beckett spectacle towards unexpected diminutions of stage image, apparitionality of the live body, and estrangements of the representational field of spectacle, result in new forms of spectatorship thrust into sensoriums no conventional theatre experience can prepare an audience for. Chapter 6 explores the hypnotic ends of these experiments. Examining the lauded Walter Asmus production of *Not I*, *Footfalls* and *Rockaby* that I saw at the Jubilee Theatre in London in 2014, I consider what it means for spectacle to be experimentally hypnotic in a contemporary context after the legacies of Franz Mesmer and Jean-Martin Charcot in the nineteenth century, and psychoanalysis's founding thinkers such as Josef Breuer and Sigmund Freud in their fraught deployment of the pseudoscientific, therapeutic technique in the twentieth. In Chapter 6, I discover an inversion of hypnotic norms enabled by immersive dramaturgy; Beckett experiments with a reverse hypnotic logic in which the figures that were once compelled to perform their pathologies in the clinic now lead a hypnotic experience with a contrary audience. The theatrical audience that supplants the clinical gaze produces a self-critical querying modality that is positioned to examine the terms of observability in the context of therapeutic self-reflection. Audiences of *Not I*, *Footfalls* and *Rockaby* are immersed in confrontations with testimonial opacity as a result, eliciting a spectatorship that must become self-critical about the preconceptions of empathetic encounter with self-representation and simulation.

After six chapters on various components of Beckett's laboratory and its collaborators, the paradoxes of live simulation motivating Beckett's turn to spectacle have been examined. Chapter 7 engages in a reappraisal of the place of divergences from authorial intent in experimental adaptations of Beckett's work not intended for performance. I advocate for renewed appreciation of medium-sensitive adaptations of Beckett prose works where they participate in the legacy of Beckettian dramaturgy's experimentalism in its emphasis of the zones of contingency in live art. Adaptation proves to be one of the most controversial and least coherent of topics in studies of Beckett's dramaturgy, not least because of Beckett's noted concern about adaptations of his prose work during his lifetime. At one point, Beckett even pejoratively described adaptation as 'adaphatrôce', that is to say, 'adaptation' understood as 'atrocity' in this evocative portmanteau word.[41] In truth, however, Beckett allowed numerous adaptations of his prose work, and contemporary theatre companies and artists have engaged in major revisions of Beckettian dramaturgy's in the contemporary by careful interrogation of medium and composition in this writer's oeuvre. The best-known example of this is the historically-significant experimental prose adaptation, Mabou Mines's *The Lost Ones* (1975–6). Attentive consideration of the hypotheses that govern Beckett's experiments in the theatre inherently present an endorsement, rather than a caution against the kind of adaptational work that define the contemporary landscape of Beckett performance. While crude readings of the value of experimental adaptation tend to merely value the escape from authorial design that adaptation entails, a more enduring interpretation of Beckettian dramaturgy's ability to cross medial divisions receives guidance from the laboratory principle that Beckett's works focus upon medial contingency. The artists sensitive to the compositional problems raised by Beckett's work have also extended the practice's logics of diminution, negation, and focalization. Even establishment figures in the modern and contemporary theatre landscape have engaged in unorthodox adaptations of Beckett material not intended for performance. Namely, the achievements and problems that I discover in Peter Brook's 2015 show, *Fragments*, a show that includes an adaptation among short theatrical pieces, consolidate the view that the concept of authorial intent remains a crucially debatable point for discussions of the dramaturgical ends of the Beckett's compositions.[42]

1

Laboratory acts without words

Samuel Beckett completed two seemingly minor works without words by 1956: *Actes sans paroles I* (*Act Without Words I*) and *Actes sans paroles II* (*Act Without Words II*). The first is a solo, the second a duo. Both are introduced by the author as mimes. *AWW I* and *II* also share a conception of the theatre as a virtual cage of performative enclosure physically and conceptually constrained. In *AWW I*, the performer cannot leave the stage due to virtual force making escape impossible. In *AWW II*, the constraint is sequential and logical, the tasks in the performance sequence being interdependent and circular and thereby lacking a terminus. Any attentive spectator realizes the irony Beckett exploits in having the mime performers perform their inability to egress from that performance: the activity of mime marks out the virtual limits of the performance enclosure at the same time as those limits are metatheatrically reimposed upon the unfortunate figures of these works. Further, the constraints of the virtual cage follow premises derived from the art of physical performance and its inherent limitations. While developed with the assumption of infinite power of virtualization through gesture, the practice of pantomime has real, material limitations that I suggest Beckett made the experimental subject of these two acts. This chapter considers how these two works offer disfigured examples of post-war pantomime. Such pantomime and its entanglement with the Parisian post-war avant-garde promised a new direction in the performing arts. These two works herald a diagrammatic process in Beckett dramaturgy that will be sustained until the late exemplar of this practice, *Quad* (1982). Beckett's mimes, and the diagramming that stems from them, present a central experimental thread in the artist's dramaturgical history.

AWW I is a piece in which the spectacle actively and comically resists the performer's escape from the stage by the wings, the wings inexplicably throwing the performer back into the performance space; through cruel guile, presenting stage props for use, only to be relinquished; and, morbidly, by denying the man's means of suicide. The comic dimension of the work lies in the false promise of escape from spectacle. S. E. Gontarski suggests that the play makes use of the ironic Tantalus myth to this end; Tantalus's punishment is confinement to temptations predesigned to be beyond reach, dangled by a mocking god.[1] Each of *AWW I*'s man's failed attempts to learn a way out of spectacle starts with suggestions made by an anonymous, offstage blow of a whistle. This indicates a false route of escape that, time and again, ends in repulsion and retraction. Beckett's stage directions amount to a self-reflexive set of dimensional limitations and commands to act, then, emanating from the house of performance. These commands also entail a predetermined failure of the mime role they simultaneously shape. Metatheatricality stands for the paradoxes of self-aware ontology, or what in the introduction was allocated the Wittgensteinian principle that we defy the walls of our language-shaped cages with futility. Ruby Cohn suggests that the play 'illustrates one of [Beckett's] favourite sayings, the Latin of seventeenth-century [Cartesian philosopher] Arnold Geulincx: "Ubi nihil vales ibi nihil velis" – where you are worth nothing, there you should want nothing'.[2] The Tantalus myth's warning about the ultimately futile destination of human desire undergoes a Cartesian revival in this play that makes poignant comedy of the human circumstance.

AWW II, again featuring silent, mime practice encountering omnipotent constraint, replaces the whistle with a 'goad'. That goad is a pointed arrow prop extended on wheels to prod the nearest performer of the two in each cycle of two interconnected, interdependent routines. Here, the metatheatrical reference to spectacle-making and the apparatus concerns the concept of routine. 'Routine' means habit, a human activity defined by repetition understood in accordance with a life. But the word also designates the theatrical term for a scripted set of repeated performance manoeuvres in accordance with a theatrical career involving a particular routine. The differences imaginable between the two conceptions of routine make a witty intersection in *AWW II*. Both mime A and mime B present daily routines that are comic routines also. The comic value conferred to the double meaning lies with the qualitative differences between 'poor' or 'high' performance of otherwise irrevocable cycles of routine behaviour. A, the poorly performing one, is pathetic and supplicant, and he prays. B, achieves his routine unselfconsciously, assiduously and precisely. A cannot stomach their food, a carrot, whereas B savours it. Nevertheless, both get dressed and undressed. Both retire to the sack they emerged from, having moved one position stage right the other has carried them to. The cycle will be repeated ad infinitum; that is the suggestion as the cycle returns to A in prayer again. The two routines also suggest a cycle of *inter*dependence and inheritance upon the performance of the other – one's high achievement is visible only in comparison with its preceding, failed other, as the two performers are also interreliant on the other's transport of them in the sack to continue the cycle. One rests as the other performs. Of course, the implication of perpetual repetition allows the audience to discern the two parts' comic difference as merely permutations of a single condition. Both remain subservient to spectacle's goad to perform, part of a situation much like *AWW I*'s scenario. Again, human will has been rendered irrelevant. So, *AWW I* and *AWW II* are ironic conversions of the pantomime virtuoso. This infinitely creative figure has been revised for what they are: the actual performer of spectacle, a living being enclosed in a virtual domain. Their physical virtuosity is also the medium of their entrapment; the box of light that once ennobled the performer's ingenuity comes to encapsulate their ontological poverty. We must now inquire about why virtuosity has become poverty. Those already suspicious of the comparison of high modernist Beckett with pantomime, a now somewhat maligned genre of performing arts, may already suspect the reasons for this corporeal practice falling into disrepute after the midcentury period.

Waiting for Godot premiered in America in 1956, the year that Beckett first dabbles in radio drama with *All That Fall*, but most relevantly to the acts, the year the author made a breakthrough in the drafting of his second and most critically accepted work for theatre, *Fin de partie* (*Endgame*). It is the year when Beckett consolidates in a profound way an international career in drama. James Knowlson, for example, writes that it is through work on this first of the acts without words in 1955 that the author realizes the 'mimic elements' in *Fin de partie*.[3] More recent scholarship shows a determined period of work on mime implicated in the production of the lauded Beckett play.[4] We will look at this evidence in detail shortly. Such an association between Beckett's most critically celebrated of plays and two apparently parodic pantomimes, at first glance, seems inexplicable. Can we really equate work done in these two minor pieces with the play Theodor Adorno once called 'a post-mortem examination of dramaturgy' and post-war drama's most fatal study of the zeitgeist: '*Endgame* studies (as if in a test-tube) the drama of the age, the age that no longer tolerates what constitutes drama'?[5] After reading the summaries of these two interrelated works, students of Beckett are unlikely to view the *AWW I* and *II* as signal examples of Beckett's or indeed any other modern theatre-maker's experimentalism. Short, negative fantasies of confined, metacritical pantomime are unlikely to occur to students of Beckett as pinnacle works in a career of experimental theatre. Should not a laboratory theatre be exploring new ways to raze the fourth wall, stimulate new forms of audience interaction, dissolve the binaries of artwork and life, and equip the performing arts with new optics for inquiry and critique into a transfigured specular architecture? The acts without words seem like dystopian opposites to such projects. The liberties for performance, imagined in the workshops of experimental performance that Elin Diamond and Herbert Blau alerted us to earlier, seem worlds apart from these acts.[6] Two comical, self-mocking and apparently critically inconsequential works of physical theatre do not seem the stuff of this history-defining modernism. These works are sometimes derided by the prominent critics of Beckett's theatre; Ruby Cohn has suggested that Beckett's wordless pieces are 'far less subtle than [his] verbal plays'.[7] Gontarski says that *AWW I* 'lacks characteristic Beckett innovation'.[8] Yet, I want to explore this very occasionality that Cohn and Gontarski – admittedly, some time ago – purpose for derisory ends. The acts without words are not Beckett's most accomplished and ambitious interventions into the theatre, but they signal a particular experimental turn to the diagram that will be dramaturgically paradigmatic for the development of this writer's theatre. Once the evaluation of taste is put aside, the acts without words' centrality to a concerted self-examination and hypothesization of what spectacle is shows that a wager was made with mime in the 1950s that will continue to bring dividends throughout his dramatic output. The diagrammatic turn shows Beckett testing out what text can hypothesize about the performing body when script's constraints upon performance are employed subtractively and with dramaturgical self-examination.

Some of the experimental activities developed in the 1960s that have come to define our view of experimental art were directly inspired by Beckett's choreographed body developed in the 1950s. These include paradigmatic shifts undertaken in the performance sphere in the workshops, companies and studios of Herbert Blau, Peter Brook, Mabou Mines and Bruce Nauman, among others. A revision of these relationships will help us to overcome a critical problem. Jonathan Kalb highlights the problem of Beckett's reception in the field of performance studies: 'Beckett is avant-garde to the conventional and conventional to the avant-garde; he straddles two milieus in a way that would seem like equivocation if he had consciously sought the position'.[9] To remedy this problem, no more helpful analogy for Beckett's theatrical experimentalism can be supplied than the very concept of *writing* acts *without words* presented in this choreographic approach developed in the 1950s. For W. B. Worthen, 'Beckett's wordless play' demonstrates 'a concise critique of the drama's writing of space, its ability to transform the nowhere of the stage in to a specific location'.[10] Worthen specifically means the play and screen work, *Quad*, but the ability to read 'play' in that phrase 'Beckett's wordless play' as synonymous with 'experiment', as in 'playing with', offers a fortuitous manner in which to analyse the very explicit paradox entertained in these two pieces.

Eleuthéria – an unproduced play by Beckett which precedes *Godot*, to be discussed in Chapter 3 – constitutes Beckett's first contribution to the brand of modern French drama 'resurgent' in the post-war theatres of Paris. According to Jacques Guicharnaud, this would in the end come to be defined by the Irishman, along with two other immigrants to France, Eugène Ionesco from Romania and Arthur Adamov from Russia.[11] Soon after completion, the play was being distributed by Beckett's literary agent Jacoba Van Velde (aka Tony Clerx) in the year of Artaud's death: 1947. The play was not accepted until 1950 by actor-director Roger Blin. Blin was the best-known inheritor of the dramaturgy of Artaud in the French theatre at that time. Blin was interested in *Eleuthéria*, along with Beckett's second complete play, *En attendant Godot* (*Waiting for Godot*). However, history would favour a production of the latter over the former.

But it is with the acts without words that Beckett realizes a performativity less entangled with this 'dispossessed' Surrealist aesthetic of *Eleuthéria* and most closely aligned with dramaturgical principles shown in Beckett's next stage play after *Godot*, *Fin de partie* (*Endgame*).[12] The acts without words were realized during the long drafting process of *Fin de partie* and represent his first experiments in imagining plays with such stringent and singular choreography. The most recent scholarship on the drafts of *Fin de partie* during 1955 dispute earlier claims that the discretely achieved *Acte sans paroles* – what would become *AWW I* – was the work Beckett had been working on to sketch *Fin de partie*'s memorable opening mime with one half of the central pseudocouple, Clov. As Mark Nixon indicates: 'The problem in charting the compositional process of these three mimes is the absence of documentation; the original manuscripts of both the *Actes sans paroles* are missing.'[13] Nixon says 'three mimes' because there is a third mime included in a manuscript dated 8 May 1956 entitled 'Mime du rêveur A', now archived at Dartmouth College. This third mime carries more evident trace of what became *Endgame*.[14] However, my task is not to chronicle origins or genealogies here; my task here is to show that the acts without words realize and present a new commitment to physical theatre. This commitment seems even clearer when we know that extensive abandoned drafts and another mime exist as part of the endeavour towards the play that became *Fin de partie*. What remains undisputed is that this new scholarship shows a determined attempt at writing mime even more multifariously hypothesized on the page than was once thought, with two discrete mimes, *AWW I* and *II*, and an abandoned *Endgame*-reminiscent fragment, 'Mime du rêveur', all being implicated work on mime that culminates in Clov's silent (but for the snickering) physical prologue. I want to examine this emergent practice as a diagrammatic choreographic treatment of the performing body.

Diagrams of performance

The compositional differences between *AWW I* and *II* suggest a progression towards the diagram, a compositional tool that will become a normal part of Beckettian dramaturgy following the latter play. Beckett's theatre and screen career choreographing performance, culminating in a work such as *Quad*, retrospectively situate the mime work of 1955–6 as formative experiments in the author's dramaturgical development. The movement from a descriptive approach in *AWW I* to the use of actual diagrams in the playscript in *AWW II* exemplifies what I view as a diagrammatic process that will problematize conventional theatrical mimesis. What does diagrammatism mean for theatrical art in general?

To choreograph is to map; to map is to formulate; to formulate is to diagram; to diagram is to write. Performers realize choreographic diagrams by internalizing the calculus of a given composition, whether recorded on paper, video, algorithm or self-devised; either way, the diagram does not actually come into being until it is performed. When Gilles Deleuze uses the term 'diagram', he uses it in a contrasting, but soon to be related, artistic domain: painting. Painter Francis Bacon, an artist whose dark pictorial realm has been compared with Beckett's before, employed enigmatic diagrams in his work.[15] Seemingly straddled between visceral realism and conceptual abstraction, Deleuze sees Bacon's diagrams as an affirmation of a revolution in figuration that opts out of the binary figural coordinates of twentieth-century painting:

> According to Bacon, [tactile-optical space] will inevitably be there, in one way or another: one has no choice in the matter (it will at least be there virtually, or in the head of the painter … and figuration will be there, preexistent or prefabricated). Now what will disrupt this space and its consequences, in a catastrophe, is the manual 'diagram', which is made up exclusively of insubordinate colour-patches and traits. And something must *emerge* from the diagram, and present itself to view. … [O]ne starts with a figurative form, a diagram intervenes and scrambles

it, and a form of a completely different nature emerges from the diagram, which is called the Figure.[16]

A diagram 'intervenes' in the representativeness of the figurative form and the figural standing-in for a referent, in other words. Neither Bacon nor Beckett seems to refer to real human situations, and yet at the same time both in some way resist abstraction in their respective visual domains. Deleuze's explanation lies with the changing relation between medium and figuration in twentieth-century art. That is to say, Deleuze advocates for understanding painting according to Bacon as an enterprise compelling new experiences of our senses, one that neither denies what painterly forms suggest, nor privileges through abstraction a conceptual order that visual art can refer to over its materiality. A diagram becomes this unresolvable relation between the field of vision and the nature of the figure captured within it. Deleuze explicitly links Bacon to Beckett in a 'common setting', which is also 'the round area, the isolator, the Depopulator' – these are diagrams too. Bacon, Deleuze urges, explores 'a situation [that] finds its equivalent only in theatre, or in a Beckett novel [*sic*] such as *Le Dépeupleur* – "inside a flattened cylinder … The light … Its yellowness"'.[17] Diagrams, in other words, are chimeras of representational architecture inflected by the medium that renders them. Diagrams are the undefinable settings and forms that Beckett figures find themselves enclosed within. Diagrams as calculations of placement. Diagrams as calculations of movement.

Let us now examine the diagrams that feature in some of Beckett's dramatic works to understand the structural motivation of this compositional transition between *AWW I* and *II* mentioned earlier. First, observe how *AWW I* has been written solely in descriptive language making no distinction between gesture, movement, characterization, argument, stage direction, or recommendation. Indeed, *AWW I* resembles a prose work with minimal narration. The scene is set thusly:

Desert. Dazzling light.
The man is flung backwards on stage from right wing. He falls, gets up immediately, dusts himself, turns aside, reflects.
Whistle from right wing.[18]

AWW II comes presented in more familiarly post-*Endgame*-style *didascalies*, which is to say, meticulously choreographic graphics. The drafting of the dimensions of the performance is less descriptively rendered; description cedes to a geometrical rigor that accounts for how the work should be performed. Split between sections entitled 'NOTE' and 'ARGUMENT', the script closes with the first of Beckett's script-set diagrams for performance. As mentioned earlier, diagrams of performance become a feature typical in later works for theatre and will be adopted as the logic for scoring television and film. Here is *AWW II*'s diagram:

POSITION I

POSITION II

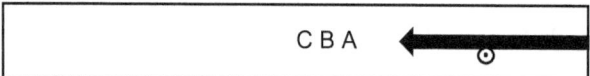

POSITION III

STAGE FRONT[19]

The 'NOTE' that precedes the diagrammatization of the layout of the play and its three interconnected scenarios gives explicit guidelines for the architectural and mechanical realization of the play: 'This mime should be played on a low and narrow platform at back of stage' to achieve a 'Frieze effect'. Characterization of the anonymous mime characters A and B is predetermined: 'A is slow, awkward (gags [i.e. jokes are] dressing and undressing), absent. B brisk, rapid, precise. The two actions therefore, though B has more to do than A, should have approximately the same duration'. The choreography is entirely mapped out, permitting no improvisation with the procedure of actions (while the question of what remains live in the performance of a given performer's version at a given time will be a crucial contingency): 'A, wearing shirt, crawls out of sack, halts, broods, prays, broods, gets to his feet, broods, takes a little bottle of pills from his shirt pocket, broods, swallows a pill, puts bottle back, broods, goes to clothes, broods', and so on.[20] Writing choreographies within a strict plot and spatial architecture constitutes a deeply paradoxical innovation in writing for the avant-garde theatre, a genre newly embracing Artaud's strident call to be free of the written word.

When one compares *AWW II*'s diagram with later works that more confidently occupy the genre of experimental theatre, the role of the diagram in Beckett's turn to composing performance texts receives clarification. That is, what becomes apparent is that Beckett's plays are also choreographies; they have dramatically figural consequences that trouble the conventional optics of stage simulation. Consider *Footfalls*, for example, written twenty years after the acts:

MAY (M), *dishevelled grey hair, worn grey wrap hiding feet, trailing.*
WOMAN'S VOICE (V) *from dark upstage.*
Strip: downstage, parallel with front, length nine steps, width one metre, a little off centre audience right.

$$L \xrightarrow{} \begin{array}{cccccccccc} r & l & r & l & r & l & r & l & r & \leftarrow \\ \rightarrow & l & r & l & r & l & r & l & r & l \end{array} R$$

Pacing: starting with right foot (r), from right (R) to left (L), with left foot (l) from L to R.
Turn: rightabout at L, leftabout at R.
Steps: clearly audibly rhythmic tread.
Lighting: dim, strongest at floor level, less on body, least on head.
Voices: both low and slow throughout.[21]

Then consider *Quad*, presented first for television in 1982 produced by Süddeutscher Rundfunk, whose mute, performer-traced geometry receives no imaginative or descriptive explanation in the textual document, but rather lengthy enumerations of how the strict calculus of the work must play out to realize it:

A piece for four players, light and percussion.

The players (1, 2, 3, 4) pace the given area, each following his particular course.
Area: square. Length of side: 6 paces.

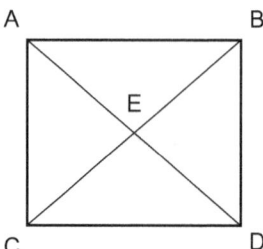

Course 1: AC, CB, BA, AD DB, BC, CD, DA
Course 2: BA, AD, DB, BC, CD, DA, AC, CB
Course 3: CD, DA, AC, CB, BA, AD, DB, BC
Course 4: DB, BC, CD, DA, AC, CB, BA, AD[22]

The diagram here is a cross-hatched box. Tellingly, a quad is also 'a playground', says Chris Ackerley.[23] The diagram is also a quincunx, a mystic symbol that looks like a five on the die. Anna McMullan describes the quincunx, following Peter Murphy, as an ironically rendered, closed allusion to the celestial sphere.[24] Such a symbol becomes ironic in a play such as *Quad*, given that its figures are incarcerated in a condition defined by repetitively tracing a symbol that should refer to an absent redemption.

Quad's deeply diagrammatic text seems to have been formulated for producers of the work only; besides the text's meticulous graphing of all elements of the work, from light, to a fixed relationship between a 'percussion' component and particular performers, to the costumes, and of course the choreographic procedure, the final section of the text provides caveats that also describe a second, embedded work, *Quad II*, also realized in the Süddeutscher Rundfunk production for television. That is, the second iteration relies upon the existence of the calculation of the first. The second piece is essentially a diminished, monochrome 'variation' of the first. This variation's very sonic quality of shuffling feet breaking the silence of the mime emerges only after the minimizing extrapolation of the piece from the rhythmic concept of the original. *Quad II* has been experimentally deduced from *Quad I*, in other words. As Knowlson writes: 'The fast percussion beats [of *Quad I*] were removed, so the only sounds that were heard were the slower shuffling steps of the weary figures and, almost inaudible, the tick of a metronome. Beckett was delighted when he saw the stunning effect'.[25] This diminishment in the second act recalls *Waiting for Godot*'s one, in which much of the world is the same except what varies within the same. The human experience of sameness, with vision and memory of time deleteriously corrupted, is brought into relief by the exposure of this ontological architecture of return.

Diagrams thus enable interdependent experiments that explore new series and new mediums. The Beckett diagram sometimes indicates the essential compositional form of a choreography such that inessential parts can be subtracted from or diminished, while enabling the figural and performative logic of the work to remain intact. Baylee Brits views this quality of *Quad* as part of a mathematical imagination. Quoting John Haynes and Knowlson's *Images of Beckett* (2003), she writes that

> in *Quad*, Beckett constructs a *mathematized* version of the unword, using numbers to exit not only the constraints of signification but also the constraints of a pre-scriptive choreography. Jim Lewis, who worked with Beckett on *Quad* at Süddeutscher Rundfunk 'recounted a conversation that he had with him in 1982, in the course of which Beckett said that every word he used seemed to him to constitute a lie and that music (in the sense of rhythm) and image were all that were left for him to create'.[26]

Mathematization of the playscript becomes one consequence of performative diagrammatization. The theatrical form that emerges would not so much follow a visual model as a mathematical calculation, the latter involving the many material components of a performance, from duration to physicality, beyond the merely visual. Mathematization also offers one way for understanding what Worthen has called a play's 'agency', especially the question of how performativity may be composed by writers to interact anew with other media.[27]

Enumeration is not numerology, of course. Let us take this opportunity to distinguish a mathematical understanding of a Beckett spectacle from a symbolic one. As Brits discusses, while the work suggests an 'occult or superstitious ritual', the piece actually emphasizes the opposite: a confined reality.[28] Brits's point that mathematization also means 'exit' from a 'pre-scriptive choreography' I take to mean that the diagram and its procedure prescribe a map but not the manner of physical achievement of the piece.[29] Online, for example, one can find enormous stylistic variations within the same constrained piece, from Pan Pan's stiff figures to Surreal SoReal's lithe ones.[30] Gontarski points out that *Quad* must be 'extra literary [i.e. extra-literary]', which is to say, 'unreadable – in any traditional literary sense'.[31] Diagrams, mathemes, numbers – they compute, refer and confer, but do not evoke a figural domain until the medial infrastructure of language involves them in a sphere. When Beckett wrote his first dramatic work intended for theatre, *Eleuthéria*, the space of play was imagined as a diversion from an industrious but excruciatingly challenging bilingual period of writing, publishing and translating that had become increasingly self-referential and also difficult for the writer to monetize.[32] The urge to temporarily divert from prose is also a *playful* diversion from the domain of reading; while a true departure from the literary domain proves unrealized in *Eleuthéria*, *AWW I* and *II* herald this deconstructive process via diagram. This process dispenses with readerly edification in the play text, and proceeds towards the extremes that we find in *Footfalls* and *Quad* and which define the late Beckett. Rather than being merely a late-period aesthetic refinement, the diagrammatic choreographic practice of Beckett exists between the acts without words.

Decisive shifts in Beckett dramaturgy often came by way of experimental trial and error. Diagrams provide the evidence of this experimental self-examination of the agency of a play text. Beckett's writing of pantomime is implicated in the trajectory towards the extremes of *Quad* and multimedia spectacle. In fact, as Anna McMullan has shown, 'J.M. Mime', an abandoned theatrical work intended for veteran Beckett actor Jack MacGowran, was a fragmentary originator of *Quad*; evidence that the author experimented with the quincunx diagram is found there.[33] Anna McMullan has called the piece a 'crucible in which several textual and *mise en scène* motifs are experimented with' – namely, those that become *Not I*, *Footfalls*, *Quad*, and a prose piece entitled 'Enough'.[34] Not only does McMullan's manuscript research here show the merit in thinking about Beckett's work as a process of experimentation, but that results emerging in that process, such as particular kinds of diagrams, prove indispensable to an understanding of Beckett in performance. Diagrams developed in the acts without words facilitated choreographic work on *Fin de partie* that also inspired this abandoned piece 'J.M. Mime'. That abandoned work leads all the way to a major Beckett achievement in screen play, *Quad II*, a work of choreography enshrined not in a live occasion but on physical performance-remediating video recording.

The diversity of contextual and medial achievements of *AWW I* and *II* affirm the diagram's availability to intermedial calculation also. Veteran performance experimenter of Beckett material, Sarah Jane Scaife, engages in a site-specific performance mode of adaptation. Her disciplinary roots lie in physical theatre: 'I went to New York to study physical theatre with Polish mime artist, Stephan Niedzialkowski, dance with Eric Hawkins, and butoh with Maureen Odo'.[35] Scaife has not made original works the focus of her career, but rather the experimental productions of Beckett's. Scaife has been presenting Beckett's acts without words since 1988 and has in recent years developed a signature site-specific application using the choreographies as vectors for understanding 'revenants' in particular places.[36] The diagrammatic quality of *AWW II* encourages this sort of motile translation to another sphere of spectacle. Beckett's diagrammatical choreography invites the application of the dramaturgy to new media and site-specific contexts.

Scaife suggests, for example, that the performance of '[*AWW II*] [can be achieved] any number of ways, maybe – different physicalities, different ethnicities, all the kinds of opposites or different ways of being in the world. They are all there in that choreography of movement'.[37] In her double-bill production of *Rough for Theatre I* and *Act Without Words II* in Dublin in 2013, the director sought a conjunction of space and sociocultural implication in real time:

> The stage for [*AWW II*] was placed along another wall so that the actors could use it performatively, during the play. The sound of the wall as it crumbled against their bodies, pieces of rubble dropping on the cardboard, provided another phenomenological experience of watching for the audience. ... This piece has great sculptural beauty, which interacts with each city in which it is placed'.[38]

That 'sculptural beauty' of the work transfers seamlessly in cinematic adaptation of the play also. This can be seen in *The Goad*, a film directed by Paul Joyce in 1965.[39] Like Scaife's, the adaptation of the play here installs the routine of two mimes in a context of disorder, here among the trash of a garbage tip. Like Scaife's version, Joyce's realization endeavours to find a contrasting sculptural symmetry in carefully conducted camera pans and leaps of movement in lines following the logics internal to the two sack figures and the passage of the goads against a backdrop of object chaos.

Then, central performance research scholar of Beckett, Phillip Zarrilli, has long been using *AWW I* to conduct his own inquiry into acting method. As a practitioner and as a pedagogue, Zarrilli finds in *AWW I* a validation of his key concept 'psychophysical' acting, a practice-based, immersive inquiry into a performer's 'bodymind'. He writes:

> I often use [*AWW I*] as a useful vehicle for the actor's application of the psychophysical process ... to problems of acting since it forces actors to return again and again to what is 'necessary' in each moment – similar to what must be done in training through the forms of a martial art. The repetition in both the Beckett score, and in form training, ideally leads to an embodied sedimentation – an experience of the inherent musicality and rhythm of the spaces between actions as one plays the nuances between.[40]

Though this view of Beckett pantomime as something to be internalized might seem beyond the remit of a mathematical appreciation, again, the assumption is that the script can be calculated and practised, rather than simply illustrated. *AWW I* is not a conventionally authored text to be resisted by experimental practitioners; *AWW I* is a calculus of experiment that attracts experimental thinkers of physical theatre such as Zarrilli who realize unanticipated possibilities by applying that calculus to their practice. Indeed, Zarrilli supports the argument that the diagrammatic quality underscores Beckett pantomime in his endorsement of *AWW I* as a medium for studying acting. Zarrilli's approach enlists various physical disciplines from non-Western contexts to rethink more holistically – indeed, metaphysically – how the performing body realizes the challenge of a play; Beckettian choreography has been critical to Zarrilli's worldly pedagogical approach to essential physical performance.[41]

Since 2013, Jonathan Heron and Nicholas Johnson's Samuel Beckett Laboratory research workshop based at Trinity College Dublin (TCD), a wide-ranging scholarly initiative bringing Beckett scholarship into closer contact with contemporary performance practice and inquiry, following a conception of Beckett in performance that they see Zarrilli's practice-based research to affirm:

> Like Zarrilli's 'metaphysical studio' before it, [the TCD laboratory] maps out the Beckettian eco-system that little bit further into the realm of praxis. … Whether 'metaphysical studios' or 'participatory laboratories', these performative environments (including installations, exhibitions and happenings) generate intercultural and interdisciplinary knowledge that can only enrich textual and archival methodologies.[42]

In Heron and Johnson's view, Beckett's writings are enriched by experimental and practice-based research. The work of this research project has been significant for the re-inclusion of testimonial accounts of working performatively through Beckett texts, enlisting not only novel work-generating sessions with figures such as Scaife, but also bringing greater attention to the contributions made to Beckett dramaturgy by performers such as Barry McGovern and Rosemary Pountney. Like Zarrilli, Heron and Johnson suggest that Beckett's plays can be *practised*. Their response to this possibility is by stimulating the scholarly and pedagogical networks that performance interfaces with, entrusting workshopping with the task of extending the potential of this calculus.

Heron and Johnson's view of laboratory concerns pedagogy and research strategy. Their concern is the future of methodology for Beckett scholarship, seeking a different compass than an author-centric view, endorsing a contrary, 'applied' view of Beckett via performance as research involving many formerly so-called unauthorized interpreters of Beckett in that context.[43] Their view of a 'laboratory', complementary with Zarrilli's studio, endorses a practice-invested study of Beckett's dramaturgy I also hope to endorse through my tracing of Beckett's diagrammatic turn. An understanding of the diagrams in Beckett's playwriting developed in this chapter hopefully carries some utility for the kind of applied research generated in Heron and Johnson's laboratory; students working in the TCD summer school workshop no doubt find Beckett understood by way of diagram more amenable to their emerging practices than Beckett the monolithic author(ity). But I now want to return to the larger theatrical history of physical performance that Beckett is transforming, a transformation from a self-confident expression of free gestural virtuosity into a self-critical art of experimental inquiry.

Beckett and the problematics of modern pantomime

In the twenty-first century, it is likely that we – indeed, Beckett scholars more than most – watch a work such as Marcel Marceau's *The Cage* with some nausea; if Beckett's theatre seems 'post-mortem', mime seems *jejune*, as this Pierrot mimics a sentimentalized terror at finding himself in a cage, and an over-expressive ecstasy at discovering an exit out.[44] Mime zestfully imagines gesture as an infinitely creative craft whereas, comparatively speaking, Beckett's spectacle tends to present gesture as futile, in decline, and captive. So, to understand what would bring Beckett to write for a subgenre of performance so apparently at odds with his dramaturgical sensibility requires that we return to the revival of pantomime in the post-war period. Here we find Beckett's own immediate associations with practitioners in a domain that had revived pantomime for new physical and figural ends.

Pantomime in the mid-1950s really should be seen for the experimentalism that galvanized it, rather than the cliché it became. Drawing physical artists to inquire after the interest of avant-garde playwrights such as Ionesco or Adamov, and include Beckett among their sphere, pantomime in Beckett's Paris context evoked the most pressing questions of what performativity represented. Deryk Mendel, who solicited the *AWW I* piece from Beckett, was a dancer and mime seeking a 'short scenario' to perform.[45] Mendel had recently performed as 'Frollo', a clown, at the cabaret Fontaine des Quatre Saisons around the time when he made the request.[46] Hans Bauer, the director of the first German production of *Endgame*, writes in an accompanying note to his 1957 production that the figural imagination governing Beckett's work selects the clown for its example over the naturalistic human; Bauer suggests this selection is made in order to resist a single Weltanschauung or world view, and that includes universal humanism: '[Beckett] re-configures the human as the clown. Which is a profound method for distancing and objectifying'.[47] Beckett's clown constitutes a nude in the genre, in a sense. Lacking the usual depersonalizing Harlequin face paint of the great mime artist Marceau, or the depersonalizing body tights used in the modern tradition of corporeal mime's founder Étienne Decroux's method, Beckett's figure is naked of the usual coverings that the genre usually employs so that its players may freely impersonate the world. The man, and A and B, seem exiled from the anonymous liberties of pantomime performers whose humanity has been concealed under make-up and estranging costume, bared to theatre lights in their fleshly everydayness. A and B of *AWW II*, for example, are dressed in plain clothes and both act out ways at failing to mimic well: A, the pathetic one, is incapable of dressing proficiently; B, the victim of routine, a 'precise'[48] character that suffers time, animatedly works against the clock to get dressed, 'a large watch' 'take[n] from shirt pocket', as he too dresses and undresses.[49] *AWW I* presents the mime with nothing to mimic but the mime's deconstructed entrapment in the virtual field. Once the free space of gestural infinitude, Beckett presents the genre cannibalizing its own restraint to the virtual, self-consciously exposed to being a human simulator without any fresh insight into the actual human predicament of performance.

Audiences thus receive a deconstructed perspective of a practice formerly seen to release theatrical performance from its bondage to words. The subject of critique is normative mimesis of human life. *AWW I* offers a kind of dystopian view of the Lefebvrian principle regarding spectacle that

> mimesis has its role and function in the domination of space. ... This role is a contradictory one, however: by assigning a model, which occupies a space, to an as-yet ill-defined desire, imitation ensures that violence (or rather counter-violence) will be done to that desire in its relationship with that space and its occupant. ... Mimesis pitches its tent in an artificial world, the world of the visual where what can be seen has absolute priority, and there simulates primary nature, immediacy, and the reality of the body.[50]

AWW I appears to work in a manner closely adhering to traditional mime, albeit stripped bare. In a letter to Pamela Mitchell on 18 August 1955, Beckett describes the man of the play as 'a mute white clown'.[51] As Jonathan Tadashi Naito writes, the style of *la pantomime blanche* developed by Jean-Baptiste Gaspard Deburau from the early nineteenth century leads directly to the modernist avant-garde of the twentieth; *la pantomime blanche* was revived in the twentieth century in the genre of 'corporeal mime', a sort of moving sculpture, developed by Jacques Copeau, favouring a stripped-down discipline of the body that would be continued by Decroux, the teacher not only of France's two most famous post-war mimes, but, at that time, France's two most famous actors in *any* genre: Marceau, and, in addition, Jean-Louis Barrault.[52] Barrault is an essential contributor to the Beckett performance archive. Indeed, the place of Barrault leads us towards a sense of the deeper influence the dramaturgical journey into corporeal paradox pantomime enables for Beckett. Barrault's involvement in Beckett's next full-length play following *Endgame*, *Oh les beaux jours* (*Happy Days*), will enable us to clarify the author's intimacy with the modern phase of pantomime in context. As Naito explains:

> *Happy Days* is a useful touchstone for considering the impact of Beckett's interest in mime on his drama in general. As is well known, the French premiere of *Oh les beaux jours* took place at the Odéon Théâtre de France in 1963 with Roger Blin serving as director and Madeleine Renaud in the role of Winnie. Less often commented upon is the fact that Renaud's husband, Jean-Louis Barrault, played the role of Willie. ... Barrault subsequently performed in several of [Beckett's] other plays, taking part in a Beckett season at the Theatre Recamier in 1970 and, perhaps most significantly, performing the silent roles in *Ohio Impromptu* and *Catastrophe* in 1983. But Barrault was not the only mime involved in the original *Oh les beaux jours*. Two decades before he directed the original production of *En attendant Godot*, Blin had studied mime, during which time he met and studied under Barrault, even appearing in several of his productions. The original Odeon *Oh les beaux jours* came about because of this previous Blin-Barrault connection. Blin's background in mime also suggests an alternative, though complementary, explanation for the convergence of mime and Beckett's drama, one that originated in performance rather than on the page.[53]

Naito maps what immediate relations to pantomime exist in Beckett's theatre. Barrault's willing self-effacement when he was one of the most famous actors in France is particularly interesting. This extraordinary gesture on the part of the star of *Les Enfants du paradis* (*Children of Paradise*) (1945) suggests a particular interest on the part of the actor in the limits of the discipline that he had come to stand for, especially its cardinal role in charting new directions in theatrical mimesis. In taking on the part of Willie in *Oh les beaux jours*, a part apparently so peripheral and largely invisible to the scopic field of this work, Barrault willingly engages in a self-obscuring practice of transfigured pantomime at a time when the actor's face was the most recognizable representation of the craft. We must remember that Barrault's celebrity is also Barrault's very own visibility as a mime in the famed role of Baptiste Debureau from *Les Enfants du paradis*, a pantomime character. Such a recognizability is importantly at odds with the mime as a practice of concealing the human face to adopt a gesturally impersonal one. In taking the role of Willie, a contrary reaffirmation of the problematic of mime is, strangely enough, reprised. I want to develop this idea of recognizing pantomime in the mid-century period in more detail, inflected by the activities of this crucial play.

In *Happy Days*, Willie spends most of his time obscured – that is, off-mound, the central setting being this rise of earth in which the protagonist, Winnie, is buried – and when onstage he either faces away, barely visible, reading a newspaper, or disappears. Willie's only movement of consequence is in that final tableau of striking self-abasement when, while ostentatiously '*dressed to kill*', he freezes 'on his hands and knees looking up at her'.[54] Such a tableau seems to affirm Deleuze's assertion that the journey of Beckett's art is the pursuit of the pure image, consolidated therefore in his screen work.[55] I dispute this suggestion's reliance on the optical by returning to Deleuze's own notion of the figure from *Francis Bacon: The Logic of Sensation*. Strikingly, the 'spasm', a conception of suspended movement contained in the figure, accounts for the premise of exposed pantomime that we discover in Beckett's spectacle:

> Movement does not explain sensation; on the contrary, it is explained by the elasticity of the sensation, its *vis elastica*. According to Beckett's or Kafka's law, there is immobility beyond movement: beyond standing up, there is sitting down, and beyond sitting down, lying down, beyond which one finally dissipates. The true acrobat is one who is consigned to immobility inside the circle. ... In short, it is not movement that explains the levels of sensation, it is the levels of sensation that explain what remains of movement. And in fact, what interests Bacon is not exactly movement, although his painting makes movement very intense and violent. But in the end, it is a movement 'in-place,' a spasm.[56]

In this sense, we might say that *Happy Days* casts the mime in a context of suspended animation. Willie is the 'true acrobat' of the living virtual field immobilized in an effort to expose a figural dimension of pantomime unseen when it appears to be putatively free in prodigious reference of scenes other than the human's true suspension. Michael Fried's analysis of tableau helps us here; tableau, he shows, draws attention to the problem of theatricality inherent in visual culture. That is, Fried shows how tableau would transition from painting to the theatre in the form of tableaux vivants. Tableaux vivants become involved in later 'absorptive' techniques that resist the explicit artificiality of the technique and eventually transition into naturalism.[57] Thus, Fried concludes, 'there can be no such thing as an absolutely antitheatrical work of art – that any composition, by being placed in certain contexts or framed in certain ways, can be made to serve theatrical ends'.[58]

Tableaus are a deeply artificial practice, freezing time and movement to render a visual form corresponding to a heightened spectatorial focus; and, yet, tableaux vivants became a technology in the stage's capacity to create more naturalistic, absorptive spectacles. Barrault plays pantomime's art of mute gesture towards a self-interrogating mimetic extreme, exploring the ends of a discipline after its incorporation into screen culture. To play Willie is to enact a deconstructive performance of mime that takes its gestural logic to a counter-mimetic end, concealing its very performer and troubling scopic norms of theatricality associated with pantomime.

AWW I's man, like Willie, is a clown who nonetheless cannot mimic anything but his own incapacities to perform. The man's gestures, like Willie's, are marshalled by commandments to perform. His reactions are reduced to timed reflections, whereas Willie follows the orders that come from Winnie. Three critical instances where the man 'looks at his hands' reflect the final poignant moment in *Happy Days* where Willie is arrested in a spasm of longing.[59] Both examples of the reduction of the pantomime mode do not naturalize mime as a result of deconstruction. Both roles present a new choreography; what stems from pantomime is this demand to perform the mimetic field to the performer's utmost capacity ironically portraying an underlying poverty of real agency. Such an irony lies within the act without words concept itself. Beckett's experiment in pantomime exposes an underlying poverty within the capacities of mimicry as it is conventionally understood.

So, while the popular genre of mime might seem to trust all too much in the mimetic possibilities of the human performer, the flip side is the Beckettian pantomime: a discipline of practised contradictoriness exposing the limits of physical simulation. Beckett's diagrammed choreographies present a virtuosic and heartfelt exhibition of human limitation as a result. The acts without words and, we shall see, Clov's opening mime, share with the Willie role an acting situation exposed to the nothingness at the heart of mimetic simulation. This is pantomime exposing its own mimetic vacuity. In this way, Beckettian pantomime marks a sort of human grace(lessness) vainly seeking out its own apotheosis; in other words, Willie seeking out his loved one, Winnie. *Happy Days* is no mere parody of pantomime for physical and visual effect. The work constitutes an act of transformed praxis. Through Beckettian pantomime, theatricality is brought to a limit point that exposes the terms of simulation. In so doing, this dramaturgical practice ennobles those frailties of human mimesis in the performance event. The debasement of Willie's humanity is also Willie's performative being, vainly striving for Winnie. Moreover, Willie's striving is also Winnie's happy day. Presumably, this physical performance is also the sympathetic spectator's happy day too.

'Gone from refuge'

AWW I followed *Fin de partie* in the George Devine-directed premiere of the latter at the Royal Court Theatre in London on the 3 April 1957, a stage and publication trend that would become a tradition many years later.[60] This interconnectedness of the two works testifies to a shared theatrical task. Naito explains that Beckett would view this act without words a 'codicil', or appended supplement, to the evening's event:

> In [a] letter [to Barney Rosset], he described *Act Without Words I* as 'in some obscure way, a codicil to *End-Game*, and as such requires that this last extremity of human meat – or bones – be there, thinking and stumbling and sweating, under our noses, like Clov about Hamm, *but gone from refuge*'. It is this idea – the possibility of using the stage to experiment with 'human meat,' or the body – that Beckett took from his mimes and applied in *Endgame*.[61]

In a sense, the man in the desert in *AWW I* is Clov taken from his 'refuge'. But we are not accustomed to estimating the codicil's significance with anything comparable to the play that it followed at the Royal Court. To better gauge the dramaturgical value of *AWW I* and *II*, it is critical that we move away from one vein of modernist thinking about Beckett dramaturgy: that Beckett's roles present examples of the ironic anti-clown. I fear that some readers might still be unclear about the discussion of irony and the pantomime figure discussed heretofore given that deconstruction can be understood with different degrees of opposition to the modality to which it has been applied. There is a critical history here that must be attended to such that my account of Beckett's diagrammatic urge towards physical performance can be distinguished from existing accounts of Beckettian theatricality and pantomime. Also, elements of existing accounts nonetheless have enormous value in the context of charting this dramaturgical practice.

Theodor Adorno's disquisition on *Endgame* presents the exemplary demonstration of the ironic anti-clown account of the Beckett figure. Adorno's view of modernist theatre comprehends this paradigm of theatre as existing in explicit hostility towards traditions of theatricality associated with pantomime; pantomime extends the logic that 'in the similarity of clowns to animals the likeness of humans to apes flashes up; the constellation animal/fool/clown is a fundamental layer of art'.[62] Adorno characterizes Beckett as the exemplary case of a modernist who uses parody to expose the post-war absurdity of this strain of popular stage mimesis reproducing the 'animal/fool/clown' model of mimesis, what Martin Puchner summarizes as 'apish mimesis'.[63] In Adorno's reckoning, then, Clov in this play represents a melancholy instantiation of the clown made alert to his own post-human condition. Quoting Adorno, Puchner elaborates that this view means that

> 'what android apes perform in the zoo collectively resembles acts of clowns'. ... [For Adorno, art] must never begin to sacrifice its constructive distance from this apish mimesis. ... Adorno's ape functions as the icon of a prehistoric mimesis, not just outside art but before art even began.[64]

Mime, like aping – in both senses of the word – entrusts faith in the powers of gestural mimesis. Such faith stands as an obstacle to modernism's hostility to popular culture, capitalism and the autonomy available to art's resistance to normative cultural logics of modernity in the view of modernism. While allied qualities can be found in the Beckett spectacle, and Adorno's reading of *Endgame* continues to be a useful way to think about the historical place of Beckettian dramaturgy, I believe there is more to the use of pantomime in Beckettian dramaturgy than hostile parody and anti-theatricalism. In other words, I endorse the idea that Beckett explores the ironies of 'apish mimesis' while at the same time resisting the idea that Beckett simply opposes this modality. I think Beckett may have relied on the physical practice undergirding pantomime for developing his practice more than Adorno gives it credit for.

Thinking back to Barrault in *Happy Days* in its final tableau, I certainly struggle to think of the image as the representation of an artist disdainful of a 'prehistoric' mimetic root. To nuance this debate, I would suggest that moments such as *Happy Days*' final tableau make a resource of the powers of virtualization in the actor in an unforeseeable situation of self-reflexive, metatheatrical crisis. It is a moment of poignant deconstruction that discovers something in mimetic simulation rather than an act of negation. The tableau – the concealed Barrault – does not simply render negative those powers, ridicule them or aspire to their annihilation. Instead, the mime can no longer refer to a world of infinite possibility. They and their tableau now make a fragilely happy day of separation and enigma in a post-crisis world of self-simulation. *Happy Days* has a place in the history of avant-garde physical theatre as a result, making profound use of the otherwise mainstream figure of Barrault. *Happy Days* is not simply a death knell to pantomime.

Similarly, Puchner has observed how Lucky's dance in Beckett's best-known play, *Waiting for Godot*, presents popular dance in the form of 'bare remnants of a once glorious art'. Puchner surmises that what results from this decreated dance is a 'human figure advanced by the anti-theatrical theatre'.[65] Lucky's parodic entanglement with pantomime differs in my view to Clov's in *Endgame*, the latter relying less on an incorporated anti-pantomime than a diagrammatic extrapolation from the practice. Lucky's entanglement with pantomime more obviously belongs to the parodic camp that Adorno, and Puchner after him, seeks to illustrate. Indeed, Lucky's entanglement has more to do with the aesthetic of vaudeville, the primary spectacle of pantomime from the nineteenth century until the cinema age, than the choreography that we find in *Endgame* and *Happy Days*. I want to visit this case to help clarify how choreographies of Lucky and Clov ultimately differ in their relation to the tradition of pantomime.

Puchner's brilliant account of *Godot*'s inglorious pantomime in Lucky's dance helps us to understand what is parodic in the Lucky role. Lucky's twice-repeated dance evidently fails to meet the standard of past, supposedly joyful achievements at a repertoire of dances, 'the farandole, the fling, the brawl, the jig, the fandango, and even the hornpipe', in the words of his master, Pozzo. Rather, Lucky's dance receives the comic designations 'The Scapegoat's Agony' and 'The Hard Stool' from Estragon and Vladimir, respectively, complementing the absurd names of popular dance forms to emphasize a comparative abjection.[66] The theme again is theatrical confinement; Pozzo bleakly replies to these suggestions that the dance should be named 'The Net. [Lucky] thinks he's entangled in a net'.[67] Such slapstick-reminiscent passages of dialogue are part of a parodic, metatheatrical preamble to Lucky's well-known logorrhoeic speech. The same speech is notable for transforming a role that, until this point in *Act One*, has essentially been a mime role without spoken word.

Lucky's dance constitutes an abject parody of the vaudeville strain of pantomime. Charlie Chaplin and Buster Keaton in film's silent era represent pantomime's next chapter after vaudeville, migrated to the next popular spectacle, silent film, followed by a further transformation in the talking pictures exemplified by Laurel and Hardy and the Marx Brothers and eventually destined for television. All these screen icons had careers on the vaudeville stage. What has been altered of the pantomime practice in *Godot* has screen vaudeville of this kind for its source. Note one curious alteration to *Godot* in the American television adaptation directed by Alan Schneider and broadcast in April 1961, featuring the original Pozzo (Kurt Kasznar) and Lucky (Alvin Epstein) from his Broadway production of 1956, a production that had featured vaudeville figure and *The Wizard of Oz*'s Cowardly Lion star, Bert Lahr.[68] The following alteration draws attention to this section of the play's particular reliance on metacommentary for Beckett's self-parody to remain perspicuous on screen; I score out the original and add the alteration:

VLADIMIR: Charming evening we're having.
ESTRAGON: Unforgettable
VLADIMIR: And it's not over.
ESTRAGON: Apparently not.
VLADIMIR: It's only beginning.
ESTRAGON: It's awful.
VLADIMIR: Worse than ~~the pantomime~~ TV.
ESTRAGON: The circus.
VLADIMIR: The music-hall.
ESTRAGON: The circus.[69]

Beckett again problematizes spectacle with a meta-commentary inflected towards the medium of confinement. Where in the Adorno paradigm of modernism we would no doubt designate this as a patent example of anti-theatricalism, I would rather emphasize the experiment in self-effacement involved that must be achieved with a particular application of medium. Indeed, the remark is too soon in the history of television to be considered anti-television. Rather, as I have argued thus far, the object of deconstruction is once again mimesis as such, an act of representation mediated most of all by the performing body. Vladimir and Estragon's dialogue comprises self-mockery and cruel retort towards the spectator who will simultaneously be amused at the music-hallish antics happening before their eyes. The scenario is deeply reliant on pantomime to achieve this disturbing yet comic recursive effect, as the television production too can only render this passage by making special use of the medium as Burgess Meredith makes his parabasis, or direct address, by looking down the lens of the camera at us as he intones 'Worse than TV'.

Similarly, Pozzo's rope, the tool used to enforce Lucky's performances, represents an exposure of the tools of spectacle-making concerned in this hyper-consciousness of medium. This rope literally commands performance. It is a precursor to the dangled props of *AWW I* and the goad of *AWW II*. Lucky's 'Net' dance amounts to a self-reflexive literalization of constraint to pantomimic spectacle. Lucky's brief and futile escape from that entanglement too highlights pantomime's collusion in the character's entrapment. Yoshiki Tajiri suggests that Lucky's manic escape from muteness not only proves to be 'a parody of academic writing' in its verbose nonsense, but in all likelihood echoes 'a mechanical figure ... inspired, consciously or unconsciously, by the broken phonograph in the Marx Brothers' film *Duck Soup* (1933)'.[70] Given that the broken machine lacks a hat, this echo of the Marx Brothers only makes sense seen in tandem with another echo from *Duck Soup*, the trading of hats gag in which Harpo and Chico jest with a disgruntled lemonade vendor. The routine has been lifted from the modern pantomime record and arguably made even funnier in *Godot* in Act Two given how extreme the latter's mechanical logic is. The comic repetition in *Godot* threatens to repeat interminably and not merely for the duration of the gag. Beckett's humour lies in its high existential stakes, imagining a world in which a figure like Harpo becomes the new Sisyphus.

As Andrew Stott observes, slapstick follows Henri Bergson's notion of comedy as the exploration of resemblances of the human subject to objects. The highlights in slapstick's history, Stott argues, often involve 'fraught interactions between the human and the machine'.[71] Normand Berlin, who was present at the 1956 production at the Golden Theater, similarly views the achievement of *Godot* as an exposed vaudeville spectacle.[72] Spectacle undergoes a rendering in *Godot* that makes explicit the fact that spectacle constitutes a threat to the biomechanical sovereignty of the performing subject, exemplified by Lucky's entanglement in pantomime. Indeed, spectacle stands for the obverse of this biomechanical sovereignty. Such sovereignty, an apparently precious quantity, ironically comes to signal the human's physical limitations and mortal finitude. While parody dominates *Godot*, we glimpse a dramaturgical trajectory out of parody in the various refinements of pantomime that reshape gags into whole choreographic practices of movement. This direction will amount to a principally experimental approach to choreography in which parody has largely been forgot. This choreography will culminate in Clov's opening mime, implicated in the fraught presentation of failed mechanicity reminiscent of physical comedy from the first half of the twentieth century from which Beckett lifted routines.

Pantomime has been the fraught centre of theories of theatrical mimesis since symbolism. Beckett, in casting mime in a choreography of the genre examining itself in recursion, inevitably positions himself in the history of avant-garde theatre following this pantomimic thread. The same thread once captured the major figure of symbolist beginnings of modernism in the work of Stephane Mallarmé. *AWW I*'s man has been rendered somewhat like Mallarmé's Pierrot of silence in *Mimique*, 'a pure medium' '*under the false appearance of a present*'.[73] Jacques Derrida's complex braiding of a discussion of this text with material from Mallarmé's unfinished *Livre*, the exemplary case of modernist closet drama for Puchner, presents the contention that self-reference in mime constitutes an influential conceptualization of simulacrum and simulation:

> We are faced then with mimicry imitating nothing ... It is in this that the mime's operation does allude, but alludes to nothing, alludes without breaking the mirror, without reaching beyond the looking-glass. '*That is law the Mime operates, whose act is confined to a perpetual allusion without breaking the ice or the mirror.*' This speculum reflects no reality; it produces mere 'reality-effects'. For this double that often makes one think of Hoffmann (mentioned by Beissier in his Preface), reality, indeed, is death. ... In this speculum with no reality, in this mirror of a mirror, a difference or dyad does exist, since there are mimes and phantoms. But it is a difference without reference, or rather a reference without a referent, without any first or last unit, a ghost that is the phantom of no flesh, wandering about without a past, without any death, birth, or presence. Mallarme thus preserves the differential structure of mimicry or *mimēsis*, but without its Platonic or metaphysical interpretation, which implies that somewhere the being of something that *is*, is being imitated.[74]

Mallarmé's pure medium in the figure of the mime appears as 'a ghost that is the phantom of no flesh'. Such a mime, standing for nothing but simulation, lies at the antipodes of Beckett's self-exposed mimic. The latter remains a living creature of spectacle finding himself performing a mimetic act that refers to the very base materiality of his own performance *of performance*. This conclusion, poised as a comment on the relation between spectacle and human representation, concords with Joseph Anderton's exploration of the Beckett human creature as 'an anti-humanist figure that emerges from a ruined humanist ideal'.[75] Such a presentation could be terribly pretentious in a less meticulous dramatist's hands. However, Beckett's pantomime can contain such provocation about mimesis in one mere gesture of reflection. That is what makes Beckett a subtle and untendentious experimentalist. The problem of theatricality has been magnified in Beckett's exposed pantomime.

Crucially, Beckett *affirms* the material figure that stands in for mimetic (im)possibility – the unpainted clowns of the acts without words, Barrault playing Willie, or the footfall that emerges from a mathematical formula – where Mallarmé imagines the other end of the spectrum, the phantom. Mallarmé concerns himself with *the concept of the mime* where Beckett develops a dramaturgy that practices the paradoxes of physical mimicry. In the acts without words, it is as if Beckett has confronted Mallarmé's mime with Simone Weil's conception of death: 'To love truth means to endure the void and, as a result, to accept death. Truth is on the side of death'.[76] The exposed mime is the real, dying mime, not the infinite play of simulation dreamt of in symbolism.

In this sense, Derrida's ingenious account of Mallarmé's pure mime suggests that the discipline of pantomime remains relevant to the physical and gestural economy of theatrical modernity and cannot be as easily dismissed as Adorno wished to. Beckett's deconstruction of mime enlists the discipline for more than the representation of an apish minimum. Pantomime represents a field of meta-mimicry that simulates mimesis and allegorizes simulation itself when drawn to self-examination. When a mime mimics, they mimic acting, whereas naturalistic acting makes no 'allusion', to adopt Derrida's term, to the act of mimesis. According to Samuel Weber, 'for a mime that *dares to speak* is no longer a mime – unless, of course, he mimes speaking'.[77] The repeal of pure mimesis is the assertion of live materiality, in other words, and the same inversion is fated for the opposite logic; the repeal of live materiality asserts the purely mimetic. Beckett exposes this fascinating paradox of the mimetic problem of the mime with plays that deliberately choreograph logics of movement and gesture that deconstruct and problematize the idealism of pure virtuality such that a hole emerges in it, a hole with contingent meaning for the spectator. The man of *AWW I* mimics the factual liveness of the mime, and such circular dramaturgical logic means that the Beckett mime terminates his self-exploration 'look[ing] at his hands'. The crux of Beckett's laboratory endeavour with performance begins with this enigma of the simulated within the unsimulated, a paradoxical avenue for theatricality after the death of faith in stage mimesis that most contemporary audiences will bring to a contemporary act of mimesis. Beckett's theatre shows that when no one believes in the mime any longer, this discipline's gestures and modalities can come to stand for the raw facticity of the subject's nonetheless ongoing practice of self-simulation.

2

Sensory deprivation

During rehearsals for the 1973 British premiere of Samuel Beckett's *Not I* (1972), actor Billie Whitelaw collapsed. Whitelaw: 'If you are blindfolded and have a hood over your face, you hyperventilate, you suffer from sensory deprivation … [As a result,] I hung on and hung on until I couldn't any longer. I just went to pieces because I was convinced I was like an astronaut tumbling out into space'.[1] Whitelaw's experience of sensory deprivation while rehearsing a play designed for her incarnation constitutes an event in Beckett's dramaturgical practice and so deserves special consideration in any history of his practice. In this episode of his career, I want to suggest that the writer learns that text can intervene into the voice's array of capacities to amplify script, and that text can broker new realizations of verbal art. As I will show, this experience compels the writer to explore the production of new apparitions in a live, haunted spectacle. This principal event in the Beckett-Whitelaw collaboration would come to enable some of the writer's most significant self-transformations.

In Beckett's work with Whitelaw, we see theatre reimagined as a tremendous resonating chamber of voice and script. The floating monologist of *Not I* is a mouth. She is a metonym of voice severed from the body and thus from the assumed unity the two usually make in the performing body, 'only her mouth could move', writes Zoe Ingalls.[2] Whitelaw's collapse from deprivational elements while rehearsing this part indicates that Beckett's late plays, written after the 1960s, proceed following a particular dramaturgical logic of sensory experiment conducted by deprivation. Importantly, such processes do not necessarily entail physical or mental suffering, like some kind of extreme method acting practice. Nor does sensory deprivation's obvious employment here, while exemplified by the Whitelaw episode, suggest that Whitelaw's own version establishes a fixed model for other actors to realize. While future actors have much to learn from Whitelaw's incarnation, I wish to expose aspects of Beckettian dramaturgy brought into relief by this collaboration rather than laud a particular example. This chapter interrogates a dramaturgical procedure tied up with the British premiere that came to modify the writer's own approach to theatre-making and in which Whitelaw was a critical collaborator. Additionally, the value of constraint as a precondition of the Beckett role receives clarification in an analysis of this episode. Whitelaw's commentary on her work with Beckett in *Not I* and two other roles that he wrote for her to play, *Footfalls*'s May (1976) and *Rockaby*'s woman (divided between W and V) (1981), together with the archive of her performances, are central to understanding not only the writer's dramaturgy but also the development of theatrical innovations in sensation and in the actor's craft that follow. I analyse the particular case of Billie Whitelaw's tumultuous rehearsal period for *Not I* as an exemplary case study for understanding Beckett's experimentation with theatre's compositional possibilities regarding sensation and sensorium. Studying the collaborative event of the plays most associated with Whitelaw exposes related questions of liveness and corporeality in post-1960s theatre in which sensory deprivation becomes the mutual circumstance of both spectator and performer. Whitelaw becomes a medium, a witness and an event to observe in the story of Beckett's changing dramaturgical direction.

Writing for Whitelaw

Billie Whitelaw, an English actor who became one of the most highly regarded performers of Beckett's theatre, was discovered by the writer as a collaborator of interest more than ten years before he wrote *Not I* in 1972. Whitelaw's voice was already stirring in Beckett's brain after he had seen her in a George Devine production of *Play* (1963) that ran from 1963 to 1965. Whitelaw recalls that

> [Beckett] had for some reason carried the sound of my voice around in his head – not my normal voice, but the voice I used in *Play*. Apparently, when he wrote *Not I* that was the voice he heard. … [A]ccording to Calder he wanted me and nobody else.[3]

The world premiere would not be realized by Whitelaw, but rather by Jessica Tandy in New York in a co-directed production involving Beckett's trusted American director, Alan Schneider, also featuring Tandy's husband, Hume Cronyn, on 22 November 1972. Nevertheless, Whitelaw's voice shaped Beckett's creation of the role. Indeed, *Eh Joe* (1966), a screenplay for television, was the first role that he had Whitelaw explicitly in mind for. It was after hearing Whitelaw in *Play*, a fast-paced work in which a spotlight conducts three figures whose heads protrude from urns to speak, that Beckett's subsequent plays engage in experiments in sensory deprivation.

Decollation of the conventional theatrical role begins this direction towards sensory deprivation, then, Whitelaw's voice emanating from a head above an urn. *Eh Joe* follows, her voice severed from the speaking body no longer a problem of liveness since all is antedated in severance in a television work featuring recorded voice. *Eh Joe* features Jack MacGowran in the role of Joe and was Beckett's intended medium for the Joe role, yet another mime role,[4] shaped almost entirely by the activity of mute listening. Yet, Whitelaw would not be available to play the Woman, and so Siân Phillips took the voice role. Whitelaw would not feature as the Woman until some years later, in 1989 under Walter Asmus's direction, with Beckett's favourite German mime – therefore a frequent Lucky – Klaus Herm.

The live decapitations really begin in *Happy Days* (1961), a role that Whitelaw would receive acclaim for her performance in 1979. Once again, this is a play featuring the theatre apparatus as a conductor. Now an alarm bell commands the transitions of activity in the work. These commands Winnie describes as 'hurt[ing] like a knife'.[5] But, once Beckett composes a live experiment explicitly for Whitelaw in 1972, the sensory outcomes of his theatre expand the excisions of role to excisions of the domain of spectatorship. The expansion of the terms of sensory deprivation to entail a shared immersement in the diminutized condition that results becomes the next stage exemplified by *Not I*. Not mounds or urns alone enclose, in other words, but a shared theatrical confinement comes to envelop all. Such is not torture or painful or even necessarily uncomfortable, at least in the case of these three plays' sensoriums. Rather, we will observe how sensory deprivation comes to heighten a sense of medium. Sensory deprivation intensifies live theatre's capacity to focalize. Winnie embedded in a hill is only an entrance into stark diminutions best associated with these three Whitelaw plays. The late theatre, for which Whitelaw stands as a sort of icon, involves more than mere happenstance collaborations. Rather, these examples demonstrate an applied experimental investment in sensation deprivation with figural and spectatorial ramifications for the medium of theatre that enables a revolution in the Beckett theatre's approach to the performer.

We saw in Chapter 1 how choreographic advents in Beckettian dramaturgy enabled the dramatically narrow choreography of *Footfalls*; in this chapter, we will have the opportunity to combine that perspective with a theory of sensory deprivation in dramaturgy. Indeed, Billie Whitelaw enables Beckett to discover a vocal dexterity and estrangement from naturalistic principles of vocal performance that will be solicited in later works. The practice of acting Beckett, we have seen, adheres neither to the institutionalized American psychological realism of the actor we call method acting, nor to devised-theatrical methodologies coming from Europe in the 1960s after

Jerzy Grotowski. Rather, as Worthen describes: 'Beckett's roles require of the actor an extraordinarily negative athleticism, the ability to endure a cramped and fatiguing stasis that reflects the restraints of Beckett's characteristically repetitive and inconsequential language'.[6] We might build from Worthen's notion of a 'negative athleticism' by engaging in a study of theatrical constraint, the problem that negative athleticism must extrapolate from. Whitelaw's acting develops strategies of movement, gesture, tone and repetition that insinuate through corporeal constraint and deprivation a haunting figural quality projecting affects of confinement to the sensorium. This projection renders supple the divide between audience and spectacle such that character predicament becomes a matter of shared sensory experience.

Let us now look carefully at the dramaturgical construction of sensory deprivation. The dramas written for Whitelaw have highly particular sensory-depriving requirements for spectacle. First, the floating monologist of *Not I* is a mouth suspended in the dark. To achieve this live image, it requires some form of an apparatus that will produce a still image. The Anthony Page production employed head clamps and suspended rostrum to enable Whitelaw to realize its distinct stage image, as shown on the cover of this book. The mouth role comprises a disembodiment and an isolation of voice from body realized by medial experimentation. Such dramaturgical investigations tie in with an affective renovation of theatricality's ends. Beckett's writing for Whitelaw signals an expansion of the affective possibilities of spectacle-making through an isolation of the actor as the problematic collision point of text and apparatus. Sensory deprivation also shows that affects concern our limitations and restrictions as human beings as much as enlargements and magnifications of our endowments. Affect provides the means for speaking of disembodiment not as an ideal, but rather as a procedure. In this way, exploring the affective ends of sensory deprivation enables us to rethink how disembodiment has been read in Beckett studies in the past. Two prevailing approaches that have some bearing on the discussion of disembodiment include the 'mind as the stage' model associated with the theatre of the absurd, and the notion of Beckett's dramaturgy as a new form of theatrical symbolism.[7] The latter I will debate in earnest in Chapter 3. Theatre's capacity for rendering an affective 'resonating chamber', to quote Brian Massumi, can in Beckett's work be charted in terms of the dramaturgy's blueprint-like strictness.[8] On the other hand, the actor's inflections of the affective specificities of this space composed for the installation of performance become the second layer of our concern in observing the behaviour of affect in its theatrical resonance.

Disembodiment has some value for phenomenological approaches to discussing Beckettian dramaturgy. Anna McMullan in *Performing Embodiment in Samuel Beckett's Drama*, for example, describes aesthetic strategies of disembodiment as practices that 'test the boundaries of embodiment in the theatre'.[9] Stanton B. Garner Jr. and Bert O. States are among the most prominent of theatre studies critics to foreground phenomenological perspectives on modern theatre, including Beckett, with the work of Maurice Merleau-Ponty situated prominently; McMullan applies this preference to a committed analysis of Beckett.[10] Here, Beckett becomes an exemplar of the apparitional ends of consciousness explained by phenomenology in its interest in subjective phenomena such as phantom limbs. We will look at these applications to Beckett in a moment. What such discussions attempt to demonstrate in sum is that the phenomenological approach to discussing modern theatre validates its long-standing interest in the re-enactment of phenomena in haunting form, phenomena which Marvin Carlson argues habitually 'return, that appear again *tonight*', an extension of apparitions that arise from human perception in general.[11]

Disembodiment can also be understood as a consequence of the diminution of form as much as the re-enactment of phenomenological experience in distilled form. Deleuze's important essay on Samuel Beckett, 'The Exhausted', conjectures that the writer's compositional play with medium both exhausts form and materializes exhausted forms, from colour in the visual field to the reservoir of energy in the performing body. For Deleuze, the objective becomes a refinement of representation towards a singular 'pure and unsullied image, one that is nothing but an image'.[12] I am concerned that Deleuze's theory puts exorbitant emphasis upon the visual domain, when in fact the sensory experimentation of this writer in live space evidently concerns the total sensorium. Whitelaw's collapse will confirm this difference, since her experience details how the Mouth role completely absorbed her to the point of vertigo. Moreover, I hope to show how this vertigo proves to be an infectious dimension of the spectators' experience of the play and an effect of an array of reconfigurations of sensory experience in performance, from tone, to volume, to diction, to the challenge of focusing upon a small lit object. Beckett's dramatic pursuit of unsullied theatrical sensation I agree is exhaustive in the Deleuzian sense. But I want to draw that visually focused argument into the context of theatre mechanics, dramaturgy, the body and spectatorship, such that we retain the value of performativity in experiments composed as deliberate challenges to the performing body. Performativity, and not screen culture, is what I view as the central determining force of these compositions.

Familiar to Beckett scholars is the aesthetic of negation.[13] Whitelaw's illuminating accounts found in *Beckett Remembering, Remembering Beckett* by Knowlson and Knowlson, and in her autobiography *Billie Whitelaw... Who He?* (1995), chronicle an extraordinary subtractive achievement with acting in what can best be described as a process of self-exposure through

Beckettian dramaturgy. Whitelaw's anecdotal contributions to this discussion draw attention to the reciprocity between the actor-vessel of sense and the problematics of a theatrical text that together come to define the theatre's 'fictive cosmos'.[14] Studying the actor exposes the somatic registration of a performance experiment also. Before conducting that analysis in earnest, I must acknowledge Steven Connor's caution about interpreter-centric readings of Beckett actors. Connor calls such readings 'tautologous', since they can incoherently suggest that the Beckett actor-collaborator discovers the freedom to do Beckett's necessary bidding.[15] A critic, in deifying a particular actor, produces an untenably tautological dramaturgical assertion about acting if they present the Beckett actor as a clairvoyant or virtuosic interpreter of an acting paradigm that at the same time forecloses the exertion of the actor's will. Indeed. I don't want to offer an account of Whitelaw's collaborations with Beckett in an effort to reinstate an ideal authorial intent or standard that can be extrapolated from the Whitelaw way of realizing Beckett. Nor do I wish to mythologize her personal closeness to the author as if contact with Beckett were some kind of charmed conduction of practice, either. The myth of personal closeness, Connor suggests, participates in a discourse of Beckett in which the writer becomes 'a myth, which can be articulated unpleasantly around mysticisms and the power that they can enshrine'.[16] I resist these options in my treatment of the Beckett-Whitelaw collaboration. For me, Whitelaw exposes a very particular affective experience of working on numerous productions of these plays. In turn, in their exposure of somatic detail and aspects of the actor's craft shaped by Beckettian material, these cases suggest that theatrical composition for Beckett by the 1970s had become an experiment profoundly concerned with sensory constraint. The actor's experience of this constraint draws into relief Peggy Phelan's concept of Beckett's mise-en-scène as a spectacle of 'seeing the unsighted ... the drama of sight', since the effects of deprivation such as vertiginous disembodiment become a dramaturgical as well as anecdotal dimension of this work.[17] Phelan's premise that spectators *feel* the paradoxical *unseeing* of the stage figure in a Beckett play is underscored by this notable actor's feeling of the act of rendering that unseeing. Like Phelan, I view these effects as part of a construction shaping an affective experience in which unseeing can be felt by spectator and performer together.

The soma of *Not I*

Play was first performed in German as *Spiel*, produced in English for the first time at the Old Vic in London in 1963. S. E. Gontarski positions *Play* as an important event in the writer's discovery of the visual field of the theatre. To introduce the short, more experimental plays of Beckett, Gontarski writes:

> With *Play* Beckett's theatre finally grew more static than active, more lyric than dramatic. ... The change is evident to anyone who has tried to read *Play, Breath, Come and Go, Ghost Trio,* ... *but the clouds* ... or especially *Quad* without access to productions. On the page, without the full visual counterpart, the works are denuded, skeletal, finally unreadable – in any traditional sense, that is, if by unreadable we mean to suggest that their primary effect is extra-linguistic.[18]

Pursuit of the extra-linguistic may be the motivation behind the diagrammatic turn in Beckett's writing explored in Chapter 1. In the post-*Play* dramaturgical paradigm of the Whitelaw plays, compositional constraint has the added value of compelling sensory deprivation most notably concerning the domain of actor mobility. *Play*'s decollation of the actors in the visual field represents part of this emerging practice. Speaking to James Knowlson, Whitelaw's account of *Play*'s shifting spotlight that cues each actors' speech she describes as 'an instrument of torture'.[19] As Angela Moorjani delineates, such an instrument applies to the different levels of live spectacle:

> (1) on the literal level, it is a mechanical spotlight; (2) on the social level, it functions as a tormentor; (3) on the psychic plane, it calls to mind a self-observing eye/I, and (4) in the anagogical realm of myth or religion, it conjures up a diabolical or divine creator-judge.[20]

The conventional spotlight thus comes to connote, in the context of *Play*, an inhuman commander and omniscient judge under whose authority characters have no recourse to silence. In this sense, Pozzo's rope has been reincarnated as the power of light, enjoying a far greater existential endowment and reach as a result. Thus Mouth in *Not I* represents the decapitational logic taken to a new extreme. Here, the light that commands performance is unwavering and the performer's head is no longer (visually) required; the mouth is sufficient to render this stage effect. In complementary fashion, Mouth's monologue presents a character tethered to a tortuous, interminable recounting of a narrative which Mouth refuses to bring to light. The play provides even less suggestion of an exterior world than that suggested in the spare narrative of adultery governing the verbalized drama of the urn-bound creatures of *Play*. Decollation is a performative reality with profound characterological and narrative consequences as much as an image.

Escape is again imagined in the narrative. Skirted by defiant paroxysm, it is never consummated. Indeed, it is through evasion that monologue's disjunctive form is realized. That is, the monologue is of course *not* the *I*. It starts and ends as a frenetic first-person narration propelled by dint of the evasion of the personal pronoun. Voice's presence too undergoes magnification by virtue of its paradoxical decollation, as her name suggests. The mouth's unnatural height and suspension in darkness emphasizes this experimental separation from physical, phenomenological and naturalistic dramatic norms; '8 feet above stage level' as it is written in the text.[21] High enough to avoid suggesting a full-bodied person standing in the dark. Still apparently a creature deducted from human affairs, Mouth does not suggest a mythic fantasy of non-human being either. Notably, in the original, unrevised text, Mouth is accompanied by a silent cloaked form, the Auditor, who stands to the rear and obliquely raises their arms during the course of the play. The Beckett mime here has become not only mute but faceless. Since Beckett amended the play to omit the Auditor, we can see that he was drawn to cut whole figures from his plays subsequent to experiments in the theatre.

Hans-Thies Lehmann in his treatise on the reconfiguration of drama in the postmodern context proposes that contemporary theatre has been shaped by a post-dramatic turn in which medium rather than text orients it. What this means is a release from the obligation to illustrate literature and instead draw attention to the practices of the performing arts themselves. Contemporary theatrical invention for Lehmann proves to be most influential in those cases where extra-literary dimensions of the materiality of spectacle have been most radically altered.[22] The kinds of experiment we see *Not I* exemplifying accord with the extra-literary concerns of post-dramatic theatre. *Not I*'s innovative liveness has an ineluctable sound component, for example, that, again, thanks to a dramaturgical experiment in maximizing decreation and physical isolation, amplifies the actor's vocal art beyond the conventional representational obligations of drama. Lehmann asserts that the new focus upon sensorium is thereby concerned as much with sound as much as vision and kinesis; theatre can be '[a] *disposition of spaces of meaning and sound-spaces* [on the postdramatic stage]'.[23] Beckett's *Not I* soundscape is one example among numerous cases of altering the theatre sensorium in the composition itself. Beckett's practice of sensory deprivation presages the contemporary postdramatic preference for scenographic and mechanical experiment of the kind we find sublimated in the aesthetics of Robert Wilson, Claude Régy or the Berliner Ensemble. Such practices are often defined by the reshaping of theatre architecture such that the scopic and sensorial norms of spectacle are rearranged. Where figures such as Wilson have explored adaptational and collage textual approaches to achieving such a theatrical art, Beckett shows that writers too can make similarly radical interventions.

This play's relation to postdramatic theatre suggests that the soundscape of *Not I* deserves extended dramaturgical analysis. *Not I* demonstrates the moment in the Beckett oeuvre in which the theatre is given due prominence as a 'sound-space', a space in which voice as transmitter of text is magnified. Whitelaw is key to exposing the role of this dimension of the work. With Whitelaw, voice comes to enable sensation deprivation through a cultivated ghoulishness that also establishes a compelling vocal practice that is practiced and embodied. Consider another of Whitelaw's anecdotes in this light. The following statement comes from the actor's reflections on remarks made by Jocelyn Herbert in *Theatre Workbook*, Herbert being a veteran designer on Beckett productions, including the British premiere of *Not I*: 'In her book, Jocelyn quotes Sam as saying: "When we were doing *Not I*, Anthony Page wanted it to go slower, but Billie and I won".'[24] The importance of this remark lies in demonstrating that Whitelaw and Beckett collaborated on the sound-space of this work, emphasizing speed that had not been anticipated in the writer's early forecasts of the duration of the play in production and faster than the play had been with Tandy. In the autobiography, Whitelaw makes additional mention of the emotive intimacy with this work that such collaboration meant. Such intimacy, like all intimacy, perhaps, had a somatic price:

> I didn't realise until much later that with the two seasons of *Not I*, I had inflamed an already damaged spine and neck. Performing in that play, all the tension that went to the back of my neck also aggravated the vertigo and nausea I'd had in my early twenties. I'd come to terms with this: the damage is something I'm stuck with. In fact, every play I did with Beckett left a little legacy behind in my state of ill-health, a price I have most willingly paid.[25]

From her perspective, Whitelaw achieved the specificities of these experimental works in a body-altering embodiment of the extraordinary attributes required for the vocal accomplishment of *Not I*. Of course, Whitelaw does not speak of the same challenges later on in production runs of these works, nor of future productions; the point is determinedly *not* that one must suffer to render these plays. Rather, Whitelaw chronicles an experience that could be characterized following Worthen as 'negative athleticism'. This athleticism involves subtraction and focalization that, like most examples of athleticism, involves degrees of adjustment, modification, practice, repetition and unpredictable somatic consequences in developing the muscularity required for the effort. Moreover, such encounters within the orbit of negative athleticism are implicated with the original 'vehement refusal of third person' premised in the script.[26] Such was a matter which Beckett and Whitelaw determined would require an inhuman velocity that at first seemed impossible. About her next major collaborations with the writer, Whitelaw remarks: 'In *Footfalls* he had told me: "Don't be too earthbound", as though the character's voice was not quite of this world. In *Rockaby*, he had told me right away to make the voice monotonous, like a lullaby'.[27] Disembodiment and monotony entail non-naturalistic and extra-linguistic achievements in vocality mirrored in the visual disembodiments found in the dramaturgy as modelled in the script. Together, a sensorium involving the sensory deprivation of the body placed in saturating darkness becomes the effect. As a consequence, we must view these records involving Whitelaw as a form of somatic, affective witness to developments in Beckettian dramaturgy. Such accounts corroborate a theory of Beckett's late theatre as an act of sensory deprivation. The profound somatic consequences of practising the dramaturgy mean a practice developing a new orientation in the sensory immersiveness of theatre.

The figural ends of this sensation-depriving experimentation are stark. McMullan sees the theatrical milieu of fragmented bodies associated with late plays such as *Not I* as a 'post-human context ... primarily associated with the increasing integration of humans and technology'.[28] For McMullan, Beckett's disembodying practice of the body is indicative of something original to the subject, following the phenomenology of Merleau-Ponty; Beckett highlights the 'incarnate subjectivity of the human body ... never coincident with the world itself'.[29] Ulrika Maude in 'The Body of Memory' similarly finds in the Beckett imaginary apparitions resembling the Merleau-Pontian concept of an incarnate incorporeality. Maude argues that 'Beckett grounds the very basics of subjectivity ... firmly in the body' as Merleau-Pontian phenomenology too bases subjectivity.[30] This line of inquiry provides one philosophical explanation for the dramaturgy of disembodiment in Beckett's late theatre. In such a view, Beckett's apparitional aesthetic serves to explore the strange figural and somatic ramifications of human subjectivity understood in its most rudimentary form. Beckett in this view reshapes character to present the true circumstances of the subject as the haunted perceiver whose own originary subjectivity, so often entangled in problematics of memory, remains life's enigma. Both Maude and McMullan's accounts evoke clinical settings as comparative models for understanding the Beckett stage also. For McMullan, the Beckett stage provides a frame for a post-human commingling of flesh and technological extension. For Maude, the tensions between the objectifying will of external agents studying the subject and the subject perceiving itself govern the ghoulish dramas of figures evidently estranged from the return of themselves in apparitional form. Contemporary phenomenology of the theatre, you can see, provides a compelling set of answers for Beckett's enigmatic scenarios. In my view, what is most interesting in the Merleau-Pontian interpretation of the subject in the Beckettian context is that it prompts us to see the dramaturgy as a simulation of principles of the very human faculty for simulation.

Rehearsals for *Not I*

We saw earlier how the stage directions of *Not I* involve the 'stage in darkness but for MOUTH, upstage audience right, about 8 feet above stage level, faintly lit from close-up and below, rest of face in shadow'; they also mention '[i]nvisible microphone'.[31] To render these directions for the British premiere at the Royal Court Theatre in 1973, Whitelaw was dressed in a hooded cloak and positioned on a rostrum, gripping what she describes as a rod, a fixed object to give her something to help balance herself in the dark. This rod became a resource of her acting practice, she indicates, as something through which she 'could force ... energy into'.[32] I assume this rod is underneath the cloak she is wearing and operates as a sort of handrail. By her account, the text demanded extraordinary physical and mnemonic effort. The text's disjunctively placed repetitions almost deliberately resist memorization: 'but the brain – ... what? ... lying? ... yes ... whether standing ... or sitting ... or kneeling ... or lying ... but the brain still ...' – lines such as these are structured in staccato. Memorization of the text requires enormous adaptation of an actor used to performing naturalistically and who can now no longer rely upon the accessible psychological shape that writing with naturalistic rhythms has following normative speech patterns.[33] Sometimes, during rehearsals, Whitelaw relates that memorizing the text seemed to be impossible. The work's cadences, its illogical repetitions, and indeed, during dress rehearsal or performance, its immersed deprivations of sensation, exacerbated the memory-disturbing disorientations internal to the work.

The experience of the actor chronicled here curiously mirrors the disorientations that are represented as subjective experience of the character Mouth in the monologue comprising *Not I*. This disorientation that the actor contends with, whether in finessed accomplishment or in flailing struggle, shapes a performativity in the role paralleling the turbulence the character Mouth is said to be experiencing. In other words, the affective elements of the work can be found in the semantic and narratological domains composing it at the same time as in the acoustic and somatic requirements of the role. Whitelaw illustrates these characteristics in athletic terms:

> I began to understand what an athlete feels like, as he goes through training. The work was painful; my ribcage protested at having to take such little breaths. Like a singer, I had to work out exactly *where* I was going to snatch breath. I was hyper-ventilating like mad and often became dizzy, staggering round and round the stage. My jaws ached. The first time I tried a run 'off the book', I closed my eyes tight so that I wouldn't be distracted by anything visual. I didn't realise that as I spoke I was going round and round in circles.[34]

Together, the derangements of the text and the derangements of the dramaturgy fuse into a single affective transfiguration that the text asks to be performed. The actor naturally experiences this during rehearsal also. This 'staggering' that she speaks of would prove to be an omen of greater difficulties to come as the production came together. During a memorable dress rehearsal, deprived of sight by the apparatus, Whitelaw fainted and almost fell from the rostrum:

> We started the dress rehearsal. After about a page and a half, I felt myself starting to tumble over the edge of the rostrum. I clung on to the bar because I thought I was going to pass out. I remained convinced as I spoke my line that I was tumbling off the edge of the rostrum and into the void of the theatre. I felt like an astronaut who has left his capsule. Half-way through the rehearsal I broke down.[35]

The first derangement of affect for the actor as she feels herself tumbling 'into the void of the theatre' is described as happening due to the apparatus required to stage the floating image in darkness. The second derangement occurs at the level of characterological embodiment, the incorporation of the resistant ontology of Mouth, a character whose roots in corporeal existence are tenuously linked to memory denied – *not* I. The third derangement applies to vocal performance: the actor must actualize at incredible speed and power the amplification of the circumstances of the other two orders of affective derangement. The compression of these three derangements into a theatrical role produced in Whitelaw actual sensations of disembodiment even in rehearsal. She felt as if she were 'floating' in 'the void of the theatre'. It goes without saying that productions of the work at the Royal Court that followed did not feature Whitelaw collapsing time and time again! The theoretical argument presented here concerns the incorporation of

Beckettian dramaturgy and experiment into the actor's practice. Whitelaw later found ways to incorporate the disembodying effects of sensory deprivation into her practice that at first proved novel. The Whitelaw astronaut event of sensation-deprived floating, if you like, suggests that Beckett's explicit constraint over the acting craft composed in a work seeking a particular sensorium has profound affective implications that reshape actor self-presence and self-consciousness. Some productions will demand more or less sensory deprivation, provide more or less actor mobility, depending upon the shape in which those productions adopt the disembodiment logic of the dramaturgical encoding of *Not I*. The Whitelaw event demonstrates a profound example of what Worthen has called the negative athleticism of the Beckett role. This event also attests to the fact that the affective constraints of production and text *collide* in the actor, a matter intensified and revolutionized in Beckett's late theatre. The actor is being experimented with as if she were in a laboratory. Few actors likely faint when playing *Not I*, but most athletes that overcome a novel physical task report changes in their technique and in their body. Indeed, *Not I* stands as a compellingly affirmative theatrical testimony to alternative forms of speech act that are possible in the contemporary theatre. Whoever the actor, whatever the apparatus and whatever the interpretation, if the play is produced following the constrained directions of the original text, the actor reprises one of the most intense and practice-modifying experiences an actor can from the repertoire of modern monologue.

Sensory deprivation in Beckett's later theatre works such as the collaborations with Whitelaw present the clearest aesthetic shift in the writer's dramaturgy after the barren milieus and orchestrated silences of *Endgame* and *Krapp's Last Tape*. From now on, scenographic ruins will give way to abyssal enclosures shaped only with light. Such a design change in the setting of Beckett's works and the lighting tradition that follows focalizes audience attention upon the sensations that have been chiselled out of an otherwise sensation-deprived milieu. Sensory deprivation for Whitelaw was understood first and foremost as a matter for reconfiguring the direction of her energies, a matter of speed and of internal balance. In her words, Whitelaw came to the conclusion that *Not I* 'would have to go faster than anything [she had] ever heard in the theatre, if possible as fast as the speed of thought, and that of course is impossible'.[36] The velocity of *Not I* is only matched in the performance oeuvre by the Beckett play preceding it, *Play*. We know that *Play* was Whitelaw's first effort at live Beckettian negative athletics. Whitelaw, through devoting herself physically and verbally to *Not I* to a degree unprecedented in her own practice, came to discover ideas of her own about the craft of acting through contact with Beckett and his script for the play. She suggests to the next actor of the work that they 'let [their] skin fall off, let [their] flesh fall off, let the muscles fall off, let the bones fall off, let everything fall off'.[37]

Beckett's feelings of culpability for Billie Whitelaw's challenges with the part are also illuminating. Sitting in on rehearsals of Anthony Page's production in 1973, Beckett remarks: 'Oh Billie, what have I done to you?'[38] Beckett's instinctual reaction was to declare himself responsible, crediting his script, then, and the dramaturgy encoded there, with this event. What is most curious about this is how unlikely that sense of responsibility would be within the dramaturgical paradigms of other writers of theatre. Would William Shakespeare take responsibility for an exhausted actor playing Hamlet? Would Caryl Churchill for an overwhelmed Marlene? Here, when the actor collapsed in the presence of the crew and a director, it was the writer who took responsibility. Beckett acknowledged, we can infer, that the affective requirements of the work for the actor and the theatrical apparatus along with it were textually preconceived, with sensory deprivation being their mutual destination.

In *Not I*, it is the voiced monologue conducting the spectator's imagination not to the implied *out*side of the representative, mimetic Chekhov stage – the reality that the realism on stage refers to – but rather further *in*side spectacle, a theatre of the mouth – dark, logorrhoeic, an 'I' that is not 'I'. For Julie Campbell, the voice holds a liminal position in relation to actual and virtual space that audiences come to inhabit: 'the voice [for Beckett] seems to live in an unreal, twilight space: the narrative play space of impossible existence/nonexistence'.[39] This negotiating liminality Beckett discovered in Whitelaw's voice as he sought to render it in *Not I*. Manipulating the liveness of that existence or nonexistence becomes the central activity of this strand of experiment in sensory deprivation. 'Live', of course, connotes two different but related meanings, distinguished by context: 'live' is a statement of experiential distinction, indicating that an event occurring before an audience happens in real time by tangible beings (rather than its alternative, 'recorded'); 'live' can also mean 'living', the contingency of which determines the outcome of a particular event of performance, just as contingency determines the result of an experiment, however predetermined the hypothetical outcome. The live subject in both senses becomes the explicit object of sensory deprivation in the Whitelaw plays, and the examinations that ensue test the elasticity that binds voice to its figural referent, and narration to its narrator. Phelan's notion that Beckett's plays pursue a 'drama of sight' can be validated by studying the mechanics of sensory deprivation in these two subsequent plays, the experiment denying the spectatorial eye access to the subject that speaks for themselves through alternative strategies of isolation from conventional sensory registration.[40]

Footfalls

In this 'unreal ... narrative play', *Footfalls*, darkness enshrouds the contorted figure in rags. That darkness is rendered consubstantial with her mother's voice, the dominant monologist of the play, another narrator visually absent from the stage and as a result inhabits it by way of haunting.[41] May, her body dimly lit in a rectangle of light that also serves as her only territory for movement, is the only lit object within the stage's nine-step-long passage enclosed in darkness. Beckett's decision to extend the choreography from seven to nine steps by the time that Whitelaw realizes the role indicates to what degree the kinetic chart of May's pacing to and fro serves a performative function; such a minor difference would be nigh on invisible within a Broadway musical dance routine and imperceptible in a production of a Chekhov piece. A pre-textual narrative of the play is revealed in the dialogue between the disembodied voice of the older woman and May. The mother, V, is purportedly in her eighties, May in her forties. In the first moments of the dialogue, we are made aware of the one who commands authority over the narrative of their share reality; once again, voice when released from the fragility of physical dominion merges with the texture of spectacle and becomes one with the envelope of darkness. Thus, like in *Eh Joe*, disembodied voice wields the seemingly absolute power of narrative:

> V: [*Pause. M resumes pacing. Four lengths. After first length, synchronous with steps.*] One two three four five six seven eight nine wheel one two three four five six seven eight nine wheel. [*Free.*] Will you not try to snatch a little sleep?[42]

Here, the voice of the mother, V, narrates the action happening before us. The voice's interest in the well-being of May is immediately countered by May's reply to her mother: 'Would you like me to inject you again?' Although the dialogue gives the impression that it is the voice, the mother, who is infirm, the only live evidence of decrepitude is the live, half-contorted May, who continually defers to her mother's narrative and wishes. Both carry in their voices the hint of what could be called a haunted quality. The sound entails a vaporous fading-out of sonority in ghostly slowness performed by both. Nonetheless, the power imbalance is vocalized; V possessing May, May with limited reply. With an unearthliness that one recalls in the ghost Ada in the radio play *Embers* (1957), May is liminally apparitional. May is at once both decrepitly real and ghostly, one questionable visual quality suggesting the other.

Following Marvin Carlson's proposition about theatre as the medium of recurrent haunting presented earlier, I suggest that May's haunting exposes the underlying mechanics of simulation. Beckett in *Footfalls* exacts an examination of simulation according to the concept that theatre is haunted by the absent things and moments, and not just the characters, that it simulates. The living human being is enveloped in the narration of their forebears, thus live presence itself is haunted. *Footfalls'* interdependent roles present forms of ungovernable liveness that fold outwards by way of the repetitions of what haunts them. Interestingly, in the Asmus production, Christine Collins, V, and Billie Whitelaw, M, in moments where the text demands this, prove to be very fine imitators of one another's voice. The mutual bond the characters share in a narrated condition divided between the enveloper and the enveloped is reflected in this occasional isomorphism. Moreover, the isomorphism attests to an inseparable reliance upon the sign of the other for materializing presence according to the sensory order of their presentation; May, through her live visual figure and observable, real-time acoustic voice; V, unobservable, thus questionably live acoustic voice. Only detectable then in live performance is this dialectic of the confident, embodied-but-absent voice, and the present, but apparitional voice. Both are present in an entirely dependent way, dependent upon the logics of live spectacle not only conveyed to us, the audience, but just as importantly for each other. The call to imitate each other which so obviously draws attention to the problematic of presence motivating the drama of this piece brings into relief the severance that lies at the heart of the pair's mutually interdependent live reality.

As with the mute diagrams of *Quad* or the *AWWI* and *II*, the live, ungovernable, irreducibly contingent dimension of spectacle in *Footfalls*, however deleteriously honed in a self-questioning, self-exposing spectacle, designates a zone of invisibility in a 'drama of sight' that escapes the domination of the narrative logic that makes May so terribly visible. The only moment of explicit disagreement May has with V lies in the latter's monologue which simulates the former's resistance, and not her own. Otherwise, traces of resistance to the diegetic authority of V can only really consist in the problematics of V's diegesis. The colons in the text below, such as in 'May: Not enough', are shown as they are in the script. Therefore, they are voiced by V; V explicitly and self-consciously dominates the terms by which diegesis figures in this theatrical narrative and this narrative is the enclosure responsible for defining May's presentation to the live field of the theatre:

V: May: Not enough. The mother: What do you mean, May, not enough, what can you possibly mean, May, not enough? May: I mean, Mother, that I must hear the feet however faint they fall. The mother: The motion alone is not enough? May: No, Mother, the motion alone is not enough, I must hear the feet, however faint they fall.[43]

Curiously, the narration reveals key elements of May's otherwise concealed self-definition and (constrained) autonomy. May is represented in the narration as defying her mother's expectations that the ability to walk and its living motion should be enough to satisfy the mother's narrative; May believes she must also hear the footfall to be present. Which is to say, May would only register her living presence if she were to hear her own footfalls, a return of that residual performative liveness consisting in *Quad*, for example, and the eternally returning component of that spectacle's diagram despite the medium that renders and alters it. Presence as provisionally conferred through sound also reprises the importance of understanding the full sensorium – here, the component of soundscape – for coming to grips with self-presence. Footfalls thereby represents a sensory registration of presence and the real that would be required to satisfy the (barely) living May. Ironically, as with *AWW I* and the man's bared humanity, spectacle irrevocably mediates this resistant, ungovernable exit from visibility. Exit from these terms of visibility ultimately remain invisible. May can only enjoy resistance to being visible from inside the mother's paradoxically dominating narrative.

This narrative about footfalls and the registration of presence calls to mind Massumi's claim that each sense faculty participate in some tandem relation with the others in the construction of a balance supporting sense perception – a faculty known as 'mesoperception'. Mesoperception, Massumi explains, is the predicate of synaesthesia's condition of possibility: 'the body's registration of the in-betweenness of the incorporeal event – *mesoperception*. Mesoperception is the synesthetic sensibility ... where inputs from all five senses meet ... and become flesh together.'[44] Thus, it appears that May, represented in her mother's monologue, harbours a critical dissatisfaction. For May, that kinetic movement alone is not enough to register presence. Rather, the body must register the milieu via at least one of the other intercalated senses – here, hearing – to register the real via its sensation. The narrator – ironically the author of this version of May – clearly cannot understand this when she asks: 'The motion alone is not enough?' Such a question coming from V substantiates the dramaturgical contrast between the finite corporeality of May and the enveloping incorporeality of V; the former's movement towards embodiment paradoxically affirms her simulation by the narrator while the latter's movement towards disembodiment affirms her dominance of spectacle through corporeal absence.

Thus, by proxy, the account of the footfall as an ungovernable but calculable sensory registration of a contingent real charts May's living resistance, however undermined it is by narration and simulation. May's resistance lies in her problematic liveness's capacity to call into question the reality of the authoritarian sound-space of V: there is no evidence of V within the scopic and corporeal domains of theatrical representation. In other words, quite simply, May opposes the narrative of the mother by simply being live and present. If only she were not defined by familial haunting. This problem signals a deeply Beckettian paradox, fashioned through a focus upon the remains of figural life. Liveness and self-presence barely register in the problematized terms of the 'drama of sight'. May, we saw, cannot express her resistance in speech. She can only embody an immobilized reality subsisting in the envelope of simulation. Sarah Balkin argues that Beckett realizes 'spectral' possibilities for stage representation by using theatre mechanics in novel ways; Whitelaw's contributions to Beckettian dramaturgy could be characterized as 'spectral'.[45] This spectral practice exposes the fragile terms of resistance available to May within the terms of her narrow mobility and predetermined narrative. Time itself is arrested in *Footfalls*, as it appears to be in so many of Beckett's plays. Narration is the central authority of the enclosure. V repeatedly intones: 'will you never have done ... revolving it all?'[46]

Footfalls is crafted out of an experiment in undecidable stage diegesis that can belong neither to one monologist nor the other. This problematization insinuated into the DNA of stage mimesis through a self-examining diegetic order results in a newly apparitional dramaturgy with hallucinatory, sense-depriving effect. In another passage, May's reference to 'Old Mrs Winter, whom the reader will remember' foregrounds the tension between narration and live time, with the past belonging to the domain of reading and the spectator imagined as a 'reader'.[47] The experiment has been conducted at the order of the narrative as much as by the apparatus. V and May share in their interreliant monologues the need to relate narratives of *the very narratives they are not physically present for* to an audience of the other. This 'drama of sight' involves heightened live embodiment problematized through a theatrical procedure of decreation that charts, again, an ungovernable point defined by its invisibility (or even impalpability) within the domain of spectacle. V speaks of the movements that she is not present for as May recalls a narrative of great similitude to hers but externalizes the conversation as if it is the exchange of another mother-daughter pair. Most importantly though, it is the similarities of the narratives, especially their similarities in imitating each other, that flags the entanglement of one questionable concept of presence with the other. May, playing the roles of Amy and Mrs Winter in her monologue, repeats the dialogue she previously had had with her mother:

May: Amy: Not there. Mrs W: But I heard you respond [...] I heard you distinctly. [*Pause*. *Resumes pacing.* [...]] Amy. [*Pause. No louder.*] Amy. [*Pause.*] Yes, Mother. [*Pause.*] Will you never have done? [*Pause.*] Will you never have done ... revolving it all?[48]

What becomes clear at the end of the play is that, along with its narratological structure, the space of live performance, the theatre, is essential to the synthesis of these two quasi-corporeal (or quasi-incorporeal) realities. Moreover, Whitelaw's original role designed by Beckett, Mouth in *Not I*, has been expanded in a sense to a new separation between corporeality and narration. Light, as with *Play*, has become a subtler 'instrument of torture', now a sublimated means of fixed confinement. The cruelty, if it is anything like *Play*, or, indeed, *Catastrophe*, lies not in its propensity for commandment as a prod to speak, but in the simplified omnipotence through which the body has boundaries established around it. May's ungovernable core is buried more deeply in spectacle than the self-reflections of the man in *AWW I* or the parabasis of Protagonist. As we shall see in *Rockaby*, vivisected time, cut between the inapprehensible moment suspended and narrated time mapping the simulated journey from beginning to end, undergoes a new examination with the use of pre-recorded voice timed to a restricted rhythm.

Rockaby

Rockaby, written in 1981, is the last play Beckett collaborated on with Whitelaw. The play premiered under the direction of Alan Schneider in Buffalo, New York, in 1981, produced in tandem with *Footfalls* in 1984 (the first recording of *Rockaby* is of this production). The production toured internationally in 1986 in a version directed by Robbie Hendry along with Rocky Greenberg. *Rockaby* was then recorded for film under Walter Asmus's direction in 1988, once again in tandem with *Footfalls*, for presentation on Channel Four in the UK. It is a play in which an old woman, W, remains in a rocking chair, while what can be assumed to be her own voice speaks of her life's final moments in pre-recorded, amplified monologue. This monologue proceeds in a gentle, undulating, hypnotic mode as if attempting to draw its listener into the domain of sleep. As with *Footfalls*, all but the figure onstage – and, in this case, her shimmering sequined black dress – is invisible. With each rock of the mechanical chair the face drifts out of view, a small spot momentarily illuminating the face with each upswing of the rocking chair. Corporeality has once again been made the subject of an experiment in the apparitional. This time, that corporeality's rhythmic disappearance and return synchronize the narrative rhythms expressed in the amplified recorded monologue with a drama of decaying light.

The duration of the rocking of this chair is timed with the recorded voice, pausing when the live figure cries out for 'more'. The strange slowness of Whitelaw's recorded voice, timed precisely to the rocks of the chair, makes for an astonishing moving image. The recorded voice, meanwhile, describes what lies before us in a recursive diegetic doubling of the stage image. The narrative appears to concern the final moments in the life of this reclining stage figure. Live exclamations of 'more' exclaimed by the woman are the only breaks in this trance of sound and light. These exclamations too decline towards a final destination. Each exclamation slowly diminishes in volume and enamour with each return. This decline suggests that the character slowly apprehends, or futilely resists, the imminent fate of the aged body. The decline in energy also conveys a desperate tone of opposition towards the void as it closes in. The impact of these intervals of voice intensifies in relation to the strictly mechanical nature of the movement onstage and the recorded speech.

In *Rockaby*, the problematic of spectacle that positions the incarnating voice reaches a limit point of constraint. Liveness, the ungovernably contingent element of the spectacle, here has been reduced to the last incalculable aspect of the diagram: time punctuated by the living performer. Despite its diminution, the explosive affect of that limited protestation for 'more' produces a profound live performance event. *Rockaby* situates live self-presence as a precious, mortal reservoir of intensity that is utterly evanescent and entirely dependent upon an inevitably deleterious visibility. While the expression may have been calculated in a durationally specific experiment, and the tone and nature of that expression anticipated to have a certain form, the event of that exclamation 'more' bridging the immobile stage figure and the spectator carries an invisible but loaded affective value that should chill most audiences of the play. For Anthony Uhlmann, the figure's immobility has a particular function. The image draws a parallel between the rocking chair W sits in and the metaphor of the cradle for Geulincx, whom Uhlmann points out Beckett read in detail. The cradle, Uhlmann writes, is a metaphor 'used by Geulincx to illustrate the notion of [humanity's] true powerlessness'; *Rockaby*'s rocking chair, with attendant lullaby-reminiscent monologue, presents a permutation of Geulincx's ontological analogy.[49] The mechanical nature of the *Rockaby* rocking chair is an essential component of this. The chair rocks the performer. Thereby the performer is enveloped in a kinetic enclosure with a prescribed rhythm for the duration of the theatrical event. The performer, like the character, has an entirely predetermined *recline* for the duration of the composition.

In 'The Exhausted,' Deleuze articulates what these immense subtractions of theatre resources such as duration and stage presence to predetermined, confined forms alter of theatricality. Such subtractions achieve a visual language that departs from the text, 'operat[ing] [not] only with images but also with spaces'.⁵⁰ In Chapter 1, I argued that this revolutionarily decreative transformation of the playscript into architectural agent was a diagrammatic compositional method of calculation that involves not only image, but the mesh of sensations converging in the sensorium of live performance. The exhaustion of W in her final hours towards her final rocked demise can be seen as a conflation of corporeal exhaustion in the fictive cosmos of the work with theatrical exhaustion, enacted in a diagrammatic attention to durational rhythm. For me, this climactic collision of the active, automated rocking chair with the nearly disappearing presence of W creates the intensification of spectatorial focus, a gaze marshalled by the *live* actor in those critical exclamations of 'more'.

The pauses in the mechanical movement of the recorded monologue and the rocking chair, which allow for the demand for 'more' of the live figure, become the only signs of incarnate life in the play. This is made apparent by juxtaposition with the apparitional recording, describing little more than what is before the spectator during the play's duration: 'till the day came / in the end came / close of a long day / sitting at her window / quiet at her window / all eyes / all sides / high and low / for a blind up / one blind up / no more / never mind a face / behind the pane / famished eyes / like hers'.⁵¹ The rhythmic release of 'more' is an exclamatory counterpoint to the scenario's otherwise slow languor. The narrative represents a narrative of dying, of course, so when W cries out for 'more' she cries out not only for more life but, paradoxically, for more dying. Stanton B. Garner Jr. analyses this dialectic of disembodiment in the late Beckett plays as a dynamism in which 'the body asserts itself as a primary field for the play of phenomenological presence and absence'.⁵² However, Garner Jr.'s analysis relies on the notion of 'normal principles of normal corporeal subjectivity, the dispossessions at the heart of self-possession'.⁵³ For Garner, these cries of 'more' made in the rocking pulse towards death thus mean self-possession, rather than radical self-abnegating exposure we have witnessed in Beckett's laboratory so far in the production of a sensory-deprived theatrical spectacle. Moreover, the *barely* of the barely perceptible difference between life rocked in a rocking chair and the injunction repeated by the recorded voice, 'rock her off' – between the virtual, seemingly perpetual repetitions of the recorded voice who never tires and the waning cries of the live subject for 'more' – is magnified and amplified by spectacle. Life, you might say, trembles into perceptibility in what has otherwise perished. '[F]uck life', expressed without special emphasis in the Whitelaw version, disappears into the void of the theatre like all else, however unanticipated. The script indicates: 'Together: echo of "rock her off", coming to rest of rock, slow fade out', all departing elements of the sensorium dissolving together.[54] Herbert Blau's theory of liveness perhaps has its profoundest commendation when applied to this play. As Blau writes, 'the body in performance *is dying in front of your eyes*. Unceasing process is out there in the flesh. Or hangs, perceptually, on the audience's breath.'[55] *Rockaby* is a live sound drama with a seemingly automated hominid figure until the appearance of that earth-shattering declaration for 'more'. The declaration becomes so moving because it affirms that the living body dying in time does indeed speak live. Indeed, with the diminishing return of this vocal motif, this crystallized expression of the living figure 'hangs … on the audience's breath'.

We have observed how a dramaturgy of experimental sensory deprivation applied to the memory play reshapes figural and performative presence and self-presence, begging for new practices of physical and verbal disclosure of the actor. This is negative athleticism, in a phrase. What is observed in *Rockaby* as a live encounter between the corporeal and the incorporeal, and the problematics of their interreliance for representing figural life, will be structured differently in a film or television work like *Eh Joe* where sound and vision are equally and inextricably recorded. To take *Eh Joe* again as an example, the minute, almost imperceptible reactions of a man in his fifties, 'practically motionless throughout', contrasts with the taunting recollections of a woman's voice who reminds him, 'Weaker and weaker till you laid her too … Others … All the others … Such love he got … God knows why … […] And look at him now … Throttling the dead in his head.'[56] Recorded visual material for television makes the voice at once a discrete female voice *and* the internal thoughts of the character in close-up. Interpretation allows this attachment to slide from one domain to the other, from the woman's story to the man's, and yet in medial terms the moving image and the overdub are intertwined as one unresolvable 'image'. The theatre allows for no such fusing. In *Rockaby*, the compressed texture of a recording, perceptibly different from the responsivity and acoustics of a live voice, fuse with the surroundings and the actions therein as a single theatrical soma in which what is live and what is pre-recorded remain desutured. Any director or theatre-maker attentive to these essential problematics within the Beckettian view of spectacle will orient a performer in a framework that reiterates these dramaturgical paradoxes. Nevertheless, Whitelaw's role after *Not I* in establishing a vocal practice that performs the 'drama of sight' and would be realized in newly imagined relations of light, figure and soundscape is compositionally significant. I reiterate: the point is not that Whitelaw sets a standard as a result. Rather, the Whitelaw collaboration over a series of plays, most notably the three that I have studied in detail, transformed Beckett's writing such that a particular dramaturgical practice became more apparent.

The spectator of *Rockaby* is drawn into increasingly heightened anticipation of the woman's only phrase independent of the recording – 'more' – her voice becoming 'a little softer each time' over its three final permutations after the opening of the play.[57] This phrase acts as a sort of theatrical equivalent to that monument to Beckettian rhetoric, 'I can't go on, I'll go on', from Beckett's key 1958 novel, *The Unnamable*.[58] To go on, in spite of time's deletions. To beg for more decline, in the case of *Rockaby*. The trajectory of the Whitelaw collaborations can be traced from *Play*. The paradigm of sensory deprivation achieved through dramaturgy was achieved explicitly in the collaboration on *Not I*. Whitelaw's negative athleticism was an influential factor in the composition of the play in the realization of new attitudes to monologue and a physical practice of haunted figuration that would forge a spectatorship solicited to attune to the dimensions of spectacle undisclosed by light and narrative. The actor, we saw in the introduction, was throughout Beckett's dramaturgical career seen as a medium to be written for. In the end, the extraordinary stagecraft, apparatuses, figural enigmas and sensory experiences of the Beckett spectacle, challenge audiences to enter a domain in which the coordinates of sensation are rearranged, as the actor-mediums too float in space, glide through light or rock off.

3

Impediment and the symbolist dramaturgical inheritance

Eleuthéria, a completed drama written in 1947 shortly before the defining drama of the twentieth century, *En attendant Godot* (*Waiting for Godot*), begins Beckett's plot to enter the live, collaborative artistic sphere of dramaturgical event we call 'theatre'. This play would not be produced in his lifetime and, as you will see, occupies a contentious place in Beckett's oeuvre because of its renunciation by the writer himself. Indeed, part of that contentiousness stems from a resemblance the play has to the contemporary scene of avant-garde theatre in Paris at the time, rather than the work's special lack of accomplishments in accordance with Beckettian standards. Due to a number of setbacks, along with the passing of Beckett's enthusiasm for this debut drama, *Eleuthéria* would eventually be foreclosed by the unrealizable situation of the piece in the year or so following its completion. The work did not survive Beckett's famously self-critical censure by the time of its tacit acceptance for the stage in 1950. That change of heart regarding the play's value would come to prohibit the work's production and publication until nearly fifty years later, along with a reluctance to provide print publication rights until after his death. But this play was not his first play.

Beckett's first play was *Human Wishes*,[1] an example of what Puchner calls 'closet drama'. Closet drama is a genre of theatre-resistant literary playwriting that reprises, in Puchner's view, the classic philosophical argument with theatre levelled by Plato in his dialogues in the *Republic*:

> The resistance to the theatre in Plato's dialogues manifests itself in two traditions of the closet drama, which one might call the *restrained* closet drama and the *exuberant* closet drama. The restrained closet drama, ranging from Plato through Milton and Swinburne to Hofmannsthal, consists of philosophical or poetic speeches and monologues, a theatre characterized by a withdrawal from and resistance to scenic action. … Goethe's *Faust II*, Flaubert's *La Tentation de Saint-Antoine*, and Wyndham Lewis's *Enemy of the Stars* are examples of such free-floating, often allegorical theatricality, whose constant changes of scenes, large

casts of characters, sudden appearances and disappearances, and strategic mixture of hallucination and reality wilfully exceed the limits of theatrical representation.[2]

Puchner argues that modernists found the page to be the most experimental domain for live art to be imagined in. This continued a mode of writing popularized during Romanticism, transforming it to realize new horizons by pursuing an anti-theatrical urge.[3] Modernists tended to prefer closet drama, Puchner argues, because it was unbounded by the limitations of the commercial stage, the craft of acting, the materiality of stagecraft and the expectations of a paying (bourgeois) audience. *Human Wishes*, an unfinished 'Johnson Fantasy' and closet drama of 1937, had it been finished and published, would have realized the most pretentious of outcomes for a young modernist: membership among the scholarly ranks of writers dabbling in exploratory private dramas about blind spots in the historiographies of literary figures, in this case of the Enlightenment figure Dr Samuel Johnson. Ruby Cohn suggests that *Human Wishes*'s abandonment lay with the play's unresolvable entanglement with realism, a sensibility Beckett was already resisting: 'historical realism [like *Human Wishes*] betrays Beckett's own developing vision. ... He could not resolve the conflict between the realistic biographical drama he had painstakingly prepared himself to write and the verbal ballet he actually found himself writing.'[4] *Human Wishes* would figure as the former type of closet drama – the restrained type – and however it is viewed, the play is not a particularly good example of closet drama. After all, the play is unfinished. It also experiments with very little of the possibilities of the page that would animate the most experimental of the symbolist closet dramatists, including Stephane Mallarmé in works such as *La Livre*, or avant-gardists such as Gertrude Stein and her *Dr Faustus Lights the Lights* (1938) that continued the symbolist experiment with the conventions of scriptwriting.

Eleuthéria too, like *Human Wishes*, still does not yet materialize the theatrical turn that *Godot* would come to enshrine for Beckett and for modern theatre. But hints of a dramaturgical revolution are found here. Unlike *Human Wishes*, *Eleuthéria* does solicit the collaboration of the contemporary performance sphere that his work of the post-war moment in Paris in the late 1940s does. The play has been seen variously as Beckett's first experiment in vaudeville parody and physical theatre that would later inform *Godot*,[5] and as a self-reflexive 'examination' of traditions of theatricality: 'there are parodies or allusions from Sophocles, Shakespeare, Molière, Corneille, Shaw, Zola, Ibsen, Hauptmann, Pirandello, Yeats, Symbolism, Surrealism, Artaud, Jarry and Socialist Realism'.[6] Some of this collage of parodied materials concerns practitioners or central figures of the contemporary theatre of his time, with the spectre of surrealism still in a state of strong but contentious influence upon the French avant-garde.

As discussed in Chapter 1, *Eleuthéria* was a deliberate attempt at writing for the avant-garde stage of post-war Paris. Although completed in 1947, the play would not be picked up by a director until 1950. Roger Blin would elect to stage *Godot* rather than *Eleuthéria*; the multi-character, interior-set *Eleuthéria* no longer proved as appealing as a crossroads-set four-hander – with additional child part – *Godot*. At this time, Beckett appears to have been an only occasional visitor of the theatre during a period otherwise defined by a 'frenzy of writing'.[7] The hopes for *Eleuthéria* were humble and the reason for writing it emotional: 'I turned to writing plays to relieve myself of the awful depression the prose led me into', Beckett commented in 1972. 'Life at the time was too demanding, too terrible, and I thought theatre would be a diversion.'[8] Theatre would be a diversion, he remarks; Beckett evidently did not know when writing *Eleuthéria* how that diversion would become the chief focus of his writing life by the end of the next decade. Beckett was a respected writer and translator at the time, but not a theatre-maker. S. E. Gontarski writes that 'Blin had heard of Beckett from the Dada poet Tristan Tzara'.[9] James Knowlson suggests that Blin and Beckett knew each other by sight from around the bohemian quarters of Montparnasse.[10] Bair's flawed account of Beckett's enthusiasm for Blin's production of August Strindberg's *Ghost Sonata* is evident when considering a letter Beckett writes to art critic Georges Duthuit suggesting that, contrary to the account in Bair's biography, Beckett initially had some concerns about the quality of Blin's work.[11] Indeed, Beckett and his partner Suzanne Deschevaux-Dumesnil's solicitation of Blin's interest seems to have preceded their having seen his Strindberg, inspired instead, it appears, by the actor-director's associations with Adamov and Artaud. Nevertheless, despite this, Blin would become Beckett's defining collaborator in Paris. But the tentativeness with which Beckett conducted his entrance to the theatre signals an ongoing tentativeness that would mark his ever-unpredictable experimentation, and the lack of a manifesto by which to proceed with it.

Most readers of *Eleuthéria* would agree with the suggestion that the play recalls Pirandello, the use of stage techniques that break the fourth wall of the stage fiction, especially one of its roles, the character Spectator, being a key resemblance to the figures from the Italian avant-gardist's work. Cohn repeats Bair's point about the play being more traditional than *Godot*, Cohn opting for the term 'well-made play', but this term is misleading if we do not couch it within the context of a particular tradition. As for me, I see *Eleuthéria* as somewhat overly conscious of the new direction of the contemporary avant-garde theatre.[12] While absurdist techniques certainly have become traditional by now, at the time, *Eleuthéria*'s peculiar and incoherent combination of an altered symbolist domestic domain, combined with epic theatre and surrealist metatheatrical devices, really situate Beckett within the post-surrealist multimedia art community of Paris, a community for whom the stage was one among many exhibition spaces. Indeed, Tim Lawrence suggests that surrealist playwright Roger Vitrac had the most direct influence upon Beckett's play; the 1928 play *Victor, ou, Les enfants au pouvoir* is the source for *Eleuthéria*'s wastrel protagonist, Victor Krap. As Lawrence elaborates:

> Vitrac's play was first produced in 1928, and was directed by Antonin Artaud, at a time when both men had moved away from the close circle of Surrealists loyal to Breton and the principles outlined in the First Manifesto of Surrealism. … Whether the play represents Surrealist drama in the strict sense has been a matter of debate; at the time Vitrac conceived of the play he may be accurately described as a dispossessed Surrealist.[13]

'[D]ispossessed' surrealism would become 'burlesque' surrealism in Beckett's liberal experimentation with an undefined post-surrealist dramaturgy. While more recently completed prose in 1946 'sicken[ed]' him, in this case *Mercier et Camier* (*Mercier and Camier*) ([1974] 1999), playwriting tenuously connected Beckett to an embryonic dramaturgy filling the venues of the Théâtres de Babylone, des Noctambules, Lancry, or de l'Œuvre at that time that was essentially trying to revive an avant-garde from the ruins of war.[14] *Mercier et Camier* represented a direction that he would continue in in prose, an abyssal passage into the indeterminacy of writing. But, for the time being, *Eleuthéria*'s diversion suggested a more public direction for the writer supplying degrees of appealing contingency to a period of inexperienced and still tentative belonging to an intercultural and intermedial avant-garde. Critic Leonard Cabell Pronko suggests that it is only this term, 'avant-garde', that captures the disparate philosophical, cultural and aesthetic approaches of those writing for the stage at the time in Paris, a time when surrealism's authority had all but perished, living on in unorthodox, post facto practices.[15] Only 'avant-garde', describes this incoherent set, a term suitable as a matter of 'convenience' and an act of 'deference to common usage' as it figures during Beckett's early theatrical career.[16] In the view of modern theatre history, the next play to arrive in Beckett's writing properly defines his entrance into the avant-garde.

Observation of a live experimentation enabled by production and the collaborations it entails, in one sense, must start with Beckett's first staged work, *Waiting for Godot*. Now that we have considered *Eleuthéria*'s entanglement with post-war avant-gardism in the Parisian context *in principle*, since the play was never actually produced in that context, we can now consider what live production actually modified of Beckett's earliest produced compositions with the arrival of *Godot*. The familiar discussion of anti-realist tendencies of this author, especially surrounding the play that forged Beckett's fame, *Godot*, will be directed to a more comparative theoretical discussion of trajectories of post-symbolist theatre such that links to conceptual and live art contexts become more visible. Katherine Worth (1978; 1999), Martin Puchner (2002), Allen Lane (1979), and Tim Lawrence (2018), among others, articulate for this study what the extent of the symbolist dramaturgical influence on Beckett might be.[17] I hope to extend this historicization of dramaturgy and aesthetics into the realm of materialist understandings of live performance and conceptual art in context; contexts that themselves are noted for the ways in which experimentation brought avant-garde tradition into uncharted territory.

Further, I hope to use the diverse history of productions of *Waiting for Godot* along with ethereal play *Ohio Impromptu* (1981) to demonstrate that the material contingencies of the stage's constraints upon human presence inspired Beckett's post-symbolist style, rather than aesthetic objectives alone. My account differs from existing claims of Beckett's theatre as an effort to pursue a negative symbolist spectacle that nevertheless aims at a pure, unbounded visionary event, even as it ends in failure. My account of the symbolist influence will show that Beckett's relationship to the mode was more critical, and also more unprogrammatic, than critics have shown heretofore. I hope to show how the playwright's negativity towards spectacle has more to do with a desire to forge new relations to audience registration of live performance than an effort to reference the dream of symbolism and its impossible-to-realize enterprise for simulation via negation.

Symbolism and avant-gardism

Theatrical space, since the 1960s, has been understood in the avant-garde as any space in which live performance event calls upon an audience. Theatrical space understood in this liberated way entails understanding the spaces created by performance as liminal spheres at once implicated in and excepted from the real, always already expropriated from social space.[18]

Samuel Weber's theorization of spectacle along these lines has an Artaudian inflection that emphasizes irruption and liminality:

> What Artaud writes in French to describe the emergence of theatre, is that 'c'est alors que le théâtre s'installe': it is then, at that moment, 'that theatre *installs* itself', *takes* its place. To '*install oneself*, however, is to *take* a place that is *already there*, to occupy it, indeed, to *expropriate* it and, in the process, to *transform* it and oneself as well. That is precisely what theatre does when it turns the site into a scene, the place into a stage [...][19]

This notion of theatre positions performativity as the generative force that brings spectacle to *install* itself in the real through an irruption that operates like a plague, possessing the living beings and rendering a 'spatial poetry' as a result. The ability to heighten the immediacy and materiality of the performance event Marvin Carlson also credits the early-twentieth-century avant-garde with, focusing on Futurist Filippo Marinetti and Pataphysics figure Alfred Jarry, artists who imagined a variety theatre such that the fourth wall became a membrane for the real theatrical encounter to breach. Among other antics, such figures of avant-gardism urged that theatre-makers 'spread a strong glue on some of the seats, so that the male or female spectator will remain stuck to the seat and make everyone laugh'.[20] These uncivil conceptions of theatricality revise it as an event of attention unbound by genre or architecture. Rather than a tradition of stage fiction, this avant-gardism arose out of discontent with the received conventions of theatricality. That discontent was mostly evidently adopted in a theatrical movement by the symbolist theatre. Symbolism was a movement these avant-gardists both shared affinities with and used as a point of departure. Puchner sees the most influential dramaturgical and ideological text in the formation of this often imagined theatre – since many of such texts remained 'closet dramas'[21] with requirements for performance impossible to materialize on stage – as Heinrich von Kleist's 'Über das Marionettentheater' ('On the Marionette Theatre') (1810).[22] Kleist's concept of performance speculated that the gestural and psychological barriers posed by actors could be overcome by automatic and artificial interventions into the mechanics of drama. The marionette offered a prototype for the symbolist dramaturgical project of realizing 'abstraction' in place of mimesis. Puchner claims that symbolists sought to follow this Kleistian formulation to 'mould bodies and their materiality in the spirit of abstract thought' via machines that would transcend the finite human organism.[23]

For Puchner, the key dramaturgical line-through between symbolist theatre and Beckett's is a shared attention to the mechanicity of the 'signifying entities' of the theatre stagecraft. Beckett, like the symbolists, he argues, sought to transform theatrical resources from their service to mimesis and serve the worthier task of abstraction; Beckett's 'precision' Puchner credits the symbolist theatre with essentially inspiring:

> The task for turning objects and gestures into signifying entities can only be accomplished if the objects and gestures begin to represent more than just themselves, if they transcend their immediate mimetic relation to the world. Attacking, suspending, or foreclosing the self-sufficient presence of objects and actors – making object and the actors' bodies talk – is therefore the prerequisite for achieving symbolism in the theatre. For this reason, symbolism had to devise ways of controlling actors, whether in the text (Mallarmé), in the theatre (Craig), or both (Yeats). Beckett inherits this symbolist project in that he too is invested in a theatre of objects and a theatre of gestures, an investment that led him to insist that everything must be staged precisely the way he wrote it and that the few selected stage props and isolated gestures be realised with utmost precision.[24]

Following this view, Beckett empties the meaningfulness of these practices as processes representing a sublimated symbolic order but retains, and even refines, their dramaturgical tools. That would lead to suggest that Beckett continues one aspect of the symbolist project, which is to purify the theatre's powers of representation promised in its mechanical potentiality, notably its hostility towards the living actor. Beckett, Puchner writes, 'holds onto what is otherwise only a kind of by-product of symbolism, namely, an emphasis on isolated gestures and objects that dissolves the human actor'.[25] Here, Beckett would seem to be amenable to the Kleistian view of the actor if he had employed something resembling the marionette theatre in his spectacle in ways that symbolists such as Craig did. Yet, Beckett did not. Consider Craig's assertions about his dramaturgical vision; they bear little resemblance to Beckettian scenography:

> 'The artist', says Flaubert, 'should be in his work like God in creation, invisible and all-powerful; he should be felt everywhere and seen nowhere'.
>
> ...
>
> Do away with the actor, and you do away with the means by which a debased stage realism is produced and flourishes. No longer would

there be a living figure to confuse us into connecting actuality and art; no longer a living figure in which the weakness and tremors of the flesh were perceptible.[26]

Omnipotent authors and scenes without 'weakness and tremors of the flesh' hardly echo Beckett's dramaturgical imagination. So, including Beckett in a canon of symbolist 'anti-theatricality' may provide some convincing material for historicizing Beckett's compositional approach in relation to the symbolist paradigm, but there are substantial caveats that arise when we engage in this comparison. Symbolist dramaturgy in a Kleistian vein evidently cannot explain Beckett's irrepressible interest in the sorts of corporealities and finitude, 'weakness[es] and tremors', that Craig wished to expunge from the theatre. Then, there is Beckett's notable reluctance to overvalue the creative ends of writing, diametrically opposed to Craig's model of omniscient authorship.

So, Beckett's spectacle does not show the unequivocal hostility to theatre-making through the actor's craft and form, nor employ an incorporation of anti-theatricalism into an order of untheatrical theatricality with any coherence, that could situate his dramaturgy as a revised symbolist practice. Rather, as we will determine, a trajectory of practice deeply self-reliant on the provisional domain of performance shaped in earlier experiments in performance are undertaken following an interest in an impeded spectacle often concerned with the brute materiality of spectacle. However, the limitations of aesthetic resemblance as a means for dramaturgical analysis are becoming more and more apparent.

To conduct my revision of the largely accepted idea of the symbolist influence on Beckett dramaturgy, I will engage in a comparative discussion of Beckett's theatre with that of his closest symbolist forebear, the figure much discussed by Worth: W. B. Yeats. Specifically, I want to probe historical productions of *Godot* and look at their use of impediment towards characterological figures, the reader or scholar figure, that in Yeats's spectacle promises visionary and abstract accounts of human life while in Beckett's present a self-recursive human entanglement with memory and text that do not rarefy the abstract and conceptual domains. Remember, writing for theatre was considered in Beckett's own words to be 'first of all recreation from work on fiction. We are dealing with a given space and with people in that space', a matter he described as 'relaxing'.[27] These remarks suggest a playfulness and an uncertainty directing his first theatrical efforts that are at odds with the visionary seriousness of a figure such as Yeats also. Apprehending this playfulness means introducing a compelling new contingency that connotes neither hostility nor adherence to the stage aesthetic but rather a materially expressive mischief with once-precious dramaturgical norms. With this point, I hope to honour Herbert Blau's principle of liveness, itself partly derived from a career experimenting with Beckett's theatre in the 1950s and 1960s, by introducing it into our understanding of Beckettian dramaturgy after symbolism. Live performance is most acutely present in the decomposition of the live performing body. As Blau writes: 'The body in performance is dying in front of your eyes. Unceasing process is out there in the flesh.'[28] We considered this point in Chapter 2 also. Such decomposition was a property that the symbolist stage was obliged to deny. Yet, Beckett emphasizes this dimension of the stage figure.

We will see how Beckett solicits the live body's vital degradation to render a figural domain in which time's depredations are a dramatic resource and narrative subject. I propose that this dimension of Beckett's post-symbolist drama seeks to impede the logics of transcendent embodiment that once endowed a Mallarmé closet drama or a Yeats visionary work with its power. Impeding embodiment distinguishes Beckett dramaturgy from the von Kleist/Yeats/Craig project of a theatre of abstraction unimpeded by human physicality. The drama of the body's impediment becomes the very centre of a Beckett work such as *Godot*. We saw in Chapter 2 how Lucky became monologuing collateral of spectacle. This kind of proposal indicates a critical departure from existing scholarship on the post-symbolist Beckett: rather than a willingly failed symbolist project, I think *Godot* and Beckett's impeded spectacle develop a dramaturgy that seeks to observe what happens to the human when their efforts to perform their being undergo impediments by time, by light, by the responsibility to appear. Beckett's resemblance to symbolist dramaturgy harbours an unresolved materialism and not the extension of the trajectory of abstraction argued by critics in the past.

Echoes: The problem of embodiment

There is some precedent in resisting the neo-symbolist view of Beckett that carries value for this discussion. For example, I hope to avoid what Ulrika Maude articulates as the assumption in the symbolist comparison that bodies were, for Beckett, 'little more than obstacles'.[29] I take heed of Maude's, but also McMullan's critiques of hermeneutic accounts of Beckett that do not acknowledge corporeality on the Beckett stage.[30] Maude and McMullan's work represents examples within a wave of new approaches to Beckett that have sought to dispose of notions found in first-wave Beckett studies that had sometimes used the symbolist heritage to imagine Beckett as a new direction in stage abstraction. Some of those notions include the 'Mind as the Stage' model of critic Martin Esslin in *Mediations: Essays on Brecht, Beckett, and the Media* (1962). Theodor Adorno's existentialist reading of *Endgame*, 'Trying to Understand *Endgame*' (1961), presents the progression out of the ruins of symbolist dramaturgy as an uptake of those signs into a more abstract domain.[31]

By contrast, in an effort to understand the particularity of Beckett's embodied apparitions in their brute facticity as anxiously live beings of spectacle, I propose that we: (a) develop an expanded theory of Beckett's theatre that includes the insensate and insensible dimensions of stagecraft, design, and concept as dimensions of a materialism of the stage; and (b) explore the human figure in Beckett's stage work as a uniquely theatrical creature, neither mere concept nor human. Where Puchner uses *AWW I* to describe the marionette-like treatment of stage props and the play's protagonist as examples of post-symbolist engagements in anti-theatricality, I will engage with *Godot*'s use of the ruins of formerly cosmic scenery to argue that the presentation of a decomposing materiality stems from a deconstructed spectacle.[32]

Symbolism is a movement significant to media across the arts, from poetry, to painting, architecture and theatre. Allen Lane writes that symbolism 'took on its classic form in about 1870 but had its roots in the sixties ... In broader terms, symbolism can be thought of as part of a philosophical idealism in revolt against a positivist, scientific attitude'.[33] Symbolism repudiates the 'positivist' and 'scientific' in aid of a metaphysically endowed 'philosophical idealism'. The movement therefore comprises a sensibility concerned with the rendering what is insensate and insentient to rational observation. Hence Allen later describes this initially mostly Francophone theatre – with Belgian Maurice Maeterlinck (1862–1949) the most significant theatrical proponent of the movement on that front, and, of course, Mallarmé, whom we saw in Chapter 1 presented as the pre-eminent conceptualist not of the movement's actual stage realization but rather its aesthetic objectives imagined in their purest form. Essentially, symbolist dramaturgy entails an 'avoidance of all *trompe l'oeil*'.[34] Importantly, though evidently sharing with symbolism this rejection of trompe l'oeil, Beckett devises a theoretical alternative to trompe l'oeil as early as 1948 in his writing on post-war painters such as Geer and Bram van Velde that bears some relation to his later theatrical practice of impediment. This theory he calls *l'empêchement-oeil*.

Beckett's sensibility of impediment was first explored in an essay entitled 'Peintres de *l'empêchement*'.[35] Beckett uses the term *l'empêchement-oeil* to describe the effect of a new mode present in the work of abstract expressionist painters Bram van Velde and Geer van Velde. For Beckett, such an aesthetic proves preferable to the false assumption of making present an idea or image through artistic expression. Quite literally, the term inverts trompe-l'oeil (deception of the eye), a mode of representation that is supposed to trick us into seeing an absent reality.

L'empêchement-oeil certainly shares with symbolism a doctrinal rejection of naturalism. Here lies the temptation of equating Beckett's dramaturgy with symbolism. Consider, for example, how Beckett's play *Happy Days* (1961) employs a set that by design explicitly problematizes the realist theatre's pretensions of trompe l'oeil; according to the stage directions, *Happy Days* should look '[v]ery pompier trompe-l'oeil backcloth to represent unbroken plain and sky receding to meet in far distance'.[36] Daniel Albright describes the result as an effort to achieve 'a kind of failed realism', another reminder that dramaturgical alternatives to realism do not necessarily adhere to the symbolist effort to expunge the material real from occluding stage symbology.[37] In *Happy Days*, the contrary appears to be true: realism appears on the Beckett stage, but in a transfigured, ruinous state detached from its absorptive reference to the world at large. What is real is made too literal, rendering a *stage* realism of unbelievable, estranged performance materiality in which poignant moments of unconsummated feeling refer to pantomime and not the more conventional reverse.[38]

In Chapter 1, a discussion of pure mime according to Mallarmé in *La Livre* represented the symbolist project at its most experimental imaginative capability. How symbolist dramaturgy was mechanically, aesthetically and incidentally rendered should be distinguished from the material realization of works by symbolist-affiliated or sympathetic writers in context. Of Beckett's plays, *Godot* bears the closest resemblance to the dramaturgy of Yeats, especially works we have evidence of Beckett referring to, such as *At the Hawk's Well* (1916). Here, symbols appear to stand in for characters, the preternatural in place of the natural, the mythic in place of the real, and the uncanny in place of the documentary on a stage otherwise denuded of naturalistic elements. Beckett both includes and disfigures these basic attributes of a formative artistic sensibility. An allusion to Yeats's play *At the Hawk's Well* appears in Beckett's *Happy Days*: 'I call to the eye of the mind.'[39] Beckett made regular visits to Dublin's Abbey Theatre and the plays of the Irish Literary Revival that were shown there before he migrated to Paris.[40] Worth takes examples such as these for proof that Beckett should be viewed as the 'heir of Yeats' and be credited for developing a new theatre of 'interior being'.[41]

Lane's characterization of symbolism accords with Worth's on the subject of interiority. Lane describes the movement's direction as an 'insistence upon the independence of art from nature ... towards a painting that "has the character of continuity with states of interior feeling" '.[42] Realism becomes the movement's philosophical opponent in the end, according to Lane:

> One of the principal characteristics that sets off the (eighteen-)eighties from the previous decade is its concern with theory, related to a common concern for meaning ... whether psychological or idealist, semi-scientific or semi-philosophical, the purpose is to establish the importance of the representation the artist has undertaken, and to establish it precisely by making it, in some way, go beyond realism.[43]

Symbolism disavows realism's monopolization of the dramaturgical direction of theatre practice in the late nineteenth century. M. A. R. Habib writes that, for symbolism, 'the struggle for unity is sublimated to the level of form, displaced to a subjective realm where it becomes a conflict of viewpoints'.[44] For Lane, similarly, formal approaches to representation such as Claude Monet's colour experimentation and Edvard Munch's scream reorder the figural domain and change how subjectivity is signified in it. Symbolism even seeks to manifest the unformed, employing a process called 'entelechy' to provide form to orders of experience that transcend the verifiable, from the mood found in the scream to unfathomable, unimaginable colour.

We must remember, however, that the underlying problems with the stable status of reality on the realist or naturalist stage is not only an imagined opponent in symbolist polemic but also the subject of self-analysis and process for realist and naturalist theatre-makers themselves. The intent to 'go beyond realism' has no single trajectory as a result. Henrik Ibsen, for example, the canonical realist playwright, if you will, who Allen remarks 'saw himself as a realist',[45] can be included as part of the symbolist movement. Consider how Aurélien Lugné-Poë, fellow painter of post-impressionist group The Nabis, stage designer at the *Théâtre de l'Oeuvre*, and champion of the symbolist theatre in Paris, along with his associates 'perceived other, more mystical values under the realist surface, and it was at the *Théâtre de l'Oeuvre* that Paris became familiar with Ibsen's plays'.[46] Sarah Balkin claims that in Lugné-Poë's treatment of the Ibsen play, *The Master Builder*, 'the occult symbolist orientation of [his] production ... brought out the de-psychologized formulation of character in [his] play, which nonetheless retains the expository dramatic speech that famously grounds Ibsen's realism'.[47] Symbolists even employed explicitly naturalistic dramaturgical devices for heightening stage reality; André Antoine of *Théâtre Libre*, staging Ibsen's *Ghosts*, 'demonstrated his belief in the power of the actual [for symbolist stagecraft]. For Antoine the set of a butcher shop had to be hung with real hams'.[48] So, while Ruby Cohn once remarked that '*En Attendant*

Godot brought the curtain down on King Ibsen', the ghost of the fallen king inevitably returns in an unpredictable fashion.⁴⁹ We cannot rely upon the resistance to realism be our cardinal vector for identifying Beckett's echoes of symbolism, then.

The only consistent statement about the nature of symbolist theatre's departure from realism and naturalism might be the movement's conceptualism. This conceptualism Lane describes as its concern with the 'theory' and 'meaning' of art's representations, entailing projects of formal experimentation 'beyond realism' and a recognizable, mobilized metatheatricality that tenders this conceptualism. For Mallarmé, symbolist dramaturgy existed only in theory; in his case, as a theory of pure mime.⁵⁰ The proto-surrealism of other key symbolists, the poets Charles Baudelaire and Arthur Rimbaud, similarly typifies the movement's contradictions between the two axes of 'concept' and 'real'. Baudelaire and Rimbaud's realization of paradoxes shaped by a disfigural representative field concerned with the stunning realities of abject life, their fascination with an inverse metaphysics of the diabolical nevertheless couched in actual, urban contexts of malaise, retain this widening contradictoriness explored by the movement. Symbolism, then, conceptualizes how the real and the actual might newly intersect through adopting tenets of avant-gardism at once Romantic and realist, and often contradictory, concerned with heightened emotional and material encounters through art.

Lane positions the problem of formalizing 'interior feeling' mentioned earlier as that which differentiates symbolism from the Romantic and idealist artists that preceded them. Lane writes, '[the] symbolist line reveals the impulse of its creator … evidence of a struggle to give shape to an impelling idea, between awareness of form and an awareness of emotion'.⁵¹ Entelechy, that is, a process of manifesting the unmanifest, becomes symbolism's central aesthetic problem. Craig was the leading technician of the symbolist theatre's dramaturgical realization, and arguably its most notable dramaturg. Craig would be Yeats's architect of stage entelechy for his poetic visions. Illustrating designs for Yeats's dramaturgy through those made for Yeats plays such as *The Hour-Glass*, 'total theatre' artist Craig would come to the attention of Yeats when the latter saw the former's symbolist design for *Dido and Aeneas* by Henry Purcell, adapted from *The Aeneid*, at the Purcell Operatic Society in London in 1901. Worth claims that this acquaintance became the single largest dramaturgical influence on Yeats. She writes: 'There is no more impressive demonstration of Yeats's almost demonic intellectual energy than the speed and thoroughness of his assimilation of Craig's ideas'.⁵² Yeats comes to assimilate Craig's dramaturgy into his theatrical imaginary. Of two sketches by Craig, 'The Heroic Age – Morning' and 'The Heroic

Age – Evening', Yeats reflects that these images 'are impressions ... of the world my people move in ... one, however, suggests to me *On Baile's Strand*, and the other *Deirdre*.'⁵³ Craig's illustrations are hardly stage blueprints. They appear more like illustrations of another world in the tradition of Piranesi. As Craig himself avows in his manifesto for a radical theatre, *On the Art of the Theatre* (1911): 'actuality ... accuracy of detail, is useless upon the stage'.⁵⁴ His sketches for *Dido and Aeneas* from 1906, and *Hamlet*, 1907 are utterly impracticable and indulge in monumentality.⁵⁵ These designs improbably shape a new theatre mechanics, composing hypotheses of spectacle in a figurative visual language. These sketches are defined by their impracticability, very much in the spirit of the impracticability of many symbolist theatre visions composed by its leading playwrights. Yeats claims that the influence of Craig is so significant to his stage art that he can no longer differentiate between his own words and the imagined scenography envisioned by Craig:

> All summer I have been playing with a little model where there is a scene capable of endless transformation, of the expression of every mood that does not require a photographic reality. Mr. Craig – who has invented all this – has permitted me to set up upon the stage of the Abbey another scene that corresponds to this, in the scale of a foot for an inch, and henceforth I shall be able, by means so simple that one laughs, to lay the events of my plays amid a grandeur like that of Babylon. ... Henceforth I can all but 'produce' my play while I write it ... allowing the scene to give the words and the words the scene. I am very grateful for he has banished a whole world that wearied me and was undignified and given me forms and lights upon which I can play as upon some stringed instrument.⁵⁶

Note grandiosity's proximity to the process of artistic composition in this self-reflection. The indistinguishability of scene and words that has emerged for Yeats in his dramaturgical imagination serve a similarly grandiose program for spectacle authored by visionaries.

I will now engage in a comparative discussion of two examples where the aesthetic similarity between Beckett's dramaturgy and Yeats's can be detected in the ways that Worth is noted for elucidating in Beckett studies. To enact a revision of how I think we should observe this resemblance, I make use of Yeats's *The Hour-Glass* and its resemblance to Beckett's *Ohio Impromptu*. There are numerous echoes of the former in the latter. The figural arrangements, the use of spectrality, apparent visual references to the painterly tradition of depicting 'the scholar', and a shared intent to symbolize the figural circumstances of the act of solitary mental reasoning feature in Beckett's piece in ways that are suspiciously alike. In *The Hour-Glass*, the scholar's uncertain future becomes a matter of divine concern, arriving in allegorical form of the character of the Angel. In *Ohio Impromptu*, by contrast, the scene itself does not suggest an allegory of redemption; it even suggests the contrary. Beckett's scenario evokes a dead zone in which the scholar exists in perpetual self-reference. This arrangement compels audiences to contemplate this scene as a metatheatrical scenario about the construction of self-consciousness through the inheritance of memory. There is no visiting Angel for Listener and Reader in Beckett's lyrical piece. There can be no afterlife for the narrative of the scholar figure who has in Beckett's scenario been entrapped in a circular narrative manifested in the doubling of the subject of that narrative. The memory drama is now irrevocably split between the doppelgänger double of a listener and a reader. Thus the refrain 'little is left to tell' becomes the profound motif for the new dramaturgical and diegetic conditions that arise in the Beckettian scene after symbolism.

Beckett's late play *Ohio Impromptu* performed in 1981 has a mise-en-scène strikingly similar to the dramaturgical sketch for *The Hour-Glass*. Although for Worth it is the room spaces of Maurice Maeterlinck that most closely resemble Beckett, Yeats's distilled Irish twilight realm most resembles the dramaturgical design of *Ohio Impromptu*. In both plays, a lit table is 'midstage'.[57] Beckett's play demands that the backdrop be in darkness, as in Yeats's play's design. Both plays open with figures seated at the table, with the one stage figure in Yeats's play multiplied to two in Beckett's, but figured as the mirror image of the other. Echoing principles of symbolist dramaturgy, both plays utilize symbolic props and minimalist stage design in a domain without setting that also resists trompe l'oeil. The split stage of *The Hour-Glass* actually recalls the space of another of Beckett's plays, *Eleuthéria*, with its split stage between character Victor's room and the Krap family salon. This use of partition, in its close resemblance, suggests that Yeats's dramaturgy is recalled throughout Beckett's career and not merely in the later *Ohio Impromptu*. We shall see how dramaturgical suggestion does not entail adherence and may even indicate critical opposition.

Yeats's *The Hour-Glass* concerns the drama of a character named Wise Man and the visit he receives from an angel which causes him to rescind his atheism. The Craig design allegorizes this split between faith and disbelief through a lighting design that distinguishes the enlightening, brightly lit portal through which the Angel character enters – the world of the miraculous – and the lamplit near-darkness of the realm of Wise Man sat at his desk reading – the world of reason. This chiaroscuro suggests a Manichean world view to suffuse the scene. Manichaeism is a theological perspective concerned with the presence and apparitionality of good and evil, a perspective Chris Ackerley characterizes as 'gnostic'. Gnosticism is associated with less orthodox formations of Christianity, and, for Beckett, a doctrine most linked to the *Confessions* of Augustine.[58] Manichaeism governs the visual imaginary of works of literature such as Dante Alighieri's *Divina Commedia*, perhaps the most influential source of this visuality in Beckett's work, along with the work of John Milton and the philosophy of Arthur Schopenhauer.[59] Yeats's stage design is explicitly Manichean. Note the inventory of objects that allegorize the Wise Man's pre-conversion faith in reason: '*An hour-glass on a bracket near the door. A creepy stool near it. Some benches. An astronomical globe. A blackboard. A large ancient map of the world on the wall. Some musical instruments.*'[60] Those props stand in shade, lingering in the gloom, only to be stunned with the bright light emanating from the insentient realm figured by the Angel that dominates the other half of the stage. Yeats's symbolism attempts a maximum of metaphoricity by a minimum of stage craft that analogizes light and dark as Manichean forces. With the updated version of *The Hour-Glass* of 1914, Yeats writes that 'The Fool [character] too, when [the play] is now played at the Abbey Theatre, wears a mask designed by Mr. Gordon Craig which makes him seem less a human being *than a principle of the mind*'.[61] Again, the Manichean dimension in Yeats's dramaturgy exalts abstraction and symbolism over materiality and the self-reference of humanity.

Certainly, Beckett's *Ohio Impromptu* employs the process of denaturalizing stage figuration employed in symbolist dramaturgy. Beckett may even be said to exacerbate this process, dissolving the once-Manichean configuration this mode of theatricality renders of the stage to draw the dramaturgy into a mode of heightened self-reference. As a result, the evacuation of the transcendental references renders the realm of the unknowable and the promise of light a circumstance of confinement and greyness that is circular rather than terminal. The Wise Man becomes two figures, Listener and Reader, and there are no pupils, fools or angels. With a kind of eternal impediment emerging between reason and the self, self-consciousness appears not in the emergence of faith, but as the site of an unmendable rift. The Manichean becomes the miniature. This diminution of the Yeats's Manichean symbolist dramaturgy divides what was best idealized in Mallarmé's imagination as a transcendental sphere of symbolic entelechy enabled by script into two negative zones of mutual separation, the narrative written and the narrative heard.[62] This diminution of the suggestive resources of symbolist stagecraft shows most powerfully in the shift in the value of characterological role from an *archetypal* scholar in Yeats's play whose wisdom is cast into doubt by the Fool and the Angel to a mere self-reader in Beckett's, whose self-knowledge only heightens sameness and repetition. *Wisdom* becomes what is *little left to tell*.

Without a Manichean differentiation between light and dark, the scene of *Ohio Impromptu* is contrastingly saturated in darkness. All is very dim. No backdrop should be visible. The two figures are sat at a table with a single-source of light and a large book. The Listener figure faces the audience and the other, Reader, sits in profile. Crucially, the light during the play does not change. The difference between listening and reading entails a difference of responsibility to the durational reading of the otherwise complete text – the dialectic divides time between rhythmic, circular duration and eternal, inert script. Listener raps his fist on the table to direct Reader's recitation of what is the play's monologue. While this punctuation of certain passages suggests a modicum of agency, by the end of the play, the audience sees how repetitions in the text confirm that there is 'little left to tell' and that the options for altering the impression of the life narrated in the book have dwindled nearly to nothingness.

For Knowlson, the scenography of this play is reminiscent of 'seventeenth-century Dutch painting', especially of Rembrandt's figures within that tradition and their long hair and long coats; Vermeer's *The Geographer* and *The Astronomer* are other suggested reference points for this scenario.[63] We might say that those props in *The Hour-Glass* such as a globe, like the astronomer's in Vermeer's painting, and a map, like the geographer's in Rembrandt's, comprise possible reference points for Yeats also. Considered in this light, Beckett miniaturization thus entails condensing these various representatives of wisdom into the sole prop of *Ohio Impromptu*, the unnaturally large stage book. The scholar figure, a painterly motif best associated with the Enlightenment as represented in Dutch painting, crystallizes in symbolist and post-symbolist dramaturgy as a progressively more metonymic and generalized scholar-figure. There is a third painting not mentioned by Knowlson that seems particular apt in this light. Theatre scenography and Rembrandt's portraiture meet most profoundly in the Faust rendered by Rembrandt in *Faust in his Study* (*c*.1652). Faust, of course, is the archetypal scholar of German folklore and the protagonist linking, in a sense, Christopher Marlowe's baroque tragedy, Goethe's closet drama, Yeats's Wise Man, Stein's modernist closet drama (in *Doctor Faustus Lights the Lights*), and Beckett's doppelgänger miniature drama of impediment.

Faust represents the diabolical pact the human threatens to make with wisdom. Deni McIntosh McHenry makes a case for understanding light in Rembrandt's painting in a mystic following a Kabbalistic interpretation tracing its resemblance to other works with enigmatic light, such as *Belshazzar's Feast* (1635), positioning Faust explicitly as an alchemist.[64] The scenographic tone and figuration of the scholar in these Rembrandt images can be seen to precede the Yeats and Beckett versions of the Reader as versions of an archetype of the scholar. Thus, we can observe how the light of inspiration, neither naturalistic nor divine in *Ohio Impromptu*, has been substantially impeded in unchanging gloom of the Beckettian scene. That impediment mirrors the circumstances of the narrative that governs the book of these two figures' lives. That is, the play has two narratives within Reader's monologue: a languid, uneventful scene accounting for lost love, and the self-reflexive lines that chronicle the bare circumstances of their predicament in which 'little is left to tell' at the end of life.[65] The accounts of the character's poverty of volition and being at terminus of 'profounds of mind' has a sonic, kinetic counterpart in Listener's punctuation of Reader's monologue through commanding knocks upon the table directing transitions.[66] These raps also remind the spectator of how little volition Reader really has as a mere recycler of an already complete narrative.

Ohio Impromptu's debt to the scenography of *The Hour-Glass* is obvious after comparative analysis. Beckett's refashioning of a dramaturgy of Manichaeism drawn from Yeats into a figural miniaturization should be seen as a departure from symbolism, rather than a continuation, I have urged. Where Yeats's play stages Wise Man's deliverance from corporeal Manichaeism as the undergirding of presence, carried away into revelatory Paradise by the Angel, Reader and Listener, Beckett's doppelgängers, are '*Unblinking. Expressionless*' during their '*Ten Seconds*' to '*Fade out.*'[67] Beckett's stymied denouement, quite unlike the cries of Wise Man in *The Hour-Glass* as he nears death, has the stark return to darkness for its conclusion.

Cosmic scenery and cosmic space

We have observed the miniaturization of a formerly symbolist mode of dramaturgy in Beckett's work through a comparative analysis of *The Hour-Glass* and *Ohio Impromptu*. But it is *Godot* more than any other play by Beckett that has traditionally enabled most of the comparative inquiry into the symbolism's influence upon Beckett's spectacle. Worth's *Samuel Beckett: Life Journeys* ultimately makes a case for Beckett's ties to the theatre of Yeats, as well as to continental figure Maeterlinck's dramaturgy, through a discussion of the cosmic reference this play especially appears to make after the symbolist theatre. She writes: 'All the scenic spaces Beckett creates become cosmic spaces where we find ourselves, in the Maeterlinckian phrase, face to face with "the vast unknown that surrounds us".'[68] The theory of impediment I have been using in this chapter undermines that proposition; the 'vast unknown' becomes less suggestive of the cosmic in a Beckett spectacle such as *Ohio Impromptu* because the coordinates once connoted by the Manichean use of light, figure, and stage prop undergo diminishment such that the Beckett domain remains irreparably opaque. This opacity occurs most of all to those that audit it, the audience, the results of the experiment in impediment being the Beckett spectacle's enduring metatheatrical concern.

We might conclude this chapter with the most familiar of symbolist evocations in the Beckett theatrical oeuvre: *Godot*'s scenography. Following the argument I have pursued thus far, we can revise Beckett's dramaturgy here as a literalization rather than energization of the figures that traditionally stand in for the cosmic in Maeterlinck or Yeats. Helpfully, this process is quite evident in *Godot*, since the play may be the most aesthetically allusive with regard to the symbolist dramaturgical tradition and, indeed, towards the Romanticist forebears of the avant-garde movement. As Dirk Van Hulle contends: 'Whereas the Romantic *Sehnsucht* is a longing for the infinite, Beckett "strives" after the infinitesimal.'[69] The experiment of dramaturgical exposition of the meagreness of the stage economy for referring to an external realm becomes a refrain in Beckett's theatre. The trajectory means escalating an increasing poverty of means in dramaturgy and drawing further attention to this circumstance.

Again, *Godot* resembles the scenography of theatrical works by Yeats. This time, Beckett alludes to the plays *The Death of Cuchulain* (1939) and *Purgatory* (1939). In *Purgatory*, we find 'A Boy, An Old Man. Scene. – A ruined house and a bare tree in the background'.[70] The two figures, the nondescript rural setting, and the bare tree could all belong in *Godot*'s 'Act One. A country road. A tree. Evening'.[71] Then there are the allusions to visual culture that Worth helpfully analyses as the inspiration for the scenography of *Godot*: Caspar David Friedrich's *Two Men Contemplating the Moon* (1819), and, potentially, *Man and Woman Observing the Moon* (1824) also, the latter being a sort of revision of the former painting. In Knowlson's biography, Ruby Cohn is said to have viewed *Man and Woman Observing the Moon* in Berlin with Beckett in 1975. Knowlson writes:

> As they were looking at Friedrich's painting ... Beckett announced unequivocally: 'This was the source of *Waiting for Godot*, you know.' ... [Beckett] may well have confused [the] two paintings ... In any case, the Berlin painting is so similar in its composition to the Dresden picture [*Two Men*] that what he said could apply equally well to either.[72]

To account for Beckett's cosmic scenery as part of a symbolist visual mode more fully, Worth couples the Friedrich image with *The Two Travellers* (1942), an impressionistic painting by close friend of Beckett's, painter Jack

Yeats, that clarifies the symbolist visual mode in its unsteady relationship to Romantic and avant-garde approaches to vision:

> Both (paintings) draw an extraordinary sense of cosmic space from the image of two figures in an empty landscape; in one, gazing up at the moon, in the other, appearing to meet in the middle of nowhere, totally isolated in natural yet mysteriously alien countryside.[73]

Worth sees an extenuation of the minimalism and barrenness of the symbolist mise-en-scène in the Beckett theatre as a return to the cosmic rendered in these ambiguous ways. Beckett's approach is thus seen as a more distant, fragmented minimalism than found on the symbolist stage. Of the cosmic trope of the 'tree of life' as rendered in *Godot*, for example, Worth notes that the tree 'is given impish pictorial expression with the shock appearance in *Act Two* of "four or five leaves" '.[74] On the shared cosmic and Romantic image of the moon, Worth writes of Peter Hall's first version of *Godot* in 1955 and later production of 1997 that they meet 'Beckett's wish for playfulness, drawing amusing chuckles as (the moon) rose with ostentatious deliberation. It was also affecting; a serene, pale golden orb silently speaking of transcendental space'.[75] This playfulness would distinguish symbolist from Romantic modes, the former allowing for ambiguity where the latter should entail visionary completeness. Here, Worth exposes a telling inconsistency in Beckett's uptake of the symbolist dramaturgical mode critical to Beckett's ever-paradoxical dramaturgy. Like the bare, 'impish' tree, the moon rising with 'ostentatious deliberation' becomes an excessive piece of stagecraft at once playful and transcendental, even less suggestive than Yeats's mythic scene.

The barest, most reduced and ruinous achievement of this symbolist trajectory using *Godot* may be the famous production directed by Walter Asmus at the Gate Theatre in Dublin in 1991. Major Irish visual artist Louis le Brocquy was the designer of the scenography, and the production featured Barry McGovern and Johnny Murphy. Photographs of the production by Tom Lawlor in the Worth book show that the tree is not even the wan twig often erected for the piece, but rather an abstract, two-dimensional object resembling more a lightning bolt upended than any Romantic crossroads arbour. Such abstraction presents Beckett in a notably symbolist vein. But then another famous production of *Godot* provides a different sense of the play as an enclosure lost to the cosmos: the famous San Quentin Workshop production of 1957. The literalization of the play's concern with human life as an incarceration in time defined by waiting presents even more strongly the departure from symbolism, and the promise of cosmic potential encoded in its dramaturgy, that comprises Beckett's impeded dramaturgy. This production follows the Lüttringhausen Prison production in Wuppertal, Germany, put on by a prisoner who translated the French into German for a show in the prison on 29 November 1953. The San Quentin production is perhaps better known because it enabled the discovery of inmate and later significant Beckett actor-collaborator Rick Cluchey. This production exemplifies the dramaturgical interpretation of Beckett and his dramaturgy for Herbert Blau, the major experimental Beckettian dramatist and thinker of the mid-century period; Blau directed this storied late-1950s production with his company, the San Francisco Actors Workshop.[76] The San Quentin production had the added evocation of fatality by being staged in the former gallows room of the prison.[77] *Godot*'s structure of interminable, impotent waiting has its real conditions foregrounded by production in a prison.

More can be said about the materialist approach to staging *Godot* as a mode that deviates from the neo-symbolist one. Incarceration as a general condition is the point of reference for Matthew Melia's argument that Beckett belongs to a tradition of avant-gardists concerned with incarceration, including Artaud and Jean Genet. The thematics of imprisonment are seen by Melia to structure a French avant-garde context transposing 'wartime techniques of cruelty and the dialect of power and control that exists between director and actor within modern theatre'.[78] Yet Melia does not refer to this telling use of the prison stage for realizing *Godot*. Melia's account of how these playwrights evoke Foucauldian visions of modern control carries new dramaturgical meaning when we consider how the transposition of *Godot* to the prison domain not only came seamlessly and creatively, but by prisoner collaboration in the very early days of staging the play, both in the cases of Lüttringhausen and San Quentin.

Prison *Godot*s mount the case for thinking about Beckett's impeded spectacle as one whose theatricality is closed off from the cosmic, rather than an evocation of it. Prison *Godot*s, in a way reminiscent of Simone Weil's ontology, suggest that the cosmic can only exist in such a raw domain if the transcendent condition is completely subtracted from the living abyss. The very scene of Beckett's *Godot* is a prison. Even if the two prisons, Lüttringhausen or San Quentin, and '[a] country road', do not seem entirely commensurable, the shared carceral circumstance of the two lies with the more critical reference points of time and repetition. *Godot* provides the theatrical means of *miniaturizing* spatial and durational confinement through the category of waiting. Perhaps this element of Beckett's experimental dramaturgy is more evident when such a play has the reality of incarceration as its material resource rather than the symbols that have accrued in theatre history to represent it.

Two images of *En attendant Godot* present the carceral *Godot* in its most basic substantiality and yet do not derive from the conventional prison landscape. Perhaps we should not be surprised by the production that they document: they belong to the premiere directed by Roger Blin at the *Théâtre de Babylone* in Paris in January 1953.[79] Melia provides the argument that Blin is the most influentially shared interlocutor of the work of three major figures of modern French drama, Beckett, Artaud and Genet.[80] Blin's dramaturgical role in providing a conduit for these theatre-makers dramaturgical innovations cannot be overstated; as these three also happened to inaugurate the French theatrical avant-garde style of post-war drama, they share Blin as their incidental dramaturg. Importantly, these three writers share an envisioning of *theatrical* imprisonment in some parallelism with real carceral imprisonment. Blin thus provides a critical dramaturgical cipher for understanding this parallelism. In the photos of the *Théâtre de Babylone* premiere, a simple tarp constitutes the production's backdrop, pulled over what seems like machinery for propping up rear lights and other theatre equipment. Theatre machinery is visibly part of the spectacle in the premiere production. Then, the space is so evidently confining the players are framed with a sort of pathetic theatricality that is also profoundly claustrophobic. We can assume the atmosphere was acutely felt by the audience present for these shows. Theatrical-mechanical profanation of the once cosmic scenery of symbolist pure mimesis results. The setting for *Godot* in this instance, perhaps even more than the prison *Godot*s, reprises the Beckettian concept of presence as a matter of incarceration. Ironically, here the theatre most resembles a jail, insofar as theatre represents the human figure incarcerated to the observational field of others. *Godot*, we are reminded, realizes a dramaturgy that transfers effortlessly to other domains of confinement. *Godot* I argue is best designed when the mechanics of simulation have been exposed, regardless of the actual context. Indeed, the applicability of *Godot* to contrasting political and social circumstances relies upon this characteristic to make best use of the actual context when the play is *actually* mounted.

Cohn once famously remarked:

> Godot has subsequently been explained as God, a diminutive god, Love, Death, Silence, Hope, De Gaulle, Pozzo, a Balzac character, a bicycle racer, Time Future, a Paris street for call-girls, a distasteful image evoked by French words containing the root god (godailler, to guzzle; godenot, runt; godelureau, bumpkin; godichon, lout). Beckett told Roger Blin that the name Godot derived from French slang words for boot – godillot, godasse ... Beckett's play tells us plainly who Godot is – the promise that is always awaited and not fulfilled, the expectation that brings two men

to the board night after night. *The plays tell us this dramatically and not discursively.*[81]

What Cohn identifies is a dramatic realization of an impediment to interpretation that spurs multiple ones. Godot is a dramatic impediment and not a symbol. He structures the action of two central characters by his absence. He is a dramatic deferral that nevertheless generates not a single interpretation – God, say – but rather a chain of signification. The variant stage illustrations of *Godot* suggest that the poverty of the stage's representational capacity in Beckett's compositional intentions encourage this manifold of possible figures. Maximalist dramaturgical productions of *Godot* have a tendency of illustrating too much as a result. The bare bars of the theatre might just be the most apt presentation of the dramaturgical vision imagined in the play. Thanks to Beckett's departures from symbolism, stage mimesis has extended its diminutions of stage materiality and reference point to entail a new dramaturgical paradigm after Mallarmé. This paradigm affirms material contingencies of performance not through a vitalism of pure mimesis but through an opaque and self-exposed theatricality. Since Godot the absent figure is character, narrative, architecture, joke, metaphysics and spatio-temporal limitation at once, Godot himself profanes the inheritance of symbolist dramaturgy with a metatheatrical enclosure in which spectators too are likely to find themselves newly incarcerated in a live present. Godot is the allegorical symbol that never turns up.

4

Dream space, the other laboratory

Samuel Beckett's early prose renders the Sisyphean burden of consciousness with a distinctly Dantean atmosphere. The novel *Dream of Fair to Middling Women* ([1932] 1992) and short story *Echo's Bones* ([1934] 2014), among other examples, present figures moving between an unshakable dark of sleep into a bothersome light of waking in playful exile. They are in exile from all the connotations that light commonly stands for. The late Beckett, by contrast, no longer entertains these exaltations of the grotesque and Joycean comic logorrhoea that charm a life of hopeless gloom. Rather, life 'vaguens' here. No longer the characterological landscape of spoiling, festering and suppuration, characters in late works such as the stage play *That Time* (1976) and the teleplay *Nacht und Träume* (*Night and Dreams*) (1983) position the abyss as a more total enclosure than the meagrely social and ironic sphere of the early prose. In these plays and works for film, the gestures that survive the darkness point to a different connotation: darkness means sleep, most of all. As a result, these emanations take on a more overtly somnolent allusiveness. Freedom in Beckett's work thus tends to appear as a thematic absurdity. Freedom is an unresolvable paradox, in tune with Martin Heidegger's refinement of the concept of the void as a zone that vaporizes ontology and lies completely beyond phenomenological experience, a representation of 'the unoccupied free [realm]'.[1] From early to late Beckett, we move from 'fighting in vain against the hideous torpor and the grit and glare of … lids … so long lapped in gloom' to the basic gestural conditions of emerging into the light of representation, or dissolving them mise en abyme.[2] Sleep, in its guises of dream, trance, ghostliness and unconsciousness, therefore provides a representational medium for understanding the active traces of what survives or approaches the void through the problematics of consciousness. These problematics emerge when we query dream, imagination, affect and other apertures that open to the inaccessible zone of pure interiority.

Explorations of nothingness following the cognitive, psychoanalytic and ontological connotations of the theme are well-established in Beckett studies.[3] Less considered is sleep as a matter of more meaning than simply as the medium for examining nothingness. That is, sleep is less often explored in Beckett as a commonplace, material circumstance that living beings undergo, and typically every day. The mundanity and regularity of the human experience of this medium and representation of void also appears to be Beckett's concern, I want to suggest. A different importance attends this line of inquiry. The gestural, materialist presentation of sleep, especially through its counterpart, sleeplessness, features in the irritations, enclosures, dramatic encumberances and self-perceptions of a host of dramatic works worthy of enquiry. I use Giorgio Agamben's theory of gesture as the 'other side of language' to assay this importance of the sleeplessness motif in Beckettian drama. Gesture, the philosopher asserts, presents 'the muteness inherent in humankind's very capacity for language, its *speechless* dwelling in language'.[4] Beckett's dream-clouded, sleepless figures existing at the edges of sleep produce gestures that expose the emergence of once-solitary spaces of interiority to a representational field. This field, however enshrouded, might crucially be observed externally, by the other, when we strive to find a form that retains this paradox of speechlessness.

Sleep's intrigues

The first register of sleep and the intrigue of its inaccessible contents is sleeplessness, prior to all moral and ontological hermeneutics regarding what sleep is. Sleeplessness is a rejection of the condition and destination of sleep, be that destination prosaic and quotidian (rest) – or absolute – (death). It is in sleep that we most resemble our origin and destination. Sleep constitutes a space of absolute continuity with self and its automaticity, a space of absolute unconsciousness. Sleep is an unwitnessed state, most of all by ourselves.

Quoting Maurice Blanchot, Herschel Farbman argues that dream 'is the pure perpetuation of insomnia – "the impossibility of sleeping" that we encounter in the very heart of sleep'.[5] Later, Farbman adds that unconscious life within the context of dream contains this inverse dimension of sleep: 'The unconscious never sleeps. If it did, there could be no dream'.[6] As such, we see in Beckett's work a repertoire of gestural and figurative states of sleeplessness that present progressively starker intimations of being at the brink between dream and life. At the same time, the Beckett cosmos on the stage appears to treat the same boundary as the always amorphous and uncertain horizon of an unlived state. Such a state is 'unoccupied', and its completeness would mean 'death'. This is the approach to the topic that Shane Weller establishes as the site of Beckett's exploration of questions of nothingness, inflected using Friedrich Nietzsche as 'the repose of deepest sleep ... the *absence of suffering*'.[7]

Weller basically positions Beckett as sympathetic to this Nietzschean view. Beckett explores human reality, in other words, as a permutation of sleeplessness. Sleeplessness in this sense comes to mean the sphere of suffering exiled from an indifferent abyss that inherently excludes subjective experience. We see avowals of such a distinction in Beckettian rhetoric, especially in some of his favourite quotations. Beckett's experimental translations of maxims by the fatalistic French aphorist Nicholas-Sébastien Roch Chamfort in Beckett's 1977 series 'Long After Chamfort' comprise some of the best-known ones. These maxims overtly equate death with sleep: 'sleep till death / healeth / come ease / this life disease'.[8] Sleep here is characterized as some kind of bedfellow of death, a comfort prior to a supposed absolute comfort from the 'life disease'. Dream problematizes the conceptual unities that Chamfort exploits for ironic effect. As a sleepless state, an insomnia inhering in sleep, dream illustrates how consciousness and self-examination throw the subject into equivocal ontological formations excluded from peace in a conceptual totality. Beckett's dramatic works that explicitly consult the subject of sleep present an aspiration for Nietzsche's 'absence of suffering' and Chamfort's healing balm of the 'life disease'. At the same time, such works acknowledge the kind of psychic conundrum posed by dream, found for example in Freud's suggestion that 'the unconscious wish … always expresses both that driving wish and the preconscious wish to sleep'.[9] As a result, Beckett's dramatic creatures tend to appear as entities whose crises are shaped by the delay of rest.

The dreamscapes of Beckett in performance can be read as allegorical presentations of an inverse side of dialectical spectacles of unconscious human life realized in material gestures of *sleeplessness*. Thus the late Beckett of experimental theatre and prose poetry, rather than situate voice and text as the infinite domain lying within states of absolute sleep, or void, instead constructs anatomies of dreamscapes and their gestures. These anatomies retain the inevitable signs of a remaining self-visibility at the brink of disappearance. By his final works of the 1980s such as teleplay *Nacht und Träume*, stage plays *Catastrophe* (1984) and *What Where* (1983), Beckett develops brightly lit autopsies of the remains of subjects and their gestures at the brink of abyss and sleep; those remains take on the appearance of floating heads, hands and animated death masks.

Among a selection of dreamscapes and commentaries on sleep in the Beckett oeuvre, I will observe Beckett's anatomies of the sleeping subject as a cartography of the human figure's proximity to void left in the traces found in gestures. Examples such as *Happy Days* (1961) and *Nacht und Träume* in which hands reach out from the dark and into the light signal zones of disappearance. We observe these interactions too in *That Time*'s Listener's periodic awakening, and in the emergence of the head into light manifest by *Catastrophe*'s Protagonist. What these examples share is the characterization of sleeplessness as the last obstacle preventing an entry into the abyss. Dismembered gesture in the context of dreamscape thus presents a parallelism between theatrical atmospherics and dream settings, a parallelism that enables an experimental sphere of figural presence to be put into play. Let us examine how *Happy Days*, *Nacht und Träume*, and *That Time*, most particularly, present gesture at the limit of the abyss.

Dream as medium

Sleep is the space in which dream, the medium of the free reign of the void, resides. Much of Beckett scholarship so far has considered Beckett's conceptualization of Beckett's dreamlike spaces in terms of their atmospherics of what is impossible to view from the eye of consciousness, belonging instead to the domain of unconsciousness. Sarah Balkin (2019), Enoch Brater (1987), Steven Connor (2014), Mary Luckhurst (2014), Ulrika Maude (2002), Jean-Michel Rabaté (1996) and Paul Sheehan (2009) have each theorized about the figural or aesthetic implications of reading Samuel Beckett's characters as ghostly apparitions that challenge norms of conscious apprehension.[10] This wide range of approaches shows, for one thing, that such apprehension belongs to a diverse set of auditors, from the audience present at a Beckett play, to other characters relating to principle ones, or as the latent concept of the dramaturgical realization of the stage work. The liminality that these apparitions bear in relation to the principles of representation that govern theatrical spectacle remains the crucial shared point; what resists full apprehension also in turn means a challenge to the norms of theatrical representation. Sleep and dream are also unextraordinary and unquestionably real; this paradox is not only meaningful for examining Beckett's gestural logics, but also appears to motivate the writer's continued to return to the dialectic of sleep and sleeplessness.

Dream is the setting or condition of characters in a number of dramatic cases: Krapp of *Krapp's Last Tape* is noted in Beckett's own theatrical notebook as 'Traumgefressener mensch', or 'Dreameaten man';[11] *That Time* involves a suspended head named in the script as 'Listener', who with closed eyes appears to be immersed in three dream narratives. These narratives are presented in pre-recorded monologues that the live head reacts to only by brief intervals of eyes opening, the final reaction being a 'smile, toothless';[12] and *Nacht und Träume*'s title is German for 'Night and Dreams', its characters being 'Dreamer' and 'His dreamt self'.[13] Of a draft version of *That Time*, James Knowlson and John Pilling make the observation that added at the side of the manuscript are the directions 'face about 8' above stage level, podium in consequence'. The only query [to the draft made by Beckett] concerns whether the old man's head should be framed by a white pillow. By typescript five, the decision has been made: 'no pillow'.[14]

That Time is explicitly set in a dreamscape, then. This archival note reveals that, by intending to have the floating head rest on a pillow, Beckett at one point wanted this space of dream to be as literal as possible. Numerous other late television and theatre works such as *Eh Joe* (1965) or *Footfalls* (1976) utilize unsituated, often recorded voices that are not live in a characterological or dramaturgical sense to suggest that apparitions of dead or disembodied voice manifest as sleepless entities of sound that do not belong to the material world but intrude upon it like voices from a dream or the subconscious. Indeed, Julie Campbell argues that Beckett's radio plays explore the very implications of voices without origin. Voices that simply emerge from the dark suggest uncertain birth, with Campbell referencing the role of psychoanalyst Carl Jung's influential notion for the young Beckett that subjectivity can be formed against conventional norms, even '*never born entirely*, and never really there'; such beings Jung once called 'ethereal children'.[15] Campbell chooses the radio play *All That Fall* (1957) for a key example of a Beckett 'dreamscape' that belongs to the apparitionality of radio. Campbell surmises that the rapt listener engages with the sound drama as if in a kind of shared dream with characters therein.[16]

Living and performing are often portrayed as synonymous conditions that arise from unpleasant awakening on the Beckett stage: in *Endgame* 'HAMM *stirs. He yawns under the handkerchief. He removes the handkerchief from his face* ... HAMM: Me – [*he yawns*] – to play', and Hamm's parents, Nagg and Nell, sleep in 'ashbins' and are coerced from them to perform. *AWW II*'s two mimes are similarly goaded from their slumber in containers, this time sacks. The Speaker of *A Piece of Monologue* seems to be delaying impending sleep to give his monologue, dressed, after all, in a 'white nightgown'.[17] Then, there are numerous instances of characters who appear to be sleeping who in fact are not. Notably, many such characters are in fact listening: *Ohio Impromptu*'s (1981) Listener, face on arm, knocks on the table at intervals in the text recited by Reader; *Rockaby*'s (1981) W, when apparently sleeping, is actually listening, which we recognize by her three, progressively fainter cries for 'more', sleeping it appears absolutely (in death) only once the stage lights go out.[18]

Numerous illustrations of sleep in Beckett's oeuvre position the interiority of sleep as a realm that, paradoxically, remains external to what is given on stage. Sleep is a condition from which the stage extracts access to demand attention. Hamm under his handkerchief has his face unveiled to start the play and re-covered to close it; Hamm's parents Nagg and Nell are hit to awaken them to perform; Nell's subsequent lack of reappearance indicates a return to sleep in its final formation, death; the two characters of *AWW II* (1959) who are goaded out of sacks must have been sleeping; Winnie's state is one of sleep before alarms wake her at the beginning of Acts I and II of *Happy Days*; and *That Time*'s periodically awakening suspended head responds to the least invasive of the goads, a short spell of silence from the otherwise constant audio narration. All such cases present waking life as an interruption of a seemingly more total, absorbent condition of sleep, in some cases literally referring to the expiration of life that sleep comes to allude to. Arbitrary, mechanical, periodical or scheduled, and interval provocations, enacted by hands, bells, object, or sometimes simply the invasion of periodic time, together suggest that the urge to perform is associated with the will to live, what in both cases is problematized by the usual morbid wit of the Beckett imagination that questions whether the will to exist is in any way elective. Beckett's theatre, in other words, provides a wide-ranging set of characterological anatomies of basic existence as conditions best defined by prohibitions and interruptions of sleep.

Those who see us sleep in our sleeplessness share in a community of observing that configures a particular division between disconnected but interreliant domains of experience. That is to say, the other sees the gestures of sleep as an opaque surface withholding a dream whose content is unobservable, a private, sleepless simulation of existence within sleep. In this sense, that exterior laboratory space of dream beyond the grasp of spectacle becomes a solitary quality, belonging to an implacable interior. Eddie Paterson suggests that the heightened solitariness of monologue in Beckett's oeuvre indicates his most radical contribution to the tradition of this subgenre of performance. Paterson argues that Beckett's becomes innovation with monologue involves the experimentation with norms of stage narration and narrative logic that ultimately 'encourage a distance between the "speaker" of the monologue and the spectator'; the effect is to 'foreground[] the theatricality of the narrative and reduc[e] the stage action to the words of a single speaker'.[19] Following Paterson, we can understand the presentation of sleepless monologue as an increasing attentiveness to the otherness lying within self-testimony, the sleepless consciousness ever referring to the sleeping self. The monologist's conventional realization of narrative as an exposure of interiority and a more truthful presentation of a formerly undisclosed self has its diegetic theatricality deconstructed. Beckett's sleepless monologues expose the otherness comprising the relation between the speaking self and the self to which the narration refers.

Apparitions of this paradoxical intimacy found in self-alienation shape many of Beckett's roles. Such roles tend to feature some form of self-reflexive doubling. For example, consider the case of the limited self-awareness suggested in Krapp's aged presence through the live character's ontological distance from the eloquent, arrogant youth narrating chronicles of his life on tape in *Krapp's Last Tape*. Then there is the dreamer's haunted situation of being plagued by an alien interrogator in the form of the Woman in *Eh Joe* who imprecates the eponymous character. Consider also the variegated, prismatic narratives of *That Time* as they distantly associate while nonetheless never reaching continuity, neither in narrative nor vocal terms. Here, the vocal performance of the 'same voice' across audio tracks, roles A, B and C, should be arranged in a 'threefold pitch' to enable them to be distinguished from each other by the spectator.[20] Unlike Beckett's radio plays in which dream provides an interactive frame for a listener to share in the dreamscape – although not to be any more authenticated by a listenership than a spectatorship – his theatre presents dream's persistent interruption and fragmentation.

I now want to focus upon critical gestures of the pursuit of a shared situation – a kind of dream – that continually unravels due to the demands of sleepless visibility, consciousness and self-examination, in the form of hands reaching out. This gesture of reaching out is most poignantly figured in *Happy Days* and *Nacht und Träume*, where the hand reaching out becomes a compassionate desire for shared dream across the gulf made by an otherwise unbridgeable solitariness.

In *Happy Days*, protagonist Winnie stuck waist-deep in a mound is awakened from sleep by a stark bell ringing 'piercingly', and begins her performance by making a strange prayer, 'World without end Amen'.[21] Beginning Act Two, Winnie, this time up to her very neck in the mound, is once again awoken by a bell. After remarking 'Hail, holy light', she reflects: 'Someone is looking at me still. [*Pause.*] Caring for me still.'[22] In one sense, Winnie is speaking about her companion Willie, who is almost entirely faceless, seated on the other side of the mound until his final crawl towards her that closes the play.[23] By implication, Winnie is also referring to the audience, the assembly of auditors who share in this 'World without end' along with her. The alarms that open both acts and spur Winnie into a final smile at the moment she appears to return to neutrality (and, perhaps, sleep) clearly signify a prohibition of slumber, punctuating the two figures' consignment to life as it is on the mound with a perpetuity that codes most manifestly as sleeplessness. In the end, Winnie reflects that prior to Willie's old-age infirmities, and presumably before Winnie was neck-deep in the mound, both were able to give each other a hand. The figurative expression becomes an actual, visible stage pun. Now, the only hand being gestured is Willie's, reaching out to Winnie. Willie's apparently eternal lack of access to Winnie in this 'World without end' may appear to undermine Winnie's happiness, but it clearly completes the image also. The gestures of two inevitably solitary dreamers are bound together in a compassionate gesture of reaching out towards each other in their sleeplessness. If cohabitation in sleep's active realm of dream is impossible – and tragically foreclosed to all living beings – the only balm to repair this permanent severance is the gesture. Beckett presents an entire gestural tableau to affirm this, allocating a profound, other-worldly image of impassable interior domains separated by the circumstances of brute existence. The spectator's exclusion from that access also punctuates this compassionate striving for the other's dream world; we complete the tableau's picture. Sleep entails the abridgement of sight. Thus, this reaching out also suggests the traversal of zones of blindness.

Trish McTighe chronicles the reappearance of this gestural trope of the failure to reach the hand's clasp in Beckett's work as the unrealized promise enclosed in a haptic aesthetic; the haptic, that is, tactile feeling in the absence of physical touch, she writes, 'drives the impulse to reach outward, to discover and demarcate the limits of the other and the limits of the self'.[24] Interiority marks the contingent sphere within the limits of the self, a domain nonetheless haptically conjured in such encounters of gestural disconnection, McTighe suggests. The gestures of sleeplessness, the smile of Winnie's 'happy days' and Willie's outstretched hand, provide the only juncture between two inaccessible interiorities. A monologist and a mime, again, prove irreparably sundered from narrative and corporeal authority, while their distance provides an occasion for a new dramaturgical experiment in forming provisional, gestural interlinkage.

The teleplay *Nacht und Träume* illustrates that the problematic of dream and its sleeplessness starts in the solipsism of the self.[25] The teleplay's capacity to realize an aesthetic of dream without problematizing corporeal presence lies with its television medium; although this chapter concerns Beckett's theatre, *Nacht und Träume*'s medial difference proves illuminating when we juxtapose this screen work with the dramaturgical mechanics of tableau that we saw with *Happy Days*. In *Nacht und Träume*, compassion is no less a problem for the divided attention to the other that is the self, and no less productive of gesture, limited to the enclosed space of a lone subject. In this surprising screen poem, two characters appear in the frame who are identical; this is somewhat in the manner of *Ohio Impromptu*. One exception is the fact that one of the figures is the 'dreamt self' of the other, the 'dreamt self' being distinguished by being 'faintly lit by kinder light than A's [the dreamer's]'.[26] Rather than existing together in time, then, here they existence in two mutually inaccessible domains that otherwise rely upon each other to appear. Although on film the character simply raises his head to stare into space, in the script it is said that 'B', the dream-self, 'raises his head further to gaze up at invisible face'.[27] Such an invisible face is experienced by the viewer as an invisible other situated in a space of darkness beyond the frame. That face is thus mutually invisible to us as it is to the characters within the screenplay.

James Knowlson claims that Beckett had Albrecht Dürer's etching of praying hands in his childhood home of Cooldrinagh, and that the *Nacht und Träume* mise-en-scène refers to this image.[28] Knowlson's reading of the hands as iconographic representation of transcendent compassion is relevant to the philosophical issue of sleeplessness's reference to compassion for the other. This time, the two figures are doppelgängers of the same self, and signal the divided otherness of the imago that is essential to subjectivity from a psychoanalytic point of view. Phenomenology too, though in a different way, posits selfhood as split, with Heidegger claiming that Dasein, Heidegger's non-reducible postulation of selfhood, has its 'being-in-time' '*at hand*'.[29] Like in *Happy Days*, sleep in *Nacht und Träume* is prohibited by outside forces, but this time by the gestural motif and medium of its speculative remedy, the hand that reaches out. The same hands return the dream-self to sleep, as well as prohibiting it. In this sense, hands in Beckett's performance oeuvre both confirm that sleeplessness reaches out to the other and its interiority of sleep in dream, as well as emerging from dream to imagine the self-bridging their otherwise ineluctable solitariness of interiority. Indeed, we must remember that sleeplessness is the condition of perceptibility within sleep, since absolute sleep can only be beyond the audit of dream as a zone beyond memory, interpretation, and cognition. *Nacht und Träume*'s hand gestures present a language of yearning for sleep and the dark.

The murmurings of lieder from Schubert's *Nacht und Träume*, providing the teleplay's only spoken language in the form of song, compels an Agambenian reading of language and gesture. In making another mute play, Beckett is exploring the compassionate gesture of hands in dream as 'the other side of language, the muteness inherent in humankind's very capacity for language, its speechless dwelling in language'.[30] *Nacht und Träume*'s carefully choreographed mime work explores the interaction between language and its originary and inherent muteness interior to the limits of consciousness. Sleepless speechlessness forms the basis of language and thus self-consciousness. The Schubert song provides the means for lyricizing the common fugue we have observed throughout this book between mime and voice; the use of song presents a new, and uncommon experiment, with sung lyric to create a paradoxical form defined by internal separation. The compassionate call in Schubert's song for a return to the night and a return to dream animates the question of a fundamental urging towards contact with otherness. Dream becomes the context for a reaching out towards one's own inaccessible self disappearing into the unconscious domain.

The mute gestures of 'no time'

Plays *That Time* and *Catastrophe* both use the face and the skull as media for gestures that mark movements in the realm of sleep, as hands did. This time the gesture suggests less a compassionate striving than a more fundamental opening. The face's eyes and mouth become the entrances to the inner void. *That Time* is a play in which the central agent of representation for the human subject represented within is the otherwise contentless interval. That is, the floating head of Listener opens his eyes during four intervals established in the play text, and this is our only interaction with a live humanity as a theatre audience. The final awakening is punctuated by an unnerving 'smile, toothless' after the previous three in which the face appears to be listening to the narrations.[31] Like Winnie's smile at the climax of *Happy Days*, *That Time*'s rictus becomes a paradoxical portal into the absolute darkness that surrounds the character; both are black. The request for 'toothlessness' ensures the mouth resembles the unlit infinity behind the floating head 'ten feet above stage level'.[32] Quoting *That Time*, we might consider Beckett's characterization of sleep then as a space of 'no time' 'gone in'.[33] The theatrical dreamscape is the allegorical materialization of 'no time' entered through tableau all the more intensified by being unspoken intervals and material traces that in every other respect *do not represent themselves*.

If gesture is a portal that might open an otherwise irreconcilable space between sleepless states, why is no such cathartic space ever arrived at in Beckett's performance oeuvre? Something remains in sleep only if in some sense it eludes representation. However, it is gesture that can notate the positionality of the figural origins of sleep, containing the problem of linguistic representation within it. Agamben's account of gesture is helpful. For Agamben, gesture is as an originary language of representation, a 'stratum of language that is not exhausted in communication and that captures language, so to speak, in its solitary moments'.[34] Gesture is linguistic, but in a mute, primordial sense. In suggesting that gesture is the solitary, mute origin of language, it is figuration like that of the toothless smile of Listener that signals the possibility of a language that might bridge the private interiority of sleepless states. As such, no reconciliation with sleep can be given language in the ordinary sense. Sleep can only be referred to with gestures. In the late prose work of Beckett's *Worstward Ho* (1983), published in the same year as *Nacht und Träume*'s television production, its narrator chants:

> Void most when almost. Worst when almost. Less then? All shades as good as gone. If then not that much more then that much less then? Less worse then? Enough. A pox on void. Unmoreable unlessable unworseable evermost almost void.[35]

Gestures populate the free realm of the void at its cusp in Beckett, where it is 'almost'. Gestures mark the positionality of the portals that chart this otherwise inaccessible domain for representation. Live gesture has special currency as a striving for sleep in stage works that heighten the rift between narration and muteness. Beckett uses gesture as a primary notational device referring to the intractable location of sleep gestured by figures who remain sleepless so long as they are visible. The void is 'most when almost', 'worst when almost', but also, critically, the space of the other.

5

Catastrophe and the politics of spectacle

The year is 1978. Samuel Beckett dedicates a poem fragment beginning 'pas à pas' ('step by step') to political philosopher Herbert Marcuse. The same year, playwright and political dissident Václav Havel, another Beckett dedicatee, formulates a similarly ontological statement about political freedom:

> People who live in the post-totalitarian system know only too well that the question of whether one or several political parties are in power, and how these parties define and label themselves, is of far less importance than the question of whether or not it is possible to live like a human being.[1]

Marcuse construes Beckett's piece as a work about hope: '[here], [t]he world has been recognized as what it is, called by its true name. Hope is beyond our power to express it.'[2] Yet, we know what Beckett thought of the subject of so-called hope. Beckett more likely thought in terms of the words of the notorious eighteenth-century aphorist Nicholas Chamfort, words that Beckett himself translates in 'Long After Chamfort': 'Hope is a knave befools us evermore, / Which till I lost no happiness was mine.'[3] '[L]iv[ing] like a human being', in the words of Havel also happened not to be the subject of high hope in Beckett's work. In fact, Marcuse's account of Beckettian hope is profoundly negative. The puzzle of Beckett's view of ontological liberation and art during times of totalitarian restriction receives some demystification from Marcuse's use of Beckett to articulate literature's political power: 'In the work of Samuel Beckett, there is no hope which can be translated into political terms, the aesthetic form excludes all accommodation and leaves literature as literature.'[4] I hope to confront the question of the politics of spectacle for Beckett by analysing the implications of the Marcusian view of him in accordance with this challenging concept of negative hope. Integrating the account of Beckett's experimental dramaturgy developed thus far in the monograph, I want to return to the play *Catastrophe* (1982), since it so obviously concerns Havel's ideas about political freedom, to confront the topic of the Beckett theatre's politics in the context of late 1970s and early 1980s theory about negation and the human.

The Havel quotation mentioned earlier presents one of the most cited comments from Havel's long essay, 'The power of the powerless'. At the essay's incipit, invoking somewhat ironically *The Communist Manifesto*, Havel intones the following: 'A spectre is haunting Eastern Europe: the spectre of what in the West is called "dissent". This spectre has not appeared out of thin air.'[5] Havel's long essay contributes some of what will become major ideas of the anti-communist movement developing in Eastern Europe that then culminate in the Velvet Revolution. At a time when the freedoms of the twenty-first century associated with liberal-humanist ideas coming out of the Velvet Revolution seem to be threatening the social freedom they once stood for, the Left is less sympathetic today to this kind of humanitarian critique of communism. Similarly, we might take exception to the insertion of the concepts of hope and freedom in interpretation of a play that, like many others by Beckett, present a more sceptical view of the likelihood of any future free of authoritarian political structure. Late capitalism after the fall of the Berlin Wall has brokered new endgames for 'liv[ing] like a human being' that prove strikingly different than those that appeared viable during times of actually existing socialism. Nonetheless, the questions raised by Havel, Beckett and Marcuse, and their interlinked views of spectacle, remain exceedingly relevant for interrogating how ideology governs the spectacle of human being.

What drove Havel's Charter 77 petition and other acts of civil disobedience against the communist regime of his time was an anti-ideological project. The petition was predicated on the premise of the freedom to make revolution, a premise that once motivated the same communist cause that later became Eastern European iterations of Stalinism. Specifically, rehearsals of an atrophied political lexicon and the same mendacious treatment of contemporary political injustices were the target of Havel's anti-ideological attitudes. Havel sought to protect the rights of individual dignity and subjective difference crushed most of all by the censorship of dissent. Beckett's works dedicated to the political thinkers Havel and Marcuse around the same time reveal his concern for what remains of human dissent. Given the political tensions between creative freedom and the governmental control of expression in Stalinist Czechoslovakia, the play can be seen to deconstruct the mechanics of ideological scenography. Chief of all problems in this catastrophe of appearance is the prohibition of co-authorship. Ideological scenography necessarily precludes the authoring of oneself in a given ideological climate, be it through crushing self-determination, through controlling the semantics of subjectivity, or, as in Havel's oft-cited example of the greengrocer, through the co-optation of free will.

The case of the greengrocer for Havel becomes a metaphor for the political lie that Eastern European communist regimes employed to manufacture the false sense of a permanent revolution when, in actuality, they were strengthening the state's control and form. Havel writes that greengrocers across Czechoslovakia were expected to show in their windows a common poster proclaiming 'Workers of the world, unite!' As such, this propagandistic use of the assertion of freedom becomes a gesture that is profoundly ironic for Havel, revealing as it does how subjects' expression of obedience can communicate through a lie of revolt. So, when the semiotics of revolt have been co-opted by the state, true revolt for Havel must take place outside of the aesthetic terms of appearance existing in ideological presentations.

We saw in the introduction to this book how plays such as *Catastrophe* present the experimental realization of a self-examining spectacle that dramatically revises the logics of stage mimesis and control. We can return to *Catastrophe* within the context of political spectacle with a refinement of that argument in this new discursive context of political theatre. With this Havellian notion that the human is the locus of dissent, we can now observe in context how the same experimental process of dramaturgy deducing human remains also deduces what remains of dissent as a result. Examining this play alongside a largely unknown poem fragment by way of an intersection point in political theory will help to elucidate how the laboratory comes to interact with political spectacle. I propose that the Beckett-Marcuse-Havel convergence reveals an intersection of negative aesthetic strategies that present the 'spectre of dissent' haunting every ideological spectacle. Magnifying dissent's absence in *Catastrophe*, Beckett consolidates the Marcusian argument about hope as a property lying outside of the terms of expression within an ideological regime. In the words of Beckett's poem fragment, hope is 'nulle part', that is 'nowhere' or 'no place'.[6] This new rumination on impossibility again directs us to negated potentiality. It is here that we will discover the conception of hope that seems so distant from the spectacle befalling Protagonist in *Catastrophe* and the internal circumstances of Beckettian, and indeed Havellian, spectacle.

The catastrophe of appearance

A society of ideological spectacle, and one which humiliates subjects through strategies of desubjectivization, remains a significant concern for political aesthetics and dissent. Notably, the ideological spectacle was the central target of Situationist International's critique and its major proponent Guy Debord's idea of *détournement*. As Jonathan Crary summarizes:

> [What was] described in the 1950s was the intensifying occupation of everyday life by consumption, organized leisure, and spectacle. In this framework, the rebellions of the late 1960s were, at least in Europe and North America, waged in part around the idea of reclaiming the terrain of everyday life from institutionalization and specialization.[7]

Beckett's tangential relation to these critiques of mass spectacularization leads to an ambiguously political reconstruction of the spectre of dissent and of what remains of human possibility within it. Curiously, Giorgio Agamben's politically charged concept of infancy in *Infancy and History: On the Destruction of Experience* was also first published in 1978. This conception of infancy uses a rethinking of the term to imagine inception as a revolutionary power, grounding what becomes a political theory of community outside of the given political and ideological construction of an established social reality. In the words of Agamben, Protagonist looks out from the authoritarian restrictions of spectacle towards an 'unpresupposable community' at the very horizon of dissent.[8] As insinuated by Havel, dissent is a 'spectre' haunting the ideological saturation of representation. Beckett stages this haunting by couching dissent in the gaze of the subject looking outwards from the spectacle.

The catastrophe flagged by the title of the play in question concerns the catastrophe of appearance. Keir Elam adopts this position, in a sense, within the particular context of classical theatre; the term 'catastrophe' is synonymous with the Ancient Greek definition for drama.[9] Drama, Elam indicates, once meant a surprise twist in Ancient Greek (καταστροφή, 'catastrophe'). Bert O. States suggests as much when he imagines that the spectacle which the audience never sees in *Catastrophe*, the show that is supposed to follow what we see as a dress rehearsal in Beckett's play, will be a tragedy.[10] Elam notes that, as late as Dr Johnson's *Dictionary* in 1755, the original meaning of catastrophe was still in use.[11] Today, catastrophe is more likely to be associated with non-human disasters, not dramatic turns. Beckett likely encourages the double entendre latent in this word. Beckett in metatheatrical experimental fashion solicits the polysemy that arrives when thinking about catastrophe as a disaster of dramatic simulation as much as a disaster of being. Together, as I pointed to in the introduction, the play concerns the disaster of being seen.

In Beckett's play, Director, the play's authoritarian figure, seeks a catastrophe which will 'have [the audience] on their feet' – we only know this much.[12]

For the character Director, such a spectacle requires an ideal – classical? – configuration of the body. To achieve this, he, his Assistant, and Luke, offstage manipulating the spotlight, undermine the Protagonist's presence as a subject. The debasement of character presence pursues an apparent intention to achieve a desired, static image of bare flesh in submission; in other words, the subject rendered an object. Notably, this exhibition of bare life establishes a theatrical simulation of the Protagonist's being which relies upon commanding the actor-figure's passivity and manipulability such that the interior life of that figure is occluded. The capacity to appear anonymously and without any subjectivizing gestures or sounds, especially from the face, fashions this human figure centre stage to the delight of Director. Beckett reduces classical catastrophe to the theatrical bones of the tragedy genre's human spectacle.

Of course, to cast bare life as a so-called Protagonist involves a catastrophic negation of subjective control. Herein lies one connection to the Havel case. While this scene can easily be associated with the event of the play's dedication, the nature of the political gesture within it remains ambiguously unstated. *Catastrophe* is dedicated to Havel as part of a larger protest against his house arrest. The work is Beckett's contribution to the petitionary efforts of the International Association for the Defence of Artists for his release. With so little of Beckett's other work coming by way of manifesto or paratextual mandate, such a dedication contributes to the play's enduring status as 'Beckett's "political" play'.[13] Yet the play's dedication troubles the very premise of petitionary theatre. If the political exposure and appropriation of human tragedy by the ideological spectacle is the subject of Beckett's critique, what can Beckett actually contribute to a petitionary effort that intends to restore an arrested playwright and thinker back on to the stage?

While Beckett wrote *Catastrophe*, Havel was under arrest for political activities in opposition to the Czechoslovakian state. Considered as some kind of critique of this, this play is curious: of all things, lacking any overt reference to political content, the play appears to indict theatre as a manipulative agent objectifying the bare life of the human, dehumanizing the figure through the language of rehearsal and exhibition. Yet, the theatre was Havel's platform too, by which to incite cultural and political change. *Catastrophe*'s dramatic events are not dramatic at all, comprising only epiphenomena in the construction of a spectacle. For most of the play's duration, it comprises of dialogue between the characters Director and Assistant as they adjust the body of the character Protagonist and light it. Director's proposal in the exhibition of the bare life of this silent, almost unmoving figure of Protagonist is to 'whiten all flesh' by theatrical means.[14]

We vaguely understand then that a spectacle of anonymous human flesh configured as the main character of some unknown drama establishes the intention of the play's authoritarian figure, Director.

Václav Havel had been banned from the theatre. Had he been made visible on stage, such occasion would have amplified the figure's capacity to catalyse change, be seen and be heard. The theatre was the last sphere that the Stalinist regime wanted Havel to appear in. The dramatist was restricted to house arrest and to creative invisibility as a result. Events after the Prague Spring of 1968 created an environment of creative restriction and censorship of works like Havel's. Stemming opposition involved counteracting the spheres of dissent and intellectual disobedience that Havel had come to be the figurehead of, typified by the Czech radical theatre. As Elam writes:

> Havel himself has frequently spoken of the relationship between his intertwined political and theatrical careers, stressing the crucial importance to both careers of the playhouse itself as an 'oppositional' structure on the outer edges of Czechoslovak society. The use of small and relatively peripheral theatres, such as the Theatre on the Balustrade, where his own early plays were performed, was not only an economic necessity but also an ideological choice, in symbolic contraposition to the large official 'stone theatres' of the state. ... The playhouses acted also and above all as strategic centres – as authentic 'theatres of operations' – in the organized resistance to the central regime.[15]

The stage was a space of dissent that Havel would be isolated from during his incarceration. Nevertheless, as a result, this political circumstance brought Havel to the global anti-authoritarian counter-stage of the international media. Beckett's dedication of *Catastrophe* to the playwright who would later become the president of Czechoslovakia does not refer to putting Havel on display; that would be counter-intuitive. The play likely has no metonymic qualities relating to displays of political violence either (unlike the later play *What Where* [1983]), although the scene itself appears to resemble a rather abstract form of torture by bodily objectification. In every conventional sense, Beckett appears to have refrained from political engagement in a play dedicated to an incredibly live political subject.

The catastrophe cannot be the arrest of Václav Havel, then. Instead, in Havel's absence from the stage, what is catastrophic is *the development of an authoritarian ideological scene in the place of dissent*. *Catastrophe*'s scenario is one in which there is no hope of dissent. Here, human subjects are shaped into live, uncritical objects of one-way contemplation. Notably, the ideological scene entails the exhibition of *bare* life, the exhibition of a subject with all identifying features concealed and desubjectivized, modified and manipulated for the sake of a preconceived figuration denuded of dynamic subjective relation. Beckett appears to be imagining what the excision from the stage of figures like Havel might bring. *Catastrophe* constitutes a kind of post-Havel nightmare in effect. Havel's arrest means Havel's absence, leaving a void to be occupied by the exhibition of desubjectivized life. In this post-Havel stage imaginary, the subject has been reduced to a perfectly manipulable marionette-like figure governed by the will of visibility for the ideological scene alone.

To achieve such a nightmarish dramaturgy of desubjectivization in the play, Director pursues an adequately lit head for the play's climax to make 'our catastrophe' that will 'have them [the audience] on their feet'.[16] Later, I will discuss the complex revolutionary implications of dissent found in the resistant look that Protagonist displays at the end of the play. For now, we should ruminate on the powerfully unambiguous quality of defiance in this look noted by any spectator who views this play. In a *Guardian* article from 2009, we read James Knowlson recounting an experience with Beckett in which the writer betrayed his own view of the denouement to Knowlson. This view accords with the unambiguous reading of defiance:

> Knowlson recalls Beckett's furious response when a critic described the ending as ambiguous. 'I can still remember sitting with him outside a cafe in Paris,' he says. The playwright pounded the table and told him: 'It's not ambiguous – he's saying, "You bastards, you haven't finished me yet!"' Knowlson thinks this reaction, and the play he dedicated to Havel, epitomise Beckett's mindset: 'Beckett is about going on, persisting; however much you reduce somebody to an object, a victim, there is this resilience and persistence of the human spirit.'[17]

Knowlson construes Protagonist's ambiguous gaze as defiant in accordance with authorial intent. What he defies, Knowlson claims, is the objectifying reduction of the subject to anonymity. However much reduced to bare life and modified flesh, Protagonist's defiance reclaims a persistent humanity. If there is hope somewhere between that gaze and the audience that registers it, such hope is provisional indeed. While this interpretation of *Catastrophe* proves to be a fitting endorsement of the Havellian view of dissent as a matter of persistent humanity, more must be said about the still ambiguous nature of hope and the many ramifications of thinking drama and catastrophe as interlinked concepts.

Marcuse and hope after catastrophe

That Frankfurt School Marxist philosopher Marcuse was a correspondent of Beckett's at one time is not common knowledge, despite the ongoing popularity of Frankfurt School-inspired interpretations of Beckett's work. In scholarship of recent years, it is Emilie Morin that repairs this situation in dedicating some of her concluding remarks on Beckett's ambiguous political imaginary to the Marcuse-Beckett connection:

> [T]he *mirlitonnade* he dedicated to Marcuse on the occasion of his eightieth birthday in 1978 comes across as a coded tribute to political activity. Beckett knew Marcuse solely as a political thinker and figurehead of the student movements: his correspondence with Adorno from 1969 reflects on the 'Marcusejugend' or Marcusian youth, and its capacity for political conspiracy. ... Like Marcuse, Beckett was well-attuned to the post-1968 thesis that everything carries a political charge. ... Even unlikely sources give a sense of this position: in her memoir, Antonia Fraser recalls an evening with Beckett and [Barbara] Bray in 1979, during which Bray defended the slogan 'everything is political', which rallied the student and labour movements long after 1968. To this Pinter objected, 'Nothing I have written, Barbara, nothing ever, is political'. And Beckett offered the reply familiar to any supporter of the 1968 movement: 'This absence of politics is in itself a political statement.'[18]

Indeed, Marcuse's correspondence with Beckett, we will see, illuminates the fraught question of a political orientation underlying *Catastrophe* as a post-1968, post-Situationist, counter-ideological dramaturgical practice predicated on an experimental urge. Consider what spurs this correspondence. Beckett dedicated the poem fragment beginning 'pas à pas', or 'step by step' to Marcuse on his eightieth birthday in 1978. Marcuse claims in his work that Beckett's political significance really exists in its capacity to 'withstand' the twentieth century's large-scale dehumanizations of what was once accepted as the human.[19] Here, Marcuse evinces a central difficulty in pinning certain Beckett scenarios to contemporary political questions of representation and aspiration. Namely, Marcuse saw Beckett as a major example of the modernist artist's negation of the contemporary world's unjust construction. Such art as Beckett's refuses to countenance such a world by way of conventional representational logics of mimesis. Marcuse's radically political view of art's power of negation puts Beckett's in the centre of a political aesthetic statement. In Marcuse's view, Beckett's work presents a representative field in which 'there is no longer any immanent justice or meaning'.[20] In this way, Marcuse echoes fellow Frankfurt School figure Theodor Adorno's view of negation in Beckett. Both agree that Beckett represents the extreme circumstances of expression after the horrors, and horrific consequences, of ideological spectacle. However, one crucial difference between the two lies in the relation mimesis has to the act of artistic negation for each of them. For Adorno, Beckett's work highlights the new terms of modern subjectivity in the wake of the Second World War and thereby the new demands put upon representation, in which

> the surplus of reality amounts to its collapse; by striking the subject dead, reality itself becomes deathly; this transition is the artfulness of all antiart, and in Beckett it is pushed to the point of the manifest annihilation of reality.[21]

In other words, Adorno views Beckett's work in a radically mimetic light. The remains of the subject here entail urgent new terms for artistic representation in a post-catastrophic state. Marcuse's extension of certain Adornian ideas such as negation lies in the degree to which mimesis is afforded any autonomous integrity. Marcuse's articulation of hope distinguishes his view from Adorno's radical negativity.

In his letter to Beckett, Marcuse formulates a version of hope he sees as congenial to explaining Beckett's work. Such a conception of hope is likely to be one of the very few that Beckett would tolerate. In this letter, Marcuse writes that '[h]ope is beyond our power to express it. But only under the *Prinzip Hoffnung* could a human being write what you [Beckett] have written'.[22] *Prinzip Hoffnung* refers to fellow Frankfurt School philosopher Ernst Bloch's 'principle of hope' from Bloch's three-volume book of the same name. Beckett's letter of reply to this notably refrains from the usual demystification of interpretation common to his reactions to readings of his work. Beckett, in this respect, conveys at least a tolerance of the association.[23] Typical, however, is Beckett's reluctance to unconditionally countenance such remarks about his own work. Beckett does not endorse or elaborate upon this idea of hope either. Nevertheless, not so much calling Beckett hopeful, Marcuse proposes that Beckett's work affirms that hope's house lies in the inexpressible. Hope here can only be referred to in its total absence from the world as it is given. What forecloses the possibility of hope, it follows, is the humiliation meted out by the ideological stage and its enforcement of a performance of bare life.

Ideology's tendentious exhibition of the human comprises the underlying critique within Beckett's figural imagination of dehumanization in the theatre. Dehumanization is the explicit allegorical concern in a play like *Catastrophe*.

Dehumanization is also subject to the counter-mimetic approaches Beckett employs as far back as *AWW I*. Even here, a metatheatrical critique of the conventions of appearance in spectacle can be found. *Catastrophe* thus resists the temptation of a counter-spectacle for Havel as a remedy to his silencing and arrest by the state. Instead, Beckett distils from Havel's political situation a different question of representation, a question that may have outlasted the particular political circumstances of the former Czechoslovakia and Havel's later rise and subsequent fall. Beckett highlights, above all, the crisis in human self-representation in ideological late capitalism such as Havel's came to announce.

I want to resist the simple reading of Protagonist's closing look of the play as it directly addresses the audience as a matter of basic defiance. More specifically, Protagonist en face enters into a new conference with the spectator by looking upon those who look upon him as a dramatic object. We know that a bent head is necessary for Director's successful catastrophe in rendering this object, especially the lighting of the head. Upon lifting the head to reveal his face, the audience hears a '[d]istant storm of applause' which may or may not compel the actual audience into clapping; soon after, the said applause 'falters, dies'.[24] Self-examination is entailed in this conference between sentient, already self-examining beings. Given that the fade out which succeeds this faltering closes the play, the actual audience must decide how they will applaud after the fictionalized version of their own faltering applause has ceased and the light fades on Protagonist's face. Interestingly, Havel in *The Power of the Powerless* describes revolt as 'any means by which a person or a group revolts against manipulation'.[25] Revolt against following convention becomes the very question that occurs to the spectator of this play. How do I resist this kind of manipulation of a political subject at the same time as being complicit in this assembly of observation and objectification, the spectator likely wonders. Objectification should be outrageous. Furthermore, Protagonist, even under terrible restriction, can never have the 'spectre of dissent' expiated from him. Even in circumstances of seemingly complete predetermined arrest by the producers of spectacle, the figure's eyes can revolt still against the corporeal manipulations and subjective humiliations that the Director has designed for him.

Herbert Blau does not refer to *Catastrophe* when he reduces the following radical theory of performance to this particular aspect of live performance. Yet, Beckett's dramaturgical premise for *Catastrophe* accords with, even allegorizes, this Blau maxim. That is, Blau argues that, after an enormous revolution in the form and medium of drama, the only essential component of dynamic live theatrical assembly that remains critical to it is '*the look of being looked at*' that realizes that liveness.[26] There are profound roots in theatre and performance for Blau's concept of 'the look of being looked at'. As we learn from Agamben in *Profanations* (2007), the look of being looked at can be found in the Greek comic convention of parabasis. Parabasis is the theatrical convention in which the chorus speaks directly to the audience, often with a discursive purpose.[27] Parabasis, Agamben claims, repairs the inherent parody of language's 'out of place' relation to the world by returning the mimetic scenario to a conference of direct address: 'parody, as paraontology, expresses language's inability to reach the thing and the impossibility of the thing finding its own name'.[28] What becomes parodic in drawing attention to the construction of the drama is at the same time felt by the classical audience as more real, since the chorus refers to them directly. Agamben seeks to make a philosophical point about language's impersonality, here, as a material belonging neither to the self as a solitary being, nor its other, the social field. This paradoxical nature of language continues to condition the personality we inevitably breathe into it in being forced to adopt it as our own voice, our own world, and our own consciousness. In other words, the parody Agamben discovers in classical theatre's conventions, to use the words of Arthur Rimbaud, is that *'Je est un autre'*, 'I is an *other*'.[29] Language speaks us as we speak it, and this separation for Agamben, as for Wittgenstein and other philosophers of language, throws up the numerous enigmas of human consciousness and experience that correlate to the problematics of simulation and self-expression found in Beckettian dramaturgy.

To return to the classical implications for *Catastrophe*, according to Agamben, parabasis enables the chorus to broach a self-reflexive discursive address with the audience that more directly solicits their sympathies than the spectacle of mimetic representation. Agamben explains that parabasis permits spectacle and spectator to change roles, and, in turn, develop a paraontological space of discursive contact in which a 'human conversation', belonging to the real domain that the theatre expropriates, becomes possible:

> In the gesture of parabasis, the representation is dissolved and actors and spectators, author and audience exchange roles. Here, the tension between stage and reality is relaxed and parody encounters what is perhaps its only resolution. ... The staged dialogue – intimately and parodically divided – opens a space off to the side (which is physically represented by the *logeion* [a point on the stage designating the place of discourse]) and thus becomes nothing more than an exchange, simply a human conversation.[30]

A 'human conversation' outside of the field of simulation, opening another, more direct intercourse – such is precisely what Marcuse noted had become imperilled in twentieth-century modernity. The same domain Havel raised for discussion as the most vital agon of post-totalitarian political arrangements. The emergence of a 'human conversation' within a parodic, comic frame like Greek comedy's dissolves the privileged space of theatrical fiction to lay bare the more foundational relations which predicate it: the sociopolitical agora that mounts the spectacle to conduct debates about power and ideology. Shakespeare employed a transformed conception of parabasis through the soliloquy which psychologized the 'human conversation' but perhaps excluded its promise of paraontological space. We can now see that those silent gestures of Beckett's theatre arrest the audience in a state of sudden apprehension. In *Catastrophe*, the play's protagonist performs a fundamental act of liveness nonetheless often concealed from view. This act harbours within it the promise of a consciousness of something that lies outside of the spectacle as it has been contrived by the objectified order manipulated by the Director and his theatrical light.

Protagonist's gaze understood as an act of parabasis achieves, in a sense, a kind of mute monologue. As Eddie Paterson writes of Beckett more broadly, 'Beckett ... separates the monologue from the dialogic text so that it gains uninterrupted focus, and employs a self that is fragmenting and radically alienated'.[31] Earlier, we read that Agamben views the convention of parabasis as an 'interruption of parody'; this assessment complements Paterson's assertion that Beckett reconfigures the dramatic subject by problematizing the generic foundations of monologue and breach a single-dimension mimetic order. An interruption in the simulation unsettles the very foundations by which monologue and dialogue, following convention, substantialize character presence, reflection and figuration. The interruption of the so-called parody of representation means a novel interruption in the figure-audience relations undergirding the spectacle most profoundly; Protagonist is no longer an object of pathos and contemplation but a dynamic subject whose very gaze suggests, in its absence from the visual field of the stage, that a paraontological order to the ideological one exists outside of the one presented.

Havel's definition of 'revolt' relates to the totalitarian order in ways akin to the manner in which the paraontological domain solicited by parabasis relates to spectacle in Agamben's view of classical theatre. Revolt is that which 'steps out of living within the lie ... [making] an attempt to *live within the truth*'.[32] Unlike classical theatre's faith in the existence of a reparative social realm, Protagonist refers to such a domain in an alienated negative capability. Disobediently raising his face such that the lit head becomes a subjectifying visage, the character opens a space for inter-examination between actor and spectator emptied of discourse and critical of the dramaturgical language supposed to scaffold a paraontological interaction. Beckettian parabasis accords with Agamben's concept of an 'unpresupposable community' and the negative concept of hope described by Marcuse; whatever human assembly might allow Protagonist freedom from the ideological spectacle's foreclosure of his autonomy necessarily lies outside the limits of the spectacle and its existing contract with spectators. Such a conversation cannot be mimetically represented. It can only be pinpointed by virtue of a provisionally subjective relation which lobbies that alternate authority to the Director's: the spectator.

The most political gesture in art concerns how the political scene itself generates certain kinds of ideological spectacle, or what Marcuse calls 'the false reality of the status-quo'.[33] *Catastrophe* presents an experiment in reforming the conventions of what Marcuse would call the 'optics' of the work of art, opposing 'the subordination of art to politics'.[34] Or, in other words, 'art itself can never become political without destroying itself, without violating its own essence, without abdicating itself'.[35] For Marcuse, art's most political function is in never being reducible for the exigencies of representation as they are coded in the present. That is to say, art's most political function lies in transforming the mimetic order.

Infancy, step by step

In Beckett's poetic dedication to Marcuse 'pas à pas' and later compiled among the *mirlitonnades*, an infant figure proceeds nowhere. The figure proves suggestive of Agamben's concept of infancy, an existence that precedes the subject's appearance and offers hope of a different world than what appears. Exploiting the homophonic nature of 'steps' ('pas') and 'not' ('pas') in French, the poem imagines a figure in contradistinction to Protagonist: a figure of infancy said to be 'obstinately' affirming *its lack of appearance*, to take Fourier's translation of 'obstinément'.[36] Like Protagonist's parabasis, 'pas à pas' refers to a figural circumstance invisible to the given, outside of the supposable ideological conditions of appearance. Unlike Protagonist, who must appear in the configuration of bare life, the tentative figure of 'pas à pas' *pre*-exists spectacle, moving in a space designated 'nowhere'.

Militonnades means a sort of playful doggerel. Their Chamfort-derived whimsy often involves an escape from the terms of existence. Such escape tends to involve some revelry in death's advantages over the conventions and self-affirmations of life. The most extreme, but also the most lyrical, of the Chamfort maxims could be the following example: 'sleep till death / healeth / come ease / this life disease'.[37] As the editors of the 2012 critical edition of Beckett's *Collected Poems* write, ' "pas à pas" revisits the pacing motif of [play] *Footfalls*'. That is to say, the piece has a footstep-like rhythmic construction while set 'nowhere' and performed 'obstinately'. 'Petits pas' (tiny steps) 'Obstinément' (obstinately) suggests a figure who persists walking in infancy, without direction or destination, existing where time and space are immaterial.

Infancy, that which 'finds its logical place in a presentation of the relationship between language and experience', is the conceptual ground of the abstract sphere between two realities. In terms of subjectivity, infancy must be irreducibly tentative. The infant figure tends towards subjectivity and thereby language, but as an infant remains a subject-to-come. Infancy, an '*experimentum linguae*', says Agamben, enables one to 'encounter only the pure exteriority of language'.[38] To visualize such a figure who would embody this conceptual relation is difficult, but *Catastrophe*'s denouement offers one possibility for imagining them. As Protagonist's eyes meet the gaze of the audience – as if he were being seen for the very first time – the bare *bios* of the figure enters the language of gesture with the raised head in defiance, shrugging off the bent-head configuration reminiscent of characters from Franz Kafka's *The Trial*. In other words, the figure's paraontological subjectivity cannot be realized, but can be vestigially suggested in an event of looking while being looked at in its infancy.

For Agamben, gesture is the infant form that expression has in the domain of language. Agamben cautions against reading gesture causally: 'If we are to understand gesture, nothing is more misleading than to picture a sphere of means directed towards an end.'[39] Gesture is the ground of our expressive being: '*Gesture is the display of mediation, the making visible of a means as such*. It makes apparent the human state of being-in-a-medium and thereby opens up the ethical dimension for human beings.'[40] Infant steps in art wilfully going nowhere suggests that resistance to the inherited conventions of representation involves obstinate infancy and the resistance to becoming visible as a subject in the terms ordained by the existing order. *Catastrophe* seems to suggest where in spectacle these infant gestures might be located: the *lifting* of the head, the fixing of the eyes upon the spectator, the conference of self-examination at the impasse of visibility.

In this sense, Beckett's presentation of bare human life in a state of catastrophe confronts the ideological terms in which the human appears. This 'anti-theatrical' presentation – to use Puchner's term – concerns the ideological spectacle most particularly, taking to task any political formation which would strip the performing subject of their co-authorship of what appears. A play such as *Catastrophe* renders the possibility of the haunting of an infant assembly impossible in the scenario of what is put before the audience. Recalling Carlson's model of theatricality discussed in Chapter 2, such a haunting becomes the conduit for the 'spectre of dissent' underlying the Havel problem. To adopt words more complementary to the dramatic construction of Protagonist's own beguiling final gaze, '*The ineffable is, in reality, infancy.*'[41] Dissent's infancy finds a medium in Beckett's theatrical deconstruction of liveness and spectatorship. Like the role of Hamlet, according to Carlson, the weight of haunting that an actor steps into when adopting the role lies with the 'density of its ghosting'.[42] In this chapter, I have traced the convergence of political aesthetic ideas in the work of Marcuse, Beckett and Havel as a combined opposition to dehumanization entailed by the ideological spectacle. I have traced what I view as the anti-ideological counter-claims of stage and gestural formulations realized by Beckettian experiment with the figural politics of conventional stage mimesis. Hope, in accordance with Marcuse's view, exists in Beckett's scenography as a potentiality outside the terms of representation as they emerge in the present. Hope's haunting of Protagonist's hopeless situation in *Catastrophe* requires that we comprehend this radically negative view of hope without any of the usual hopefulness that our existing self-criticism bringing us to our auditorium seats is sufficient; such is the object of Protagonist's mute redressal. Human dissent of the Beckettian kind remains only when the spectator has been surrendered to that unnerving anxiety that would connect one look of being looked at to another in a mutually examining liveness.

6

Hypnosis: A theory of Beckett spectatorship

A figure wrapped in off-white fabric and apparently floating on a strip of light hung in the air trembles into appearance. She paces one, two, then three steps. She continues. She 'wheels' after the ninth.[1] The stage is invisible due to the darkness, a strip of light giving the impression that she is levitating beyond any stage floor. Your position, audience member, by relation too seems unmoored. Where is the ground? Are you both, character and spectator, suspended in air? You sit in the stalls, but where is the stage? You can fix neither yourself nor the character in a confidently grounded relation. The character calls for her mother and receives a deathly, spectral reply: 'Yes, May.' 'Were you asleep?' asks the just visible figure. 'Deep asleep,' replies the disembodied voice. 'I heard you in my deep sleep.'[2] The pace, the voices, the seeming translucency of the ghostly figure immersed in the impenetrable darkness are intoxicating. You want to shut your eyes, want to be in the dark. 'Will you not try to snatch a little sleep?' asks the voice of May's mother.[3] Yes, you do want to 'snatch a little sleep'. No, the question wasn't directed at you. But you hear it this way all the same.

You are at the Duchess Theatre in London on 3 February 2014, wrestling with the hypnotics of a work you have long anticipated seeing in the flesh. Lisa Dwan plays the part of *Footfalls*'s May in a trilogy of Beckett plays directed by Walter Asmus: *Not I* (1972), *Footfalls* (1976) and *Rockaby* (1981). These three plays have become a contemporary theatrical trilogy representative of Beckett's late theatre.[4]

What becomes of such a spectator enclosed in the immersive spaces of these three celebrated late plays by Samuel Beckett? I was this spectator, for a time. Such a question emerges from a specific encounter of mine in 2014 – following an experience that is likely to be felt in common by audiences who attended the production during its multiple runs and world tour. In this chapter, I would to return to plays discussed in the context of sensory deprivation in Chapter 2 by engaging in a very different methodological analysis that privileges the act of spectatorship. This possibility was in fact promised by the premise of sensory deprivation, the idea that immersive experience of vertiginous aspects of these plays confers special value to the affective construction of these notable examples of the late Beckett theatre and can be felt in common by actors and spectators. Such experience should be of interest to Beckett scholarship, since such experience is no accident, but rather solicited by the agency, to use W. B. Worthen's characterization of the playscript, insisting in the compositions of Beckett's theatre.[5] The discoveries made about experimentalism in the chapters that followed Chapter 2 – impediment and the problem of symbolism in Chapter 3; sleeplessness, consciousness and medium in Chapter 4; and the politics of liveness in Chapter 5 – now permit a fuller understanding of spectatorship in light of the experimental contingencies of the dramaturgy. The ends of that experience in common direct this chapter into quite a different domain: the clinical laboratories of historical psychoanalysis. The ensuing examination of hypnosis in relation to Beckett's theatre enables immersive dramaturgical strategies and the attention-manipulating techniques of historical psychoanalysis and clinical therapy to converge. Most of all, we shall see how the concept of hypnosis, especially the problems of the term, evoke the critical and hermeneutic implications of live spectatorship under the experimental influence of Beckett's dramaturgy.

Beckettian dramaturgy has a hypnotic effect. Whatever ambiguous definitions exist for the concept of hypnosis itself, the assertion of hypnotics in Beckett's theatre is nonetheless unambiguous. That hypnotic effect emerged in the late period after many unanticipated events throughout the course of Beckett's stage career, as we have seen. The varied success with mime and mime artists, a changing, escalating deployment of the stage diagram, an expanding separation between performer body and soundscape, and a deeper engagement with the paradoxes of unconsciousness that emerge with inquiries into sleep as a category of human experience all inform a dramaturgy that has become by the late 1970s a deeply hypnotic craft. Indeed, that trajectory extends after Beckett's death, and even after Billie Whitelaw's more recent passing also. In Chapter 2, we looked closely at Whitelaw. This chapter makes special use of actor Lisa Dwan's realization of the latent, hypnotic experiment conducted with *us*, the audience, within the posthumous trajectory of Beckettian dramaturgy.

There is a difference between Beckett criticism which 'goes to the theatre' and that which encounters Beckett on the page alone. The spectator, and the affective consequences of a play's agency registered by them, become essential components of a study of the former kind. What affect designates comprises not an observable 'thing', as Brian Massumi asserts, but feeling as 'an event, or a dimension of every event'.[6] Hypnosis can be described as a simulated affect event, involving an intentional staging of the event of feeling such that the hypnotized subject's autonomy is compromised by the affective event and is made, in some way, to surrender to it. Put another way, depending upon the nature of the deployment of this contested mode of suggestion, hypnosis presents suggestive monological performance into therapeutic service.

Let us think more about what hypnosis is purported to be. Hypnosis, when believed in by the patient, audience, analysand or auditor presents a notion of affect that implies that the human subject's faculty of attention is eminently suggestible. To analyse a particular instance of spectatorial hypnosis from a critical, performance theoretical point of view is to rethink the process of dramaturgy as a force of suggestion. I cannot help but think back to Marvin Carlson's model of haunting, the original basis of theatrical simulation, discussed in Chapter 2. Carlson promised that intense experiences of theatre would entail a paradoxical possession of the live assembly in which the actor and audience are possessed by virtual things. The merging of an audience into that moment of possession of the actual by the virtual, and the interreliant stimulation of those forces into event, invites hypnotic interpretations of dramaturgy. Hypnotic experience must be a possible component of any significant event of immersive spectacle if by immersion we mean the suggestion that what is virtualized in a performance is felt to be actual. Conversely, hypnotic effect can be observed where actual forces compel powerful virtual experience, such as immersion in a memory or narrative. The two are evidently interdependent. In the view of disciplines that believe in the full spectrum of human suggestibility, the hypnotized person's interpretative faculties can be said to give way to the virtual; self-awareness gives way to imagination and empathy. Given hypnosis's discreditable connotations as an act of pseudo-scientific, even performative suggestion that relies on subjective belief in the process, we might conclude that its pretensions to actual self-witnessing of unseen memories, for example, suggest that the activity actually produces a kind of 'false witness'. I use this concept following Léon Chertok and Isabelle Stengers's characterization of the term in the context of clinical practices associated with psychoanalysis.[7] Hypnotic self-witnessing thus entails a self-deception, then, but a deception quite natural to fictions of self-discovery. Hypnotic dramaturgy simulates remembrance, and in this sense, Beckett's dramas experiment with the narratives and counter-narratives deployed by a subject's own private theatre. In other words, the notion that hypnosis can help us to better uncover the past constitutes self-deception that conforms to the varying kinds of narrative construction that tend to govern the modern subject. We might first consider how such fictions of self-discovery are driven by a view of remembrance as a manipulable and manipulative quantity, echoing most of all Beckett's interest in the work of Marcel Proust.

Self-discovery as the tentative and mutable concern of the memory narrative features as the increasingly recursive concern of Beckett's late theatre. Of all the Beckett literary influences, Beckettians are aware that Beckett's view of the memory narrative has for his deepest influence Proust's *À la recherche du temps perdu*. This work is the subject of Beckett's only scholarly monograph, *Proust* (1931), written during that short period in which such a career was still being entertained by the writer.[8] Proustian conceptions of involuntary memory and the sensory ciphers of returning to remembrance's questionable depths curiously recall the assumptions of the hypnotist. Remembrance constitutes an immersive, coercive fiction of vast importance for the construction of the subject, far beyond the grasp of conscious recollection. Dramaturgical and narrative constructions based upon the effort to extenuate the false self-witnessing that emerges in practices of hypnotic suggestion bind Proustian affinities in Beckett to psychoanalytic ones, triangulating a set of concerns that we will explore in the context of spectatorship.

Such a formulation of memory's spectatorial ends in drama recalls the Proustian alignment of narrative and memory. Beckett himself writes of the Proustian formulation of remembering's active role in shaping the narratives comprising the subject that 'the most successful evocative experiment can only project the *echo* of a past sensation'.[9] Thus, these narratives that dispose the subject in particular ways through a texture of experience ever modified by memory's entanglement in time position sensation in an originary role from which memory, hardened into the prejudices of habit, wrestles with the implacable generator of it all, time: 'Memory and Habit', Beckett writes, 'are attributes of the Time cancer.'[10] What he means is that time remains indomitable, while memory and habit are human extrapolations – echoes of sensations – propelled and at the same time depleted by the march of time. What distinguishes the actual past from its representation in memory is that, in the latter case, echoes come to shape fictive recollections of sensations that chart the memory. In this way, like memory and habit, self-witnessing can be rethought as an inevitably false form of witnessing. Indeed, to remember, in the Proustian equation, is to *simulate* past events; such simulations shape the remembering subject. As Beckett argues later in *Proust*,

> Being an act of intellection, [memory] is conditioned by the prejudices of the intelligence which abstracts from any given sensation, as being

illogical and insignificant, a discordant and frivolous intruder, whatever word or gesture, sound or perfume, cannot be fitted into the puzzle of a concept. ... [N]o amount of voluntary manipulation can reconstitute in its integrity an impression that the will has – so to speak – buckled into incoherence.[11]

In a sense, hypnosis extends the Proustian affective framework described here: a sensation from the past 'is conditioned by the prejudices of the intelligence', and sensations by their nature are 'illogical and insignificant' until they are remembered. Hypnosis recalls the Proustian equation because it, too, presents the voluntary recovery of memory as 'conditioned' by the act of its 'intellection'. In fact, hypnosis *employs*, in a manipulative way, this formulation of memory. Hypnosis makes a resource of the voluntary and involuntary processes of memory towards modifying those entanglements to achieve therapeutic or clinical ends. Indeed, for popular therapeutic hypnosis deployed in clinics across the Western world today, the supposition exists that memories can even be invented. Should you want to give up smoking, for example, clinics that use hypnosis propose to lodge unconscious resistances to the act of smoking to derail your habit. Hypnosis for some, therefore, means the deliberate invention of false memory, and therefore false witnessing.

The domains of artifice and fictitiousness, however, do not discredit the subjective discoveries that hypno-therapy, say, or psychoanalysis, or even Marcel's narrative mode of remembrance wish to present to revise our understanding of memory narrative, affect and drama. I hope to endorse the contrary, in fact. False witnessing can reveal 'the false appearances of *real* life', to invoke Stengers.[12] The three plays in question in this chapter construct an impressive architectural and compositional theatricality that engages audiences in a simulation of those false appearances central to the construction of the subject found variously in modern instances of the memory narrative. Indeed, uncovering self-witnessing's 'false appearances' comprises the primary task of psychoanalysis as it developed in the late nineteenth century. This will direct my first inquiry into the convergence of fictional and clinical concerns considered thus far. More particularly, returning to the theatre of so-called hysteria, central to Jean-Martin Charcot, and then Josef Breuer's theorizations of false witnessing, with Blanche Wittman and Anna O. featuring as significant patients among the discipline's historical figures, an interface between hypnosis, clinical practices of psychoanalysis and the fraught category of memory's witness in Beckett's work can be better assayed.

In Beckett scholarship, concepts of mental pathology and alterity are viewed as particularly germane to the playwright's representations of subjectivity. Shane Weller, for example, draws a parallel between Anna O. and the characters of the theatrical trilogy: 'The female figures in Beckett's later plays certainly exhibit such functional disorganization of speech [as clinical hysterics], and they may even be said to enact what Breuer's patient, Anna O., terms the hysteric's "private theater".'[13] Examinations of hysteria's theatricality have been most influentially conducted in theatre studies in Elin Diamond's *Unmaking Mimesis: Essays on Feminism and Theatre* (1997). This book determines that performance modalities understood as hysterical offer 'a *different* mimesis – one in which the actor's body becomes a material signifier that speaks not for, but before, the referent'.[14] For Diamond, the gestures appearing in alternative forms of mimesis associated with psychopathology have a truth of their own that often escapes the enclosure erected by clinical and representationally normalized forms of testimonial spectacle. The nuances of this psychoanalytic and representational problem will be discussed more concertedly in the accounts of Charcot, Breuer and Freud shortly. Remember too that I posed the suggestion at the beginning of this book that Beckett fits among those artists Diamond views in the continuum of experimental theatre from the post-war period. We now see that this same continuum harbours practices formerly understood as 'hysterical' that Diamond urges generate ways 'to release the body's unauthorized truths'.[15] In this sense, I hope to continue Diamond's work on this problematic of theatrical mimesis with Beckett's late trilogy and the Dwan-Asmus production to demonstrate this.

My interest lies in a different dimension of psychoanalysis's parallels with the theatre. I am interested in the fraught application of hypnotic suggestion and the problems of the hypnotic theatre that was the clinic. In Breuer and Freud's *Studies on Hysteria: The Standard Edition of the Complete Psychological Works of Sigmund Freud*, hypnosis explicitly serves to recover encrypted memory: 'As a rule it is necessary to hypnotize the patient and to arouse his memories under hypnosis of the time at which the symptom made its first appearance,' they write.[16] But – as Freud would later claim, after becoming a major critic of the very technique he had once affirmed – hypnosis engenders the very narratives of trauma it purports merely to uncover. In Anna O.'s case, for example, her 'tendency to auto-hypnotic *absences*', entailing hallucinations, disengagement and nausea, among other maladies, meant that hypnosis encouraged the very production of false witnessing that psychoanalysis sought to overcome.[17] In dramaturgy such as Beckett's, we seem to be in a 'private theatre' comparable to Anna O.'s immersed in hallucinatory absences from the self. Indeed, Beckett's emphasis in *Not I*, *Footfalls*, and *Rockaby* appears to lie with the same affects of 'auto-hypnotic absences' that troubled psychoanalytic interpretation. Further, these plays appear to problematize psychoanalysis's construction and interpretation of such affects.

Consider media theorist Jonathan Crary's articulation of hypnosis, which understands the technique as an 'extreme model of a technology of attention'.[18] As Crary historicizes, hypnosis entered the common lexicon as a model of attention, pertinent to new, often modern, industrial and technological coercions of subjective attention. Not incidentally, it is in this epoch also that saw the popular rise of the psychoanalyst's interpretation of the subject as a desiring instrument or machine. Such advents are dynamically related and, indeed, historically interdependent.

In Chapter 1, we considered how sensory deprivation shaped the play's dramaturgical mandate for actor and audience. We can now see how that experimental trajectory over the course of collaboration with Whitelaw generated what we can now theorize as a hypnotic theatricality.

In production, Beckett's hypnotic plays modify the attention of the spectator who registers the fictive terms of these scenarios' narratives of self-witnessing. By extension, these three plays aim for a suggestible spectator who undergoes a sensory manipulation that is sensitive to the stage fictions being simulated. Such entanglements with virtualization are immersive, in other words. The spectatorial experience solicited by these three plays can be described as hypnotic; hypnotic I generally define as having one's mental state suggestively altered beyond conscious volition.[19] What this suggestion means for the perceiving mind could generally be defined as an 'altered state', according to Graham Wagstaff.[20]

James Knowlson notes that *Footfalls* 'grew out of Beckett's long-standing interest in abnormal psychology'.[21] May's mechanical but spectral movement, and her antagonism towards her mother's narrative, reveal some of this clinical interest in a special subjective circumstance. My own experience of these plays suggests that, thanks to the hypnotically immersive dramaturgical sphere realized in the play's design and exemplarily achieved in the Asmus production, the imperatives to sleep cast upon May are similarly felt by the spectator. Rather than urging a diagnostic role for the audience as a result, I suspect that the reason for this sort of dramaturgical realization lies more with the premise that audiences might be able to feel something of what a subject such as May feels. The suggestive, even 'false' framing of both character and narrative dissolves the fourth wall. Such a divide conventionally sustains affective and intellectual distance for the spectator; here, an immersive theatrical experience results from a dramaturgy that overflows that divide, enabling the spectator's empathic identification with sensations and narrative problems of a critically compromised, but intensely empathic, simulation of the confinement to a particular memory narrative.

Let us now study aspects of the discipline of hypnosis. In the following section, I will historicize the place that the hypnotic theatre of the clinic developed in early neurology, the precursor to psychology and psychoanalysis. I will also trace the more substantial links that Beckett's theatre makes with the psychoanalytic corpus, especially its relation to the practice of hypnosis therein.

Hypnosis carries connotations of questionable practices of therapy today. Even better, hypnosis connotes bad theatre. How do we reconcile such connotations with Beckett's lyrical spectacle and why would we even seek to? Allow me to clarify matters pertaining to the popular clinical definition of the technique. We saw earlier how Wagstaff provides the general theory that 'hypnosis is an altered state of consciousness'.[22] Theorists and practitioners differ on the status of the subject's will in such an altered condition – especially regarding the subjective ends of this technique in achieving altered states of consciousness and drive. Like the theatregoer, the hypnotic arrangement is brokered in an ostensibly consensual agreement; a hypnotized individual is supposed to be one who seeks out the experience. Theatrical hypnosis adheres to this principle also.

The real circumstances of hypnosis, both in practice and in theory, undermine the assumption of absolute consent, however. In a sense, the hypnotized subject more closely resembles an unwilling, unwitting actor. As we will examine shortly, nineteenth-century neurologists such as Charcot used hypnosis expressly to arrest often resistant subjective will to putatively ensure that their analyses were *objective* and not disrupted by resistance from patients. As such, the problematics of clinical hypnosis used for psychoanalytical ends very much questions the underlying principle of consent assumed in a clinical context that come to justify the acceptability of practices of hypnotic therapy, or post-hypnotic therapeutic practices of psychoanalysis that nevertheless have the technique of therapeutically overcoming patient resistance as their root.

Charcot in nineteenth-century psychopathology deployed the technique with the purpose of objectifying and pacifying the subject for the sake of sometimes public medical observation. Different stances exist regarding the intended ends of the hypnotic experiment for the subject in the historical deployment of this contentious vein of therapy. My definition of hypnotic experience begins with the practical account provided by Wagstaff, since it is concerned with the appearance of 'altered state[s] of consciousness' whatever the context, and can thus be critiqued with the proper inflection governing whatever the context at hand happens to be. This applicability will be essential as we blur the lines between clinic and theatre in subsequent sections.

Do we observe the states of consciousness in the self altered by a suggestive activity of remembrance conducted by an outside party in *Rockaby*? Certainly. Beckett's hypnotic characterization of the split figure of the woman in this play involves a rudimentary presentation of subjective alterability through artifice and the sensorium. Moreover, the play concerns itself with how the subject's artificial *self*-presentation – the poetic, hypnotic repetition of her final moments – leads us to reality: the remains of the subject at death's door. Thus, in *Rockaby*, a memory drama takes place in a *hypnotic* relation. This involves the remains of one's life surrendered to and altered by the affective autonomy, and otherness, of one's memories. Wagstaff's conception of hypnosis undermines the idea that one's will alone determines one's subjective being, given that the subject's consciousness is eminently alterable. Such a view is in keeping with the hypnotic principle of human suggestibility. Will can be bypassed by way of technique. W's consciousness is altered by V's. Beckett's theatrical emphasis upon the otherness inherent in subjectivity and self-perception, the I as an-other, enables the effect of the exposed rupture to open to the spectatorial field, and engulf them in a sympathetic immersion in the circumstances of simulation.

Long before the denouement of the play, that is, when W's request for more does not arrive, the audience anticipates sleep's equation with death. This is not a subtext of the play, but rather the guiding principle of it.[23] Knowlson writes that a painting by Beckett's friend Jack Yeats entitled *Sleep* was hung in the writer's library, depicting 'an old woman sitting by the window with her head drooping low onto her chest. ... [T]he woman could be asleep for ever'.[24] The image vividly conjures the scenario of *Rockaby*. The association of death with sleep itself is classical. Hypnos (Somnus in Roman mythology) was the son of Nyx and Erebus – that is, night and darkness – and lived in 'the lazy stream of Lethe', or forgetfulness.[25] Sleep is an environment of forgetfulness, of compromised memory, child of night and dark cast upon cognitive, as well as ontological and symbolic, domains.

With sleep, time, and forgetfulness establishing habitual subcategories in the natural life cycle of the subject, can free will be said to have any significance for memory after the advent of the hypnosis concept? Beckett's dark humour explains the paradoxical function of W's paroxysm, 'More'. That is, we know that to ask for more life (as opposed to honouring the end) ensures the continuation of W's dying. Indeed, considered either way, both V and W inevitably urge the end of their lives: V in the attempt to witness the death scene by a narrated remembrance of her final moments; W by asking for 'more' of V's narration, continued remembrance of dying, and therefore more of a life defined by its proximity to impending death. If consciousness can be altered, how might we distinguish between the will that is our own and the will compelled by external influences? Hypnosis presents a formulation that denies this sovereignty of will in the subject.

W's disembodied voice, V, compels, 'time she stopped'. This refrain echoes the mechanical chair, whose autonomy – Beckett specifies that the chair is '[c]ontrolled mechanically without assistance from W'[26] – likens it, if not to the hypnotist's pendulum, then to a kind of metronome. The chair anchors the play's sonic and visual elements, which are synchronized to achieve a hypnotic rhythm. Subjective will appears to be surrendered to implacable, external forces. We saw in Chapter 2 how Anthony Uhlmann suggests that the radical Cartesian idea of 'true powerlessness' associated with Arnold Geulincx finds its analogue in the automated chair.[27] W's willpower can only be marked by the manner in which she echoes this irrefutable movement; the autonomic processes that underpin her existence mark W's being in the world and propel her through time. Free will is immaterial and futile here. Whether willed or under a spell, hypnosis thus involves a similar stripping of the subject's assumed sovereignty of will. Hypnosis, like Cartesianism, views the subject as an affective machine. The understanding of this machine differs greatly between Cartesianism and hypnosis, of course, especially as the latter is understood by post-psychoanalytic affect theory.

If hypnosis has a Cartesian forbear, it nonetheless considers affect in ways that Descartes and others would have to reject. Indeed, hypnosis emerged as an explanation for results gained by accident in the eighteenth century. The technique is an affective remainder in the wake of a scientific problem. That is, Franz Mesmer, father of mesmerism, believed in animal magnetism. His experiments, involving a machine called a *baquet*, explored the unconscious affective relations between subjects in a mutual manifestation in 'phlogiston,' a still-theoretical liquid said to reside in animal bodies. In fact, the *baquet* and Mesmer's belief made a hypnotic whole, achieving some of the symptoms Mesmer sought in the name of science. When Antoine-Laurent Lavoisier and other commissioners disputed the existence of phlogiston, they enabled the discovery that *affective*, not chemical, results were due to hypnotic suggestions made by Mesmer himself in his clinical theatre, rather than actual physical interactions.[28] And so his scientific failure came to reveal a modified view of the subject. Experimenting with subjective responses manipulated by belief and affect revealed the extent to which affective susceptibility figures in areas of consciousness such as memory and will formerly understood to be sovereign faculties of an essential soul.

Importantly, hypnosis delegates renewed significance to the question of the imaginative capacity of a subject. For example, in a trance, through the combined power of the hypnotized subject's imagination and the hypnotist's leading suggestions, a subject can commit to psychic tasks otherwise not possible consciously, such as recovering a lost memory or giving up smoking. Following this simplified definition, we can conclude that not only hypnotists establish hypnotic relations; rather, hypnotic relations are possible in any number of circumstances involving attention, from watching television, to performing a repetitive task, to daydreaming. Recall that, for Crary, hypnosis represents an 'extreme model of a technology of attention'.[29] Hypnosis arose out of discoveries about autonomic systems within humans, which corresponded with new industrial systems that in their turn automated human function and utility. One of Beckett's favourite performers, Charlie Chaplin, allegorizes this trait of modernity in *Modern Times* (1936) as Chaplin's will and gestural vocabulary undergo manipulation by the factory's machines to comic effect. This pre-eminent example of slapstick and thus modern pantomime presents the biomechanical entanglement that the modern body underwent in relation to automation. The industrial framework undergirding these advents in modern biomechanics coincide with hypnosis's wide medical application in the nineteenth century. Human attention at this time was quite simply being redefined as a utility. Crary provides three categories of attention relevant to hypnosis in this historical moment:

> (1) Attention as a *reflex* process, part of a mechanical adaptation of an organism to stimuli in an environment. Important here is the evolutionary legacy of attention, and its origins in *involuntary* and instinctive perceptual responses. (2) Attention as determined by the operations of various *automatic* or unconscious processes or forces, a position articulated in many ways, beginning with Schopenhauer, Janet, Freud, and numerous others. (3) Finally, attention as a decisive, *voluntary* activity of the subject, an expression of its autonomous power to actively organise and impose itself on a perceived world. But even those who defended the latter position, like [William] James or Bergson, readily acknowledged the proximity of and blurred limits between voluntary attentiveness and automatic or involuntary states.[30]

The following application of hypnotic principles for understanding spectatorship in Beckett's late theatre will aim to implicitly refer to all three dynamics of attention – the reflexive, automatic, and voluntary registers of it – so as to explore the full range of dramaturgical influences over attention explored in Beckett's problematized hypnotic spectacle.

Not I: Against intelligibility

Now that the mechanics of hypnotic spectacle and its consequences for spectatorship have been discussed, more elusive questions regarding subjectivity and the theatrical presentation of characters from the psychoanalytic corpus may be engaged. Specifically, I want to discuss the inherently theatrical nature of clinics such as Charcot's Salpêtrière clinic and the theatrical subtexts for subjectivity inhering in diagnostic contexts associated with hypnotic activities. Subjectivities that are defined by psychoanalytic terminology retain the terms of disobedience and fictitiousness by which they were performed in the clinic when we revise the phenomena arising out of that particular spectacle. I will focus on how these subjectivities elude diagnosis in the theatrical context, and thus how a comparable theatricality might be observed in a Beckettian situation. Beckett's dramaturgy deploys techniques that bear some resemblance to those used by analysts, for whom hypnosis once encouraged self-discovery in its patients to solicit responses from unconscious tendencies found in the patient's psyche. I want also to consider the special significance of Lisa Dwan's performance of these three Beckett plays to examine these comparative theatrical engagements with hypnotic dramaturgy. *Not I* in particular will receive considerable reappraisal.

With Dwan in the role of Mouth, *Not I* illuminates parallels between the psychoanalytic corpus and dramaturgies of self-witnessing. One achievement of this 2014 production is that the hypnotic spectatorship solicited by Asmus's production trains attention on the play's sonic power and away from its narrative. Perceived through a modified spectatorship, character becomes less a category of analysis than a corporeal force with which to be reckoned. Although Beckett's fragmented narrative remains, of course, a spectator's appreciation of this memory play becomes more a matter of rapt submission to the physicality of speech and (compromised) self-witnessing. Mouth repudiates a clinical interpretation or observation, and Dwan's embodiment reaches a level of command of this repudiation unseen in the performance archive of this play. In Dwan's noisy, almost unintelligibly fast performance, Mouth undermines a diagnostic spectatorship in favour of one that is affectively overwhelmed. In this way, Dwan's version manifests a new iteration of Beckett's request for a version at the 'speed of thought', a request we learnt about in Chapter 2.[31] The resulting loss of intelligibility through speed emphasizes the play's hypnotic soundscape of verbal noise over clear recital of the character's memory narrative.

What kind of subject is *Not I*'s Mouth? She certainly seems to emerge from a psychoanalytic imagination of fragmentary, traumatized, unresolved subjectivity. For one thing, the character seems to have unfinished business involving an encrypted trauma set in a pastoral scene. The overt rejection of the personal pronoun 'I', which motivates Mouth's incessant cycles of thought, indicates a problem in self-identification and even conspicuous false witnessing. Recalling two key figures from the psychoanalytic corpus, Anna O. and Blanche Wittman, the play associates the mind with noise, conscious thought with barely controlled eruptions of memory. The play's rejection of clinical analysis thus has hypnotic and performative dimensions. Let us first view the workings of hypnotic elements in the characterization of Mouth. Then, let us observe the opening of this characterization into scenography and the relationship the play structures between spectator and spectacle.

Not I's only character, Mouth, is a figure not fully given.[32] Mouth is a fragment, a metonym, an orifice floating above the stage in the dark. Mouth signifies herself in erratic, apparently unconscious, which is to say, unintentional, ways, even rejecting the identity attributed to 'I'. Mouth is an explicitly false witness. Although Mouth is said to be 'speechless all her days', the play positions the spectator in a different relation to her; she is configured, if you will, as a figure of speech.[33] In being incommensurate with narratives of subjectivity which might interpret her – indeed, in being overtly hostile to them – Mouth recalls pathological subjectivities from the psychoanalytic corpus. As Ulrika Maude shows, Beckett's characterization of Mouth suggests neurological concepts of human disorder.[34] Helpfully, Maude notes the significance of neurological discussions in querying absolute boundaries between free will and its others. She writes: 'Neurological disorders which present with motor or linguistic automatism confound and collapse distinctions between voluntary and involuntary action, ability and disability, ... the body and the mind'.[35] The apparent automatism of Mouth's speech aligns with her elusiveness as a diagnosable subject.

Mouth also appears to be under (self-)interrogation: her defiant attitude directs itself towards a coercive agent less visible than the interrogating spotlight that compels the similar monologues in Beckett's earlier *Play* (1963). The audience is encouraged to understand this agent – the 'she' Mouth speaks of – as the self itself, a character riven by self-interrogation and rejection. Such a split suggests in turn that certain moments of her monologue's narrative are undeniably self-reflexive: 'found herself in the dark ... and if not exactly ... insentient ... insentient ... for she could still hear the buzzing'.[36] Along with the question of her consciousness of making speech – her 'insentien[ce],' as she describes it – the play equates speech itself with noise, and thought itself with buzzing. Mouth is a figure characterized by figments of memory that float and resist single narrative coherence; echoes suggest a coherent referent, as in, for example, 'wandering in a field … looking aimlessly for cowslips'; but nothing consolidates with any coherence.[37] These delinked associations, ellipses and non sequiturs collectively cast doubt on the reliability of the figure's self-witnessing. The audience thus becomes conscious of a fragmentary subjectivity before them referred to but not cohering into a single referent. Through what is unsaid, through what is absent, and through the emotional excesses that testify to traumatic obfuscation through narrative, Mouth's presence asks for a spectator's imaginative 'recomposition'.[38]

When Mary Bryden characterizes Mouth's testimony as 'mesmerizing', she invites more than an aesthetic reading of mesmeric atmosphere to examine it.[39] Bryden's account of mesmerized attention implies that Mouth's sonic and narratorial effect achieves a figure that modifies spectatorship: 'The Mouth encountered by the viewer is the overwhelming enunciator, the mesmerizing vocaliser who, the antithesis of dumbness herself, instead *imposes dumbness* and *commands attentiveness*'.[40] By recognizing how the enunciator's mesmerism 'imposes dumbness' and 'commands attentiveness', Bryden equates the rapt (and customary) silence of the spectator with the surrendering of attention. Bryden pursues a Deleuzian conclusion about stage image as a result. This pure image of vocal independence subverting normative subjectivity, especially gendered subjectivity, effects in a Deleuzian sense what Diamond described earlier as a 'different mimesis' following the figure's resistance to normative apprehension. We can integrate Bryden's theory of imposed dumbness into the theory of hypnotic spectatorship: Mouth is an entity formerly diagnosed as dumb and unheard, a clinical voice, if you like, escaping the dualism of mind torn from body. What results is the hypnotic contract inverted, with the role of the witness reversed, the mimetic field shaped not by diagnosis but instead by the urges of the self-examining subject. A soundscape results, with the stage image of a mouth as its emanating point. Thanks to this inversion, the spectator finds herself in an environment within which she can be immersed and mesmerized by Mouth, rather than the clinical gaze that would render such a figure categorically interpretable but mute.

The experimental Salpêtrière clinic of Jean-Martin Charcot took a neurological approach towards hysteria that would later revise its findings about the disorder as a psychological malady. This journey from neurology to psychology essentially establishes a pivotal moment in the development of psychology and psychoanalysis. Hypnosis was used here to control the unruly patient–subject by disarming the subject's conscious resistances and purportedly reaching the unconscious mind. Such an approach assumed that the process of recovery led by the hypnotist–neurologist was capable of scientific objectivity. The symptoms associated with hysteria came, in turn, through hypnosis: the solicitation of certain responses in the subject by guidance from the hypnotist–neurologist seeking symptoms. The case of Charcot's patient Blanche Wittman reveals the truly *theatrical* nature of self-witnessing in this clinic, as well as the manipulative role of the analyst. Though intended as serious clinical presentations of medical discovery, Diamond describes the exhibitions that featured in this clinic as 'worthy of the best sensational melodramas'.[41] Wittman's opposition to being diagnosed we can now see demonstrates elements of an affective autonomy striving for liberation. This attempt at agency in the confinement of the clinical imaginary exceeded diagnostic interpretation for the clinical theatre even as it paradoxically found its announcement and disclosure within it. These are some of the clinical and affective problems of presentation for unruly subjective formations that I hope to associate with Beckett's three challenging plays.

In Charcot's clinic, analysis was performed on live subjects for an audience of fellow analysts and students. The clinic in this sense was inherently theatrical, not unlike Mesmer's. Charisma was as much a methodological tool as a disciplinary credential in the interpretation of disturbances such as bodily contortions and paroxysms of voice attributed to hysteria. Citing an episode in Charcot's Salpêtrière clinic found in Michel Foucault's *The History of Sexuality,* Diamond observes how the intersection of hysterical narrative in melodrama and the melodrama of the so-called hysteric's live testimony reinforced a 'scopophilic position' that simulated the very symptoms it purported to objectively expose.[42] What Charcot would confidently diagnose in the company of an interested, even salaciously involved audience had to include the innate performance of the subject under analysis. This performance included negative, defiant and sleight-of-hand responses to being analysed and pressured to perform that cast serious doubt upon the pretensions of objectivity that the clinic sought to represent.

Felicia McCarren notes how dissimulation by patients was normal: 'Hysterical patients at the Salpêtrière imitated the symptoms of epileptics and others who were in the wards with them, and even those patients whose physical symptoms Charcot could prove psychically created were often thought to be faking'.[43] The clinic's suggestions of disorder were themselves informed by the patient's opposition to analysis and to clinical objectification. McCarren notes, for example, that Wittman was considered a false witness to her own mental disturbances: she showed hysterical 'antagonism in the face of mistreatment'.[44] In fact, this diagnosis came in response to Wittman's protests against a student, present at her analysis, who suggested she take off her clothes.[45] The notion of consent, of volition, is critically undermined by revisions of the very structure of this early neurological clinic's ambitions to expose the subject; its very diagnoses of resistance to therapy as a pathological tendency inadvertently point to anti-mimetic strategies that critique the pathologizing clinical theatre.

Beckett's Mouth in *Not I* – like *Footfalls*'s May and *Rockaby*'s W – generates a counter-mimetic strategy to the scopophilic, objectifying theatre of affect found in early clinics of neurology and psychology that replays historical examples of resistance to pathologizing hermeneutics of clinical reason. Mouth recalls *AWW I*'s man from Chapter 1, whose resistance to performance resembled experimental failures found in the laboratory of Wolfgang Köhler. The mise en scène of a play such as *Not I* is constructed using the affective terms that would be doomed to diagnostic resolution in the clinic, but in Beckett retain their irresolution.

Self-deception as the central drama of the memory narrative, from Proust, to early neurology, to psychoanalysis, and now Beckett, when exposed sympathetically can solicit a new testimonial order by other mimetic means with different spectatorial conclusions. Beckett's theatre specifically discourages clinical judgements regarding the subject, I argue. The scopophilia of the clinic is evidently resisted. Rather, hypnotizing affective forms of suffering and remembering echo through the chamber of the theatre *in resistance to being an I-voice* and thus as an objectifiable, corporeal, complete subject. If there is psychoanalytic value to such an imaginative enterprise, it is to encourage spectators to draw on their own affective and sensory intuitions to experience these private theatres. That diagnoses and a coherent pathological interpretation would be possible in this domain, as it was assumed to be in the coercive Salpêtrière clinic, undergoes profound questioning here. Rather, Beckett's hypnotic dramaturgy provides a scenographic frame for a new theatre of subjective gestures conventionally ostracized from empathetic attention to emerge.

Beckett's micro-novel *Ill Seen Ill Said* shares much with the hypnotic spectacle of *Rockaby*. The two were written and published within a year of each other: the former as *Mal vu mal dit*, written between October 1980 and its publication date with Minuit in March 1981; the latter completed by August 1980 after a solicitation by Daniel Labeille in March 1980 for the State University of New York Beckett Festival in April 1981.[46] They share an occupation with the narrative problem of a woman said to be disappearing, passing in and out of light. *Ill Seen Ill Said* even features a 'ghostly chair' with the character situated at times at the window.[47] Then, the 'Lick chops and basta' phrase from the micro-novel is another example of that novelly lyrical vulgarity that finds Beckett's characters' tongues when they swear, just as in *Rockaby*'s 'fuck life' remark.[48] Helpfully, Adam Piette suggests that the micro-novel offers a 'radical endgame' of 'mourning' and 'post-mortem questioning'.[49] This proves to be a compelling way to describe *Rockaby*'s counter-mimetic and 'post-mortem' spectatorial field.

As Knowlson suggests, the focal character of this prose work 'may be a ghost, a memory, a fiction, or a mixture of all three'.[50] Here we find that triumvirate of entangled concerns of self-simulation in testimonial dramaturgy which we have come to associate with hypnotic approaches to narrative and sensorium – haunting, memory, fictionality. Piette concludes that this 'endgame' is the same in both Proust and Beckett: they render 'the death of the subject as affective source'.[51] We might say that the face of W too, along with her cry for 'More', is also such an 'affective source'. Piette's remarks resonate with the idea that a hypnotic relation engenders an intensified proximity between spectacle and spectator when the hypnotic link has been released from governance by a one-way coercion to open to sympathetic auditors. An audience no longer becomes the scopophile, but rather the listener whose experience is determined by the commandments of the affective unrest enclosed in the problematic figure. The result is a theatrical mimesis governed by alterity, an alterity that resists the pathologizing gaze and instead enables more open affective commerce with the face.

Piette suggests that such spectatorial encounter with this enigmatic 'affective source' insinuates a new ethical consciousness. Quoting Emmanuel Levinas, he writes that 'all ethics begins with the summons to responsibility (and the performance of affective responses) occasioned by the "ethical proximity" of the face of the other'.[52] So, counter-mimetic strategies in the testimonial memory drama can present counter-narrative solicitations of new forms of empathy. Co-suffering, rather than diagnosis, motivates Beckett's refashioning of the subject's affective trouble formerly associated with the clinic in my view. Beckett's laboratory again supplies an alternative facticity to deterministic examples, generated through self-reflexive simulation. The significance of the Royal Court production lies in its expansion of the terms of this counter-diagnostic manoeuvre.

Let us now integrate particularities of the Dwan-Asmus production into the discussion of hypnotic dramaturgy so far. We saw in Chapter 2, how Anthony Page's production of *Not I* in 1973 starring Billie Whitelaw, a head clamp and a chair on a rostrum achieved the striking image essential to the play. But in Asmus's production, Dwan isolates Beckett's Mouth differently. A video from a BBC interview in 2013 shows that the actor is fixed into a board that holds her mouth in place but allows jostling behind the spectacle. This is an improvement upon the earlier version of the apparatus in its channelling of energy outside of the field of the spectator's vision.[53] Dwan's device appears to have been designed by the actor herself, since her use of it in fact precedes Asmus's production. She performed the role as early as July 2005, at the Battersea Arts Centre under the directorship of Natalie Abrahami, where the work was performed alongside *Play*. Dwan's version retains the same unmoving focal point as in Whitelaw's virtuosic performance, immortalized on film: a tiny focal point in the dark firing a verbal assault of recollections. As argued in Chapter 2, this focal point, difficult to see, creates an effect of vertigo for the audience that emerges out of the sensory deprivation of performer and audience alike that the image requires for realization. In attempting to hold this stage image in place in total darkness, the spectator likely experiences some degree of vertigo that could be said to simulate Mouth's chaotic private theatre. My prologue to this chapter attests to my own experience of this. Dwan's labour of unprecedented speed increases the vertiginous effect. Mutual vertigo, again, an affective circumstance that the clinic would deem pathological, suggests the kind of modified attention that we have so far assessed in terms of hypnotic technique.

Paul Taylor writes of the 2014 production that 'Dwan's 9 minute performance is the quickest on record'.[54] Particularly in Dwan's nine-minute rendition, a virtuosic performance of the role takes advantage of the spectator's affective proneness to the referent of the play, a subjective problematic involving memory, suffering, and traumatic encryption. In contrast to *Rockaby*, the solicitation for an audience to bear witness is less elegiac and more aggressive. The play's dramaturgical arrangement orchestrates a hypnotic simulation of disorder which retains the problems of self-witnessing entailed in such subjective formations, including the unresolved issues of such formations' intelligibility for outside observation. But we are not asked to observe disorders. We are asked to experience self-simulation.

Dwan has acknowledged the importance of Whitelaw's legacy on her own practice of this trilogy. When she first met Whitelaw in 2006, Dwan notes the following:

> [W]e bonded immediately, like two shell-shocked war veterans. ... Soon she was conducting me over her kitchen table. 'I can't read or write music', she said, 'but if I were a musician, I'd have put a crotchet here instead of a quaver'. She recalled what Beckett had told her: '"You can't

go fast enough for me." Also, "If the word has several syllables, use them. Ev-er-y-thing. No-thing."[55]

Upon being asked to perform the work in 2009, she again consulted with Whitelaw for further 'sessions'. So rather than an effort to supersede Whitelaw's version, Dwan's virtuosic, accelerated but more unintelligible version of the work should be seen as an extension of Whitelaw's first-hand experience of the play transmitted between performers and developing anew. Dwan identified more strongly with Beckett's cue that one 'can't go fast enough for [him]', willing to sacrifice syllabic clarity to achieve this speed. Performing Mouth, Dwan reflects, is like 'driving down the motorway the wrong way with no handbrake. Nothing is as scary.'[56] Her performance's achievement of a rushing flow – glissando instead of staccato, to increase speed – and with a new musicality, presents an escalated interpretation of the part testing the intelligibility of a play already invested in an experiment in theatrical intelligibility.

Dwan's reflections emphasize the performance's athletic challenges: she relates that her whole body 'vibrates', that she even 'gyrates' when she performs Mouth.[57] These physiological challenges concern herself (in interpreting more extremely Beckett's request for the monologue to be recited at the 'speed of thought') but spectators, too (who train their eyesight so extremely on a single point). In her own words, 'there is not a single aspect of *Not I* that isn't difficult'.[58] The difference in metaphors used by Dwan and Whitelaw to describe the role is instructive. Dwan's focus on the 'speed of thought' using vehicular metaphors shows her emphasis upon the vertiginous quality of the work. If Whitelaw's rhythmic precision arrested the spectatorial imagination in its consistency, Dwan's 'no handbrake' version dizzies us. Her performance is more like a chant than Whitelaw's, in the sense that a chant reduces words to their hypnotic effect beyond the semantic sense of the words used. Noise thus has a critically hypnotic function. To bring the play towards the sonic horizon of noise is to approach a terrain where sense gives way to soundscape.

The spectatorship that arises out of this encounter, like that in *Rockaby* or *Footfalls*, encourages the other's care towards the false witnessing of Mouth. Tellingly, Knowlson notes that the Auditor, a silent black-hooded figure in Beckett's script of *Not I* later excised in Whitelaw production, represents Mouth's 'silent witness': 'The spectator has his or her surrogate representative on stage.'[59] Perhaps the decision to jettison this 'silent witness' in production lay in this figure's overly didactic solicitation to bear witness; we, the spectator, must overcome the silence of auditing the suffering subject, the Auditor seems to suggest. Such commandments work against Beckett's preference for decreative practices that powerfully call on responses to reassemble the ruinous form that the real adopts, or, indeed, to let alone the ruinous form of the real and allow it to retain its integrity. Nevertheless, we see the desire to frame the theatre as a means towards a new kind of spectatorship that would encounter these kinds of apparitions that flee the clinic, an encouragement of care for problematic subjects who might not otherwise elicit empathy. This care for false witnessing requires its audience to accept the integrity of the witness's self-expression so that their affective trouble for analysis can resonate rather than simply be resolved. Yes, a spectator can dismiss the spectacle and avoid being hypnotized, just like other forms of coercive suggestion like advertising or charismatic speeches. But, if we allow hypnotic techniques to permeate us, our immersion in the soundscape of the work, our proximity to its compromised intelligibility, and our sense of intimacy with the narrative, asks us to answer a solicitation to deeper engagement and self-identification.

I return to the ethical question of affective proximity and appearance to conclude this chapter. In *Not I, Footfalls* and *Rockaby*, each subject's stage presence is staked in the truthful presentation of the nonetheless fictive theatre of memory. The characters' capacity to be seen relies upon fictions of selfhood developed against forms of subjective closure: opposition to a mother's narrative (May in *Footfalls*), a refusal to say 'I' (Mouth in *Not I*), or a contradictory demand for 'More' dying (W in *Rockaby*). Such a paradigm of the subject may not be unique to these plays in Beckett's oeuvre. But these plays do represent a pinnacle in the stagecraft of (true) false witnessing, with the Asmus and Dwan production realizing their extreme possibilities on stage anew. The alternative, we can speculate, would be the clinical laboratory. There, reason, especially psychoanalytic reason, consigns subjects such as Mouth, May and W to closure: Mouth to erasure, May to the confines of her mother's imagination, W to the facticity of her death. The affective particularity of these exhibitions reveals the characters' delinquency in relation to the forces that might otherwise push them into invisibility, or the sort of objectified hypervisibility that disturbed Blanche Wittman. We have seen how the spectator's co-suffering involves recognizing the not-I of Mouth in her compromised intelligibility. We have seen how the memory of W, compromised by the 'Time cancer', gets her 'More' time, however finite, bartered with the audience's belief in her fictively interminable rocking.

Without empathy, these subjectivities cannot appear in this way at all. Paul Rae has noted this issue to be a more general phenomenon of the Beckett theatre, tracing characters' reliance on empathic spectatorship in the much earlier play, *Waiting for Godot*. Rae surmises that a latent humanism exists in Beckett's theatre corresponding to the basic capacity to be seen:

> 'At me too someone is looking', says Vladimir. It's a red herring for him but bait for us. While the characters struggle to identify sufficient value in each other to be recognised as human, the audience bears witness to their plight, and finds, in the poetry and the pratfalls, grounds on which to mark the characters as having appeared.[60]

Like Didi and Gogo in Rae's analysis, W, May and Mouth may not be visible to themselves. They depend on the audience's registration of feeling and recognition in order to be seen as they see themselves, a self-witnessing that is deeply fraught. Sometimes this registration entails that the spectator seeks to view the unknown, the apparently false, and the incomprehensible. Characterization on these terms can be said to require a newly challenged spectator, one open to hypnotic modification by a dramaturgical means that, we have seen, insinuates in spectators a recursive, self-reflexive inquiry into the nature of testimony and self-consciousness. We can recall Gontarski's idea that Beckett revises the question of characters' 'thereness' in soliciting such spectatorship.[61] Chertok and Stengers would call the Beckett spectator as I have formulated it here a 'perplexed author[]' whose perplexity has drawn them to critique received models of simulation.[62] The Beckett spectator that consents to hypnotic experience comes to register the perplexity of remembrance sensorially and intimately, immersed in memory's echoes and the sensations they induce. Here, then, the act of spectatorship becomes responsible for the 'recomposition' of affects otherwise unseen or heard that adhere to norms of clinical or theatrical visibility.[63] Spectatorship of Beckett's altered kind allows these figures to go on in the memory.

7

Adaphatrôce, or the contentious fringes of Beckett's dramaturgy

Major works in the history of scholarship on Beckett in performance tend to concur about Mabou Mines's production of *The Lost Ones* presented in New York in 1975 and Europe in 1976. Jonathan Kalb describes the production as 'an enormous and utterly unforeseen international success, both critical and popular, and … a kind of avant-garde legend'.[1] Ruby Cohn describes its final effect in performance to be 'too intense for applause … a reaction that Beckett actors should cherish, whatever the genre'.[2] As an adaptation of a prose work, the production confounds our theorization of the experimental Beckett as much as it informs it. This production suggests that the experimental impulse identified with Beckett exists in a transversal, that is, diagonal, orientation across practice, theory and archive both within and without explicitly performative texts. We must confront this transversality across media and the compositional practices of Beckett's theatre pieces to properly account for the enduring value that this major example has for understanding experimental Beckettian dramaturgy.

The original prose work, *The Lost Ones*, first written in French as *Le Dépeupleur* between 1966 and 1970 and published in English translation in 1972, is itself an experiment in miniaturization. The story is comprised of a narrative that charts a society of two hundred bodies mutually invisible to one another in an enclosed cylinder 'fifty metres round and sixteen high'.[3] The individuals within are characterized as being in search of a loved one and circulating via a calculation of social despondency in four states, from motion to ontological paralysis, the latter state Beckett evocatively referring to as 'in the attitude which wrung from Dante one of his rare wan smiles'.[4] S. E. Gontarski asserts that the piece presents a central example of the 'closed space' narrative that would become the preoccupation of the experimental prose that followed, shaped by a kind of 'seeing in a closed space where the homophones "scene" and "seen" are coeval'.[5]

We know that the decreative logic employed in these prose works was a miniaturizing one by following the trajectory of writing that *The Lost Ones* marks. Works directly related to its writing, such as 'Bing', are even more diminutive than this important prose piece.[6] I want to show how Mabou Mines's production's attention to the experimental urge of Beckett dramaturgy demonstrates that the production has become historically entangled with the dramaturgical heritage of this writer. So, while not a Beckett theatre work, the profound influence this adaptation has had upon the trajectory of Beckettian dramaturgy shows that fidelity to the history of so-called authorized Beckett productions while the writer was alive does not sufficiently explain the nature of this dramaturgy. To consider Mabou Mines's, and indeed a number of other crucial realizers' contributions to expanding upon the experimental urge in Beckett's dramaturgy, begs for a new critical approach. The alternative critical approach that I suggest here is the one initiated from the outset: we must understand Beckett's theatre as a laboratory for experiments in theatre practice. Beckett's interactions with the makers of transversal examples such as the Mabou Mines *Lost Ones* suggest that Beckett had a special, if anxious interest in the experiment with medium that adaptation of his prose works inevitably involved. Then, the Beckett laboratory in its posthumous incarnations must come to include adaptation as a central means for inquiring anew into this dramaturgy's fringes. Limit works by Beckett, such as *Breath* (1969), can be rethought within the late-twentieth-century experimental performance landscape when we study their complementarity to the ways in which adaptation extends the logics of medial experiment most evidently composed by the writer in the figureless soundscape of that work. Adaptation inherently questions intention. What I discover in this chapter is not that the negotiation with Beckettian intention was a matter of vexation for the writer. Rather, I discover that adaptation became a serious subject of self-reflection for Beckett. Reassessing adaptation's role during Beckett's life will enable a more amenable revision of the posthumous experimentality of Beckettian dramaturgy that follows.

Those who know the story of Lee Breuer's directorship and David Warrilow's immersive, transformed recital of the prose work *The Lost Ones* understand how little of a definitive practice was involved in validating the rights to this company's approach to adapting the work. Much transpired by chance. Warrilow had rights to give a reading of the prose text. This reading later became a somewhat elaborately installed reading in the Mabou Mines company design and dramaturgical realization of the reading setting beyond the original remit. This design's cylinder performance space enveloping spectator and monologist Warrilow alike, along with the other actor-contributors Linda Wolf, William Raymond and Ellen McElduff installed in the space, essentially produced an immersive theatre experience in which spectators became not only actors but the characters within the ghoulish narrative.

Beckett's willingness to negotiate with this company is somewhat miraculous. No one was more ambivalent about adaptation than Beckett himself. The writer's opinion of adaptations of his work for different media comes usefully summarized in a letter to Barney Rossett regarding the radio play *All That Fall*. As we have observed across a changing array of dramaturgical practices, the sensory implications of a medium intended for experimentation are indispensable to the understanding of Beckett writing for media. Thus, the materiality of a work was a matter the writer vehemently sought to protect when it was being considered for adaptation in a different medium than it was first intended for:

> *All That Fall* is a specifically radio play, or rather radio text, for voices, not bodies. I have already refused to have it 'staged' and I cannot think of it in such terms ... Even the reduced dimension it will receive from the simplest and most static of readings ... will be destructive of whatever quality it may have and which depends on the whole thing's *coming out of the dark*.[7]

Arguments have been made to the effect that, somewhat unintentionally, Mabou Mines's experimental adaptation evaded committing *adaphatrôce* in this immersive monologue because it utilized a theatricality that was already disclosed in the prose itself. To adopt Beckett's words, *The Lost Ones* somehow managed to emerge out of the dark in a way complementary to the mode of presentation particular to the page work in the opinion of the writer. Kalb suggests that

> there *is* a certain theatricality to the act of reading Beckett's prose fiction despite the fact that it is a solitary act. It is this quality of demonstrative reflexivity, which Knowlson and Pilling compare with painting in their wonderful phrase, 'frescoes of the skull,' but if the theatre was originally a 'seeing place,' as etymologists tell us, then that skull may be just as easily likened to a stage. It should not be surprising that such texts appeal to directors with the historical avant-gardist ambition to question age-old mimetic models of theatre, such as Aristotle's, and the perceptual habits that accompany them. What is surprising is when those directors assume that the solitary theatricality of reading is directly transferable to the public circumstances of the stage.[8]

While Kalb's remarks about theatricality are borne out by attention to the deconstructed nature of narration in the prose, we do need to address other aspects of the unlikely dramaturgical success achieved by a company attempting an adaptation of Beckett's prose where the writing explicitly resists spectacle and even the visual domain.

For one thing, the tiny figurines that materialize the lost figures[9] of this claustrophobic prose work certainly have never been suggested in any Beckett script; the insightfulness of Mabou Mines's idea begs the question why. Having notable Beckett actor Warrilow manipulate barely visible figurines while using the original text to narrate their circumstances somehow demonstrates a strong consonance with the figural criteria attending *l'empêchement-oeil* found in Beckett's best-known scenographies. As a result, any adaptation must attempt to dramatize a Dantean microcosm omnisciently narrated without any promise of an outside realm if it is to adhere to the claustrophobic atmosphere of the prose work. The first component of Mabou Mines's innovations in adapting Beckett is Lee Breuer's directorship and its attention to the philosophical problem of vision for Beckett's work. As Lois Oppenheim writes in *The Painted Word: Samuel Beckett's Dialogue with Art*:

> *The Lost Ones* ... sustains the visual analogy: The problem of ontological relativism (the relation world imposes on Being) is that of art (it is the origin, in fact, of its insufficiency or failure) and this fiction, like *Bing* (which derived from early drafts of it), depicts the search for a 'way out', a way beyond the subject-object association. It does so even more emphatically: Projecting the confinement of the over two hundred 'little people of searchers', the text avoids description of enclosure to *be* it.[10]

Oppenheim therefore suggests that prose work *The Lost Ones* itself involves a decreative strategy to render a figural value to uncertain narration, problematizing its figures' visibility to a reader, imagining the problematic of no 'way out' of the 'subject-object association' that confers to narrative voice its presumed authority. The avoidance of description of a world beyond this enclosure mentioned by Oppenheim – in fact, an *impossibility* to describe it, tied up in the closed space narrative's logic of 'no apertures' attributable to *The Unnamable* and later prose works – renders an enclosure thanks to an immersive narrative strategy for *negating* the impression of an outside realm. The prose work 'avoids description of enclosure to *be* it'; Mabou Mines's immersive set realizes this by having the spectators cohabitate with monologist and the figurines he narrates in a confined cylindrical space. This immersion both reproduces the claustrophobic reading experience stimulated by this best-known example of Beckett's closed space pieces, and at the same time establishes a theatre-specific practice of decreation that comparably resists the mimetic field and the subject-object relations that usually govern live performance. Crucially, then, the figurine recreation in the Mabou Mines production of the enigmatic narrator-character relation from the original work demonstrates a remarkable consciousness of not only a Beckett aesthetic, but also the philosophical and textual problems for visibility, presence, and authority enclosed in this self-interrogating work.

Beckett the Heinrich von Kleist enthusiast never did bring real figurines or puppets into his own theatre of death, even when that relevant contemporary of his, Polish theatre innovator Tadeusz Kantor, did so in his famed work *The Dead Class* in the very same year that *The Lost Ones* featured in New York's West Village.[11] Yet, the theatrical solution devised by Mabou Mines sustains Beckettian dramaturgy's decreative practice. Here, elements of acting transfigure the subject through collectively experienced subtraction, entailing sensory deprivation, corporeal exposure and focalization. Through adaptation, Mabou Mines casts Beckett dramaturgy more evidently into the experimental contemporary performance context of the 1970s. But this was not exactly achieved by transgression of intention. Instead, Mabou Mines elaborate upon the laboratory tendencies that we have seen to orient the Beckett dramaturgical project with an insight into and experience with Beckett's writing for performance applied to a work not conceived for theatre, as we shall soon observe. Besides a successful transposition of a quality in the prose that Kalb identifies as amenable to theatrical rendition, this production also demonstrates how practice has been transmitted and fostered in Beckettian dramaturgy by a company recognized in theatre history for its application to the writer's larger theatrical aims.

As Iris Smith Fischer notes, from 1965 onwards, the collective of actors that would become Mabou Mines treated the performance of Beckett as the engagement in a new, unpredictable self-discovery of a new discipline:

> The discipline invoked by Beckett's writing made sense to young artists working their way toward a new concept of performance. His texts encouraged discipline without requiring dogma. Akalaitis, who had studied in the 1960s with a variety of acting teachers, found the Stanislavskian director-actor relationship manipulative and unproductive and was ready for a different kind of discipline. Breuer and Maleczech had learned a great deal working with Herbert Blau in San Francisco. With R.G. Davis, Breuer had interesting discussions about Brecht. ... In 1970 seeking freedom and self-determination did not mean failing to engage in disciplined practices. As Beckett knew, the writer or actor must cultivate an 'inner force' in each piece in order to operate on his or her own artistic terms. ... Without adopting Beckett's view of life or his aesthetic, by performing his work the members of Mabou Mines learned much about cultivating an inner force.[12]

As we read in Smith Fischer's book, Warrilow had been a literary editor in Paris before pursuing a career as an actor in New York; from the beginning, the notion of a career in acting had followed a pursuit of performing Beckett, materializing in his first ever role playing M1 in *Play* in 1965 in this company of performers that would become Mabou Mines.[13] Thus, since 1965, members of the company have been developing their own theatre workshop with a commitment to the Beckettian challenge to theatre in years when the contingency of that dramaturgy was most acutely contentious. This commitment enabled them to consider Beckettian dramaturgy among a range of disciplinary interests that also included Stanislavski and Grotowski, despite contradictions these practices inevitably encounter when mixed together.

Unfortunately, Mabou Mines member JoAnne Akalaitis's directorship has been associated with the most rancorous of disputes between the Beckett Estate and experimental groups adapting his work: the subway-set *Endgame*, a production Beckett deplored.[14] This was not a Mabou Mines production, however, but rather created by Akalaitis with the American Repertory Theater Company. This production's critical reputation misconstrues the place of experimental adaptation and, by relation, Mabou Mines in charting the fringes of Beckett dramaturgy. The company has had an otherwise indisputable place in realizing the challenge to spectacle and the focalization of experiment within the finite resources of stagecraft that we have seen to govern Beckettian dramaturgy thus far. Beckettian dramaturgy as a practice to be learnt, in terms of what Smith Fischer calls a 'discipline', undergoes an exemplary representation in the example of the mid-1970s *The Lost Ones*. Perhaps the amenability of *The Lost Ones* to a disciplined adaptation also occurs due to the original prose text's concern with the larger implications of spectacle:

> *Le Dépeupleur* and some of the other short prose texts of the 1960s owe a lot to his recent work in film and television. A determined effort is made to 'see' the entire structure and organization of the cylinder and to describe the workings of the 'abode as precisely as the 'eye of the mind' (or the lens of a camera) will allow. Beckett's obsession with vision and with problems associated with vision – an obsession only partly influenced by his own declining sight – also affects the 'seeing' and the describing. He referred himself to one section in an early manuscript as 'une grande myopie' ('a great myopia'), and deterioration of vision in the cylinder is still stressed in the published version. The whole text could be defined as 'myopic'.[15]

We can say that with Mabou Mines's *Lost Ones* that a dramaturgy of myopia was employed to translate the problematics of vision underlying the tale's narration in a way that entailed a theatre architecture rendering the same claustrophobic quality. The place of theatricality in relation to a writing of myopia suggests the context of writing the vanishing point that characterized Beckett's writing in the 1950s more generally. In the context of spectacle, the coordinates of presence – a concept of what is verifiably *there* – must lie in a different configuration for a live, physical, ephemeral medium compared with the textual, linguistic context of a prose work.

When the figure is rendered invisible in the spectacle, this critically questionable component of the Beckett spectacle defines what constitutes a dramaturgy of myopia. Beckett consulted this hypothetical notion of invisible figuration with a figureless theatrical event roughly in the middle of his theatrical career in the form of play *Breath*. In accordance with Beckettian custom, the title betrays the experiment: *Breath* mounts a self-examination of spectacle comprised of the live performance figure's most essential resource, a resource ironically their least visible: the entire lifespan of the breath from birth to death. *Breath* is an installation *for* the theatre, an installation *of* the theatre; the script even asks that the voice be recorded, rather than amplified live. The work nonetheless confirms Weber's Artaud-inspired concept of theatre as an immanently-installed spectacle at its most basic level. The few distinguishing features that differentiate *Breath* from installation art affirm the work's performativity: *Breath* is a live, durational performance experience for the senses at its most reduced. The work's intermedial quality and resemblance to installation art nonetheless come to reiterate the play's essential, crystallized performativity. As Sozita Godouna explores:

> Audiences can watch *Breath* onstage, but it can also be presented as an installation (of rubbish) or as a sound piece in a gallery space. It is possible to present the piece in situations in a context where viewers can be walking around it and as an installation that can be circled, departed from or returned to at one's will (provided that this durational encounter last for thirty-five seconds). The experimentation with aesthetic and conceptual aspects of duration and repetition, through the minimal duration of one of the shortest plays ever written, manifests a decisive moment in the history of theatrical experimentation, in part because of the new relationship it developed towards the formal possibilities of the theatrical event. Beckett reduces his medium to its most basic form of objecthood by staging a play with theatre's basic essentials and by exposing the components of theatre in skeletal form.[16]

Breath in time, then, is all that distinguishes this play from non-durational installation art, but that distinction is everything. The objects, and the circumstances in which they are observed, undergo a performance defined only by the liveness of being present to a pre-recorded, pre-established staging of the last predicate of live performance. Beckett-influenced theatre-maker and composer Heiner Goebbels and his work *Stifters Dinge* (2007) take this premise further, with a fully automated and pre-recorded live event of sound, image and object performed before an audience with a kinetic machinic installation taking the place of the once-figural focal point. Nevertheless, the two works expose the same indissoluble essential that remains live in automated performance works: the living spectator. *Breath* remains live insofar as a breathing audience registers it. Without the provisionality of the time in which the work plays out, it would be a work of installation art whose duration would be merely elective, and the expiration of the work no longer structurally important.

The dense human baggage of this term 'expiration' appears to motivate Beckett's stark performance experiment here. *Breath* opens and closes with 'recorded vagitus' breathing figural life into the detritus-dominated scene – 'vagitus' meaning infant crying – punctuating the inspiration and expiration components of the work's duration.[17] The term 'vagitus' recalls *Malone Dies*, in which Malone remarks on the subject of breath to bring attention to the equivocal border between life and death unified in this word 'expiration':

> Decidedly it will never have been given to me to finish anything. One must not be greedy. But is this how one chokes? Presumably. And the rattle, what about the rattle? Perhaps it is not de rigeur after all. To have vagitated and not be bloody well able to rattle. How life dulls the power to protest to be sure. I wonder what my last words will be, written, the others do not endure, but vanish, into thin air.[18]

The semantic intersection point of *Malone Dies* with *Breath* involves the ability of the principle of breath to stand in for two (supposed) opposites, life and death. The poetic justice, or what Ricks calls the mot juste, in finding not one but two mordant linguistic proofs for a shared position seems to *inspire* this expression in the writer. *Vagitus* refers to the human's first voiced breath; the death *rattle*, another expiration, also alludes to the infant's toy rattle.[19] *Breath*, then, consummates Malone's speculation that the fate of language is a return to base materiality. This means a return to 'thin air'. The irony belongs to so many of Beckett's mot juste as their persuasiveness arrives in their stunning, self-cancelling paradox. The result of this word game becomes a sort of conceptual and linguistic suspension in which a reaffirmed sense of the invulnerability reserved to inalterable truths as death and life is achieved. Moreover, the suspended compaction of two irreconcilable registers for breath, reappearing in *vagitate* or *rattle*, signals that breath, rather than being the concept represented by an irreconcilable but essential relation at the heart of paradoxical life, constitutes the original representer, the animator, if you will, of the very possibility of the paradox. As Thomas Ford writes of the Romantic concept of breath: 'Breath becomes a medium of poetic self-reference, but a medium of a peculiar kind: one that hovers between medium and form, between matter and meaning; one inscribed within an atmospheric condition of perpetual self-erasure.'[20] Beckett's rattle comparably hovers over the remains of what expiration traverses but still passes through. The design of Beckett's most structurally experimental play asks that the stage detritus feature 'no verticals, all scattered and lying'. These are the remains of breath's reference point. The detritus becomes the ruined figural ground of a vocal performance at minimum of human performance.

Daniel Katz illuminates a critical dimension of the compositional dimension of the Beckett laboratory: Beckett's roles are *written*, composed as particular agential problems for inhabitation, adoption, incorporation and play. Katz writes: 'the structuring role often occupied by the "subject" in the prose is taken by the literal materiality of the scenic space in the theatre ... in many respects the "subject" of the prose is replaced not by the "character" but by the *stage* in the theatre.'[21] The transfigured phenomenology of a Beckett narrator subject might strike us as comparable in both media – 'we are constantly reminded that ... the "no one" that is (not) speaking is riven by desires and drives which pain [that is, hurt the narrator] precisely by being not its/his own'.[22] When we transpose this idea to the theatre, following the same logic, a laboratory theatre suddenly makes the inscriptional forces external to the subject more apparent and possibly more influential; the spectator, most of all, becomes a chief problematic of the appearance of the self-witnessing character's visibility to themselves.

Gontarski has called this phenomenon of the Beckett subject on stage the 'theatrical problem' of 'how to represent in language and stage images the incomplete being, the *être manqué*.'[23] This 'untranslatable' entity of the *être manqué* designates a figure of 'incomplete being' that we have seen first appear in Beckett's life when the writer attended Jung's Tavistock Lectures with Wilfred Bion. Luke Thurston surmises that the *être manqué* constitutes a figure that would become a critical problematic invoked in Beckett's approach to language:

> In an exchange with Lawrence Harvey, Beckett ... described his sense of 'a presence, embryonic, undeveloped, of a self that might have been but

never got born, an *être manqué*. ... The 'presence' tentatively evoked by Beckett, his struggle to signify which terminates (inconclusively) with *être manqué*, is thus ... a matter of names and of the insignificant, or rather of that which insists through and *beyond* signification.[24]

Thurston pursues a psychoanalytic interpretation of Beckett's writerly attitudes that I have not been pursuing in this monograph, not least because, like his allusions to Cartesian thought, in my view, Beckett's references tend to stimulate questions rather than pose answers. Most efforts to pin particular philosophical, clinical or phenomenological ideas to Beckett as ideas adhered to tend not to be sustainable as attitudes per se. The stage, in my view, becomes Beckett's conjuration of a domain specially prepared for the occupation of the *être manqué*.

Peter Brook's (anti-)theatricality

So far, we have been discussing the contemporary field of adaptation and production contemporary with Beckett while he was alive, with which he had some input or means of comment or rejoinder. Now, I want to show how the dramaturgy of Beckett's laboratory is sustained in illuminating examples of posthumous contemporary performance adaptation that Beckett was not involved with. Of all productions in recent memory so attuned to rendering in a dramaturgically coherent way this decreative thread through Beckett's work, none is so explicitly invested, for better and for worse, in the physical theatrical trajectory as Peter Brook's *Fragments*. It is a problematic production. In fact, the show's inability to push the dramaturgical experimentalism of Beckett forwards animates my line of argument as much as the production's achievements. Adaptation's modifications to the experimental pantomime practice discussed in Chapter 1 reward an interrogation into the rights of transversal engagements with Beckett's experimental dramaturgy for the ways in which it rewards a return to the origins of Beckett's first materialized inquiries into stage mimesis. Most of all, I want to show how Brook's adaptations reveal that the omission of the impeded, sensation-deprived, and self-examining dramaturgy of Beckett charted in this monograph imperils its experimental trajectory. We shall see how Brook's confidently present pantomime Beckett omits the ambivalent contingency of Beckettian dramaturgy that unsettles stage presence.

Brook's rarefied physical theatre practice is rooted in pantomime. *Fragments* best demonstrates this, partly for how little it concerns the bowler hat and whiteface aesthetic of the practice. Brook's entanglement in that moment of physical theatre and experimentalism in the 1950s and 1960s referred to earlier constitutes his concerted engagement with the body as the essential vector for theatrical mimicry. Indeed, the Brook view of Beckett presents a key example of Martin Puchner's notion that pantomime-affiliated dance in Beckett comes to generate 'a theatre struck by a radicalized anti-theatricalism'.[25]

Brook's anti-theatricalism sheds all the accoutrements of modern spectacle-making to situate physical theatre without words – in other words, what historically has been called pantomime – as a kind of continuation of a forgotten theatrical urge better understood as a primordial, ahistorical, essential performing body. Brook's influential concept of theatre as 'the empty space' enshrined in a manifesto of the same name establishes at the end of the 1960s one of the cardinal shifts in theatre studies and performance practice from a discipline concerned with dramatizing plays to a discipline concerned with a total art of performance. For Brook, the cultural import of the Western theatre at that time, unnaturally severed from its roots in myth, ritual and festival, was anathema to theatre's true possibility in accordance with a deeper intercultural heritage:

> A man walks across this empty space whilst someone else is watching him, and this is all that is needed for an act of theatre to be engaged. Yet when we talk about theatre this is not quite what we mean. Red curtains, spotlights, blank verse, laughter, darkness, these are all confusedly superimposed in a messy image covered by one all-purpose word.[26]

The rudiments of the performing arts free of the usual decorative and spectacular armature became Brook's adventure. Brook sought to encourage a view in which the formerly isolated Western theatre, often confined to a literary incarceration, could be critiqued and advanced. Brook's program was informed by a much broader world theatre context and longer performing arts heritage than what appears in the records of canonical authors; he had the pre-Socratic sphere of myth as the imagined resource for the revival of drama. For Puchner, Brook's theory represents a historically influential distillation of the problem of theatricality to the central matter of the actor:

> Peter Brook's necessary and sufficient definition of theatre ... is based on the existence of an actor and an audience member: 'A man walks across this empty space ... [etcetera]'. This dependence of the theatre on the actor turns an anti-mimetic critique into an anti-theatrical one. While the mimetic arts such as painting or photography, can become anti-mimetic without questioning their own material condition – paint,

canvas, celluloid – the theatre, if it feels the need to abandon mimesis, must turn against its own material, namely, the human performer.[27]

Puchner's assessment situates Brook's practice within the modernist critique of popular culture that also encouraged paradigmatic developments of closet drama, diegetic theatre, and poetic theatre before it, forged out of anti-theatrical responses to mimetic and diegetic norms found in melodrama and naturalism. Brook is anti-theatrical in this line due to his candid rejection of the public theatre in the name of a universal one. Brook removes all the non-essential components of stagecraft and theatre culture until only the performer's energy for virtualization is left in an effort to purify the craft. This leaves performance to be mounted any place that this essential energy can be harnessed and exhibited.

Brook's tightrope exercise provides ample representation of his theory of theatricality and the ways in which mimesis pertains to it. This exercise reinforces in practice form the empty space concept and thus the director's faith in the powers of theatrical mimesis associated with it. A 2014 documentary on Brook presents this exercise as a metonym for a life's theory of drama. The exercise, mundane in application, has a total actor-based program of theatrical mimesis as its objective. Performers repeatedly walk along a flat surface as if along a tightrope in the attempt of transforming the core of the performing body into an innate mimicry of the fiction of a less stable point.[28] Brook's theory involves a sort of fundamental pantomime; mimicry is brought down to its most originary level, to the autonomic level of the proprioceptive body trying to keep its balance. Proficient acting would be distinguished from less proficient by the capacity for the given actor to trick *themselves* into thinking a tightrope were indeed beneath their feet. The greatest actor for Brook is the mime that can fool themselves. Let us now consider how Brook realizes Beckett following these principles of a total acting art.

Fragments

In order of appearance, *Rough for Theatre I*, *Rockaby*, *AWW II*, *Neither* and *Come and Go* are presented in an occasion of theatre called *Fragments*, co-directed by Brook with Marie-Hélène Estienne, featuring the performers Jos Houben, Marcello Magni and Kathryn Hunter in the 2015 iteration that I am referring to.[29] *Come and Go* brings the three performers together for a comic closing, three performers who were otherwise playing in duos for *Rough for Theatre I* and *AWW II* (Houben and Magni) and solo for *Rockaby* and *Neither* (Hunter). The production was first shown in Paris in 2006 with Houben and Magni, but not with Hunter. In its account in review, this 2006 production resembles in some ways the 2015 production.³⁰

Fragments exemplifies a utilization of Beckett dramaturgy confident in the powers of what is essentially pantomime to render a spectacle. Critically, however, the show omits Beckett's fundamental dramaturgical transfiguration of mimetic norms, especially the decreative treatment of stage presence. While a deconstructive turn to fundamentals such as light and corporeality are characteristic of Beckett *and* Brook's dramaturgies, the processes of deconstruction could not be more different. Beckett's characteristically ambivalent dramaturgical practice has basically been ignored in Brook's adaptation. Here, my concordance with W. B. Worthen on Beckett's mute plays diverges slightly. Where Worthen asserts that *Quad* uncovers a 'barely identifiable' but 'essential theatricality' 'cognate' with declarations in Brook's *The Empty Space*, I agree with the association between the two in the architectonic terms of Worthen's articulation. However, the extrapolation of the problem of pantomime in Beckett's dramaturgy suggests a limit to this association. Brook's faith in a universalizable, free space for the performer that the pursuit of 'essential theatricality' should entail lies at odds with Beckett's exhausted performer.³¹ Indeed, Brook's practice is essentially a rarefied mime practice. Of mime, we have seen Beckett make an experimental opportunity that explicitly problematizes and immobilizes the practice's mimetic faculty, rather than strengthening its ability to virtualize. Brook's dramaturgy trusts in mimesis whereas Beckett's questions it.

As a show, *Fragments* showcases Brook's belief that the performer's virtualization of spectacle between the audience and the performer's live body exposes the essence of performance. No set appears, costumes are essentially functional and non-representative, and very few props appear; those that do having their specificity deliberately nullified. The goad employed in *AWW II*, for example, to prod the performers into performing is a large white cone that notably drops from the flies rather than the familiar vaudeville source of the wings. The goad thus suggests no real identity of its own stemming from any particular tradition or origin. For Brook, the most radical achievement of his own practice is one in which performer and audience are unified in faith in the performance assembled before them. Lacking all design ornamentation, since apparatus would encumber this essentialism, *Fragments* stages one play after another with a minimum of stage artifice as a result. Almost unnoticeable lighting changes mark the transition between plays and tend to be imperceptible. The transitions are also unacknowledged by the players, who return from the wings to enter the sacks for *AWW II*, for example; these transitions happen not in character but informally as performers ready to perform the work. The effect of the latter approach is less Beckettian, or, indeed, Brechtian – the most obvious echo of this staging technique – than an example of old-fashioned pantomime informality and self-reflexivity. Kathryn Hunter even remains in the same costume she wore for *Rockaby* to play the voice of *Neither*. When she transitions to the part of Vi in *Come and Go* at the close of *Neither*, Magni and Houben bring her costume change for her to put on before the audience over the top of what she is wearing.

The opportunity of physical performance provided by Beckett's occasional works motivates the dramaturgy of *Fragments*. The players confidently take up the opportunity to portray a light, athletic Beckett. *Rough for Theatre I* is clownish, the playful violence of disagreement between the two characters played for laughs, superseding concern for much of the verbal dimension of the work; the desperate state of these characters living among 'Ruins', as it states in the text, receives no visual, sonic, or performative registration. This oversight follows the clownish theatrical rendering, such that A's 'folding-stool' and B's wheelchair both mere stage props, cubes much like those that tend to be used in *AWW I*, for example, which also features in *Fragments*.[32] *Come and Go*, a play Beckett introduces as a 'dramaticule' in the script, is again played humorously. This version may follow the minutiae of the Beckett diagram in terms of action, line, costume, and gesture, but it does not follow the significance of the diagram for characterization; the particular *differences* of the performers are focal points of this version, not their mathematical *equivalency* in this geometric rendering of rumour and admission within a friendship suggestively built on schadenfreude, secrecy and ineffectual non-disclosure. *Fragments* suggests that Brook views his own practice and Beckett's deconstructed spectacle to be parallel practices of the empty space principle of anti-theatrical physical performance. When applied to Beckett, I find the implied premise proves mostly inadmissible to the experimental view of Beckettian dramaturgy. The effect rather more resembles the popular Beckett. The popular Beckett I would describe as a vein of performative interpretation of Beckett that high-budget productions of *Godot* tend to follow, for example, in which the humour in such work becomes the chief dramaturgical end. Similarly, the Beckett-Estienne production makes a notably playful pantomimic spectacle of an essentialized, stripped-back performance dramaturgy in which the transmission of humour provides the highest praise to the physical achievements of the works. This is perhaps most evident in *Fragments*' version of *AWW II*. Here, the mimes have a slapstick proficiency that celebrates, rather than deconstructs, pantomime's mimetic possibility, in line with Brook's signature tightrope exercise. Character A should be miserable about the routine he is confined to and character B's routine should evoke misery, confronting spectators with an unresolvable paradox that both solicits and precludes laughter. Yet, both *laughable* situations are not rendered nakedly enough to achieve that ambivalent spectatorial feeling. In Brook's version, we simply laugh at the accomplished physical achievement of two similarly funny routines.

The omission of paradox and ambivalence in this essentialist Beckett realizes a curious physical dramaturgy that fails to transfigure spectacle of the order of Mabou Mines's *The Lost Ones*, or indeed other similarly experimental productions that pursue Beckett spectacle into the domains of the performative in miniature modelled by Beckettian dramaturgy. The laboratory quality of Beckett's spectacle, rooted in decreation, does emerge in the strongest piece within *Fragments*: the adaptation of *Neither*. The term inspiring the work, 'neither', promises inscrutability and a paradoxical act of non-being suspending the question of presence in unresolvable formal unity that recalls the unrealizable protagonists of modernist and proto-modernist prose, such as Herman Melville's Bartleby or Kafka's Joseph K. The effect this work insinuates in the Brook practice should be interesting to all who query the famous figure's method, given that adopting such an inherently ambivalent work should inevitably problematize the positivist investment in mime observed thus far.

Beckett's fragment *Neither* was a mischievous but earnest gift of a libretto for Morton Feldman's no doubt similarly mischievous inquiry about collaborating on an opera with the writer. The result of this encounter is not an anti opera as such, however, since it does not openly lampoon or oppose the conventions of the genre. Opera, Beckett admitted to the composer when meeting him, was not to his taste.[33] If *The Lost Ones* bridged a new kind of immersed exposure to the meat of the diegetic voice in Warrilow's disrobing, we might say that the Brook adaptation of *Neither* exposes the bones by realizing a figural problem in the form of Hunter's undecidedly physical diegetic mode.

Let us first re-examine the content of this short text. Curiously, both *Neither* and *The Lost Ones* concern a bare rendition of creaturely life. However, the mimetic framework of the former is entirely different to the latter; *Neither* is a more confident, even rhetorical, statement regarding creaturely life, philosophizing about the condition of life of the kind observed in the cylinder of *The Lost Ones*. While not bearing any trace of a choreography, *Neither* imagines a pacing sort of ambivalence – 'from impenetrable self to impenetrable unself by way of neither / as between two lit refuges'.[34] These lines likely recall the better known aspects of *The Unnamable* for most Beckett readers. They chronicle a kind of limited creaturely existence:

> It's a lot to expect of one creature, it's a lot to ask, that he should first behave as if he were not, then as if he were, before being admitted to that peace where he neither is, nor is not, and where the language dies that permits of such expressions. Two falsehoods, two trappings, to be borne to the end, before I can be let loose, alone, in the unthinkable unspeakable, where I have not ceased to be, where they will not let me be.[35]

The domain imagined is patent Dante homage. Such a homage is also of the experimental order we have seen heretofore. The ambivalent ontology that results accords with Beckett's lifelong interest in the purgatorial condition as analogy for 'the vicious circle of humanity', what in 1929 essay 'Dante ... Bruno . Vico . . Joyce' is described in the following stratified manner:

> Hell is the static lifelessness of unrelieved viciousness. Paradise the static lifelessness of unrelieved immaculation. Purgatory a flood of movement and vitality released by the conjunction of these two elements.[36]

Indeed, Brook and Etienne's pacing choreography of Hunter likely draws attention to another purgatorial parallel, namely, *Neither*'s relationship to *Footfalls*. Beckett was calculating the number of footsteps Hildegard Schmahl would take for this play in a production at the Schiller-Theater Werkstatt in September 1976 as he transposed the piece's new nine-step procedure developed in the Billie Whitelaw version at the Royal Court in 1973 to the Berlin stage.[37] Feldman had visited Beckett at the theatre as he advised on its production, possibly even mid-calculation of the footfalls. Thus, *Neither* works as a veritable exegesis for that play of repetitions representing 'life-long stretches of walking', an elucidation the author provided to Schmahl at the time.[38] The exegesis operates without any diagrammed performance design. *Neither* has no such detail, no trace of dramaturgical implication at all. Credit is due to the Hunter incarnation of this important adaptation in realizing an ambivalence unseen in the more confident pantomimic works in *Fragments*.

Neither represents Beckett's only experiment in opera. The work mounts a resistance to theatrical form's accommodations of performativity. Given its complete lack of dramaturgical construction, the fragment remains excluded from the so-called dramatic works. The ambivalence it presents to spectacle, in undermining the Brook faith in mime, makes it the only meaningful contribution of the *Fragments* show to the continuation of the laboratory urge consisting in Beckettian dramaturgy. There is an additional, vital connection between *Neither* and the Mabou Mines *The Lost Ones*. That September in 1976 was indeed a curious month of visits by experimentalists visiting from America; Mabou Mines were showing their adaptations of Beckett prose works in Berlin at the Akademie der Künste at the same time. This is how Beckett had occasion that to look at the innovative set for their acclaimed version of *The Lost Ones* that Alan Schneider had seen in New York and reported to him about. Beckett never saw the production, only the set. But this intersection with the company provided him with confidence in Mabou Mines to grant them permission to adapt other works not written for the stage in the future. This was thanks most especially to his now deepening relationships with Warrilow, for whom he later wrote a monologue for, entitled *A Piece of Monologue* (1979). Also, he was able to deepen his connection to another Mabou Mines member, Fred Neumann, whose requests to be the performer-adaptor of other challenging prose works Beckett approved. These adaptations comprised much of the company's success where other companies failed to receive approval.[39] We are reminded once again of how important it is to include certain experimental adaptations of Beckett work not intended for the theatre in the history of Beckettian dramaturgy. *Neither* belongs to that experimental tradition, comprising a sort of reply to an experimental composer's request for an opera.

Feldman's score for *Neither* echoes the daring of Mabou Mines's experimentalism in its willingness to encroach upon uncharted relations to Beckett's writing. Brook adapts the writing fragment, not the Feldman work. Consulting Feldman's piece reveals the kind of adaptational attitude that truly honours Beckett's experimentalism. This piece achieves a rare adaptation of Beckett's compositional logic to music, making insightful musical counterpoint to this fragment of paradoxical being.[40] Calling the work an excellent example of Feldman's 'lyricism without melody', for example, Catherine Laws comprehends the libretto as: 'an endless process within which everything shadows everything else. Just as Beckett's text maps the endless searching that it describes, so the near patterning and near symmetries of Feldman's music perform that same process'.[41] Michael Coffey describes the fragment's suggested world in terms of proportions of light: 'the Caravaggio light of Beckett's imagination, light always half in shadow and half in a thin, dying light'.[42] With Hunter in an adaptive process attempting to realize an apparitional enigma that suggests no clear character or body, Brook and Etienne similarly employ a chiaroscuro logic to revise their use of mime. Suspended between shadow and light, stripped bare to a monologue that rests at no centre, the reduction comes to expose a resonant frame in the figure in Hunter. The monologue itself casts doubt upon its monologist's presence as it commentates the figures own vacillation between dark and light. Hunter's memorable carriage in performance is critical to this achievement. Dominated by arms that hang long from the torso, with physical control that suggests the agility of an acrobat and the control of a Noh actor – a physicality also exploited in her Puck in Julie Taymor's *A Midsummer Night's Dream* (2014), as it happens – the actor's moving form crafts an animated figure situated unquestionably in the realm of figuration sought after in the stripped-back pantomime that we find in Beckett's acts without words elsewhere.

Coupling Hunter's tremendous rasp with this striking frame, the result realizes the usual challenge to representation that Beckett's text challenges of the scopic domain: an embodied unity that signals disjunction. The same register of disjunction can be appreciated in MacGowran's prose narrator from his show of prose recitals, *Beginning to End* (1965), philosophical and baritone while pitiably diminished and twisted in an enveloping greatcoat.[43] Indeed, MacGowran, another of the recognized voices of Beckett's prose in adaptation, provides a cipher for understanding strategies of prose adaptation in more ways than one: like Hunter, he too made a career in the Shakespearean pantomimic Fool role, most notably in whose but Brook's own revolutionary film *King Lear*, known by many as the video record of the revolutionary (Paul) Scofield *Lear* (1971). As Jordan R. Young notes:

> In adapting *Lear* for contemporary audiences, [] Brook took inspiration in Jan Kott's essay, '*King Lear* or *Endgame*' – in which the Polish critic found in Beckett a grotesquerie that was a mutant of Greek and Elizabethan tragedy; and in the mouth of Shakespeare's motley-clad sage, the surreal language of the modern theatre.[44]

MacGowran's stage medley of prose and performance works, *End of Day* (1962), was first shown in Dublin and then London. It was noted for its controversial use of pantomime and considered unsatisfactory by Beckett, was later much revised and improved with the help of the writer in the reimagined evening of solo-performed Beckett recital, *Beginning to End*.[45] Mime was an encumbrance for MacGowran's adaptation process later resolved by revisionary work on Beckett dramaturgy with the writer himself. Moreover, that subtraction of the problematic of mime in the MacGowran adaptation bespeaks the fraught integrity with which Beckett saw in silent acts; Beckett's efforts to reconcile with this problem in his 'J.M. Mime' following his dissatisfactions with *End of Day* suggest an enduring desire to test, and not excise, mute gesture with this important actor, even after once failing in the endeavour.

Hunter's *Neither* exceeds the limitations of the pantomime trajectory by realizing a dramaturgy of figural ambivalence, a hallmark, we have seen, of experimental adaptations of Beckett prose. In this way, *Neither* recalls another contemporary example of adaptation, again at the fringes of Beckett's dramaturgy: Kris Verdonck's projection theatre work, 'HUMINID'.[46] 'HUMINID' is one component among three in theatre-installation hybrid, *Actor #1*. In the 'HUMINID' section, a featureless doll of small stature works as a screen for the projection of a monologue by an actor reciting a collage-homage of 'Lessness', another prose work like *Neither* concerned with the ambivalence of 'refuge'. Hunter's figural contribution comes not by way of projection, but rather through the '*une fugue statique*', or static fugue, that she realizes live, a self-enclosed, physical dialectic of small bone frame and ominous voice suspended in counterpoint in which the one casts the other into doubt.[47] If what we inferred to be static in the Beckett diagram in a work such as *Quad* heretofore meant an inert form paradoxically charted by calculated movement, similarly, *Neither* suspends a disappearing but perceptible image of ambivalence between light and dark in an unconfirmable, but figure-conferred, middle. A featureless doll enables this conjunction of projection, voice, text, and apparitionality in Verdonck's piece, remediating the heightened presence of monologue with a dramaturgical gesture in tune with Beckettian diminution through disjunct. Peter Eckersall, Helena Grehan and Edward Scheer characterize this production in terms of a new media dramaturgy that employs intersecting media-inflected materialities to generate a virtual real:

> [Verdonck's] is a dramaturgy of composite materialities where there are several processes of layering at play at once – of actor to film and then via projection onto the 3D surface, and of spectators onto the projection and back to their idea of the 'real' actor as they attempt to negotiate their reading of, and response to, this figure.[48]

As Eckersall, Grehan, and Scheer indicate, such a fugue's remediation 'generates a desire to engage, to connect with and respond to this intriguing figure who appears to be both subject and object'.[49] This assertion recalls Carlson, who announced that such medial reconfigurations of presence and sensorium have been the stuff of the changing specular coordinates of what is called theatricality throughout its history. Vocal and corporeal disjunction can escalate how real, and how haunting, theatre can become.[50]

Hunter's monologue, without the aid of remediation, has its own intriguing figural qualities that afford another memorable apparition to the field of adaptations of spectacle-resistant prose works by Beckett. The exposure of medium encoded in *Neither* animates a figural enigma that at once seems to verbalize and efface an *être manqué* suspended 'between two lit refuges' in a static fugue. Hunter's achievement is an impressive example of what Worthen has called 'negative athleticism'. This is a style of acting cultivated by Beckettian dramaturgy involving careful deconstruction of vocal and physical norms of performance.[51] Comparatively, despite the undeniable capabilities of this performer, Hunter's *Rockaby* interferes with that figure's undecidability as present or absent due to the psychological realism used to characterize this version of the role; her *Rockaby* comprises of a naturalistic version of the implied character embedded in the live component of the monologue, gesturally and verbally spelling out the play's vague narrative of final hours in one's room. While *Rockaby* demands the same degree of performative equivocation as *Neither*, as we saw in Chapter 2, Hunter's overplayed 'senior' W, combined with the V part as a schizoid second voice without the recorded separation the text demands, relegates the effect of Beckett's text to the more mundane hermeneutic territory of self-narration in idleness. Beckett's static fugue has not been corporealized. So, it is *Neither*, though an adaptation, that carries the spirit of Beckett experimentalism in its choreographic and figural make-up; a diagram distilled from pantomime in which a performer can realize an examination of their own stage presence.

Blau's critique of Brook *pace* Cage is valid recourse to the *Fragments* show: there is no such thing as empty space, and therefore no pure mime.[52] *Neither*'s achievement lies in what it encourages Brook to concede: theatricality is a human labour whose powers of mimesis are finitely brokered by an irresolvable, unpredictable material real. Ironically, the adaptation of an inherently spectacle-resistant pseudo-libretto within *Fragments* meets the dramaturgical mandate of Beckett's self-experimenting performativity. Yet, contrastingly, the other pieces which are Beckett *plays* do not instigate sufficient self-analysis in the Brook mode to become experimental. Brook was perhaps too confident in an assumed parallelism between his practice and Beckett's. *Rough for Theatre I* and *Come and Go* resemble Brook-method training workshops and not the Feldman-Beckett of *Neither* or the ambivalent figure found in Brook's own adaptation of the fragment. Historically, Brook's dramaturgical attentiveness to the pantomimic body were uncovered through experimentalism, highlighting multiplicity in the performing real, sought through opening the concept of theatre to its wider performance significance belonging to a collective performing humanity. A fellow traveller among the figures of the movement of anthropological and philosophical deconstruction of theatricality that inaugurated performance studies, announced in work such as that of Schechner or Turner, Brook shows how the pantomimic trajectory in performances of Beckett is rewarded by experimentation but fraught with adaptational danger.

As Adam Alston and Martin Welston observe, adaptations do not necessarily amount to transgressions or departures from the mandates of this dramaturgy but can even involve the 'literal reading[s] of Beckett's intentions'.[53] *The Lost Ones* by Mabou Mines constitutes a breaking of ground in a related sense, since, like Pan Pan's achievement in their surmisal, this production also developed a scenographic architecture that left the diegetic constraints of the original text intact but renovated spectacle sufficiently enough to house the diegesis such that the production successfully presented the mimetically fraught enclosure of the narrative in a new medium.[54]

Cast your mind back to the unorthodox practices of dance or mime achieved in *Beckett Walk* and *Quad* charted in the introduction to this book. Exhaustive movement in Beckett's laboratory, whether hypothesized using an architecture surrounding it or inserted via isolated gesture, tests the remains of what is contingently present in performance. Kathryn Chiong evocatively describes the motif of repetition in Nauman's work as a concern with what Jean-Luc Nancy calls the vestige, a property whose proper response should be *waiting*, a matter 'which Nauman and Beckett both insist on, pointing always to the end, traversing it but never arriving there, a perpetual nonpenetration'.[55] Simone Weil once wrote that 'no poetry concerning the people is authentic if fatigue does not figure in it, and the hunger and thirst which come from fatigue'.[56] We spectators wait for these exhaustive performances to finish, having no formal beginning or end to orient ourselves by, and this waiting enables the unseen to gradually emerge in the meagre poetry of what remains. In Gilles Deleuze's notion of exhaustion, experiment comes to explore an 'infinitesimal' contingent dimension beyond vision and comprehension; this infinitesimal part is encoded in the opacities and diminutions typically concealed by spectacle.[57] For Blau, that infinitesimal part is called the 'unforeseen', Andrew Gibson 'the remainder', and Steven Connor 'radical finitude' – these are all names for what eludes representation and the mimetic.[58]

The *Beckett Walk*, the choreographic diagrams of *Endgame*, the acts without words, *Footfalls*, *Quad*, the cry for 'more', the look of parabasis, the face of the listener, the *Fragments Neither* – these varying performative figurations constitute a vestigial activity that is radically paradoxical. Jean Martin, who, among his many contributions to the Beckett performance archive, played Krapp in *Krapp's Last Tape* in 1970 remarks in a letter to Martha Fehsenfeld and Dougald McMillan that '[Beckett] has always insisted on the fact that Krapp is debris'.[59] Debris – that is to say, the vestige, always already questionably present. What is all the more human, then, is Krapp's response to being looked at as a live figure before an audience. At the play's finale, as he sits '*motionless staring before him*', he listens as '[*t*]*he tape runs on in silence*'.[60] In Rick Cluchey's performance, Krapp stares roughly at the audience. In Patrick Magee's, Krapp stares visibly towards the floor.[61] The gesture almost manages parabasis with the audience in both,[62] and yet the gaze is always somehow off. This disjunction befits the role, a role that demands that the actor create as opaque a face as possible in an effort to convey the enormous indeterminacy of feeling concealed in that face. William E. Gruber proposes that 'that mimetic act [of motionless listening] perhaps marks the limit of Krapp's self-understanding'.[63] The paradox of self-observation in mediatized form brings about a heightened sense of what we cannot represent to ourselves. The truth of this narration is what is at issue for Krapp as he tests himself with recordings. Like the mimes of the acts without words, Krapp's live testimony through the eyes, or a new performer of Beckett adapting that rhetorical riddle, *Neither*, neither for spectacle nor the page, the true result of the Beckett experiment becomes what escapes performance as these figures hesitate to represent. Beckett's static fugues are experimental figures of potential life at the brink of disappearance into dark, into light.

Notes

Introduction

1. Deirdre Bair, *Samuel Beckett: A Biography* (New York: Harcourt Brace Jovanovich, 1978), 433.
2. Ibid., 487.
3. Herbert Blau, *Sails of the Herring Fleet: Essays on Samuel Beckett* (Ann Arbor: University of Michigan Press, 2000), 59.
4. Viewable on UbuWeb: Bruce Nauman, '*Slow Angle Walk (Beckett Walk)* (1968)', UbuWeb, http://ubu.com/film/nauman_beckett.html. Also on the UbuWeb file for Nauman can be found other diagrammatic experiments in repetition, such as *Dance or Walk on the Perimeter of a Square* (1967), http://ubu.com/film/nauman_perimeter.html, or *Revolving Upside Down* (1969), http://ubu.com/film/nauman_revolving.html. *Slow Angle Walk (Beckett Walk)* is the most committed to a choreography concerned with the finite possibilities allowed by a particular manoeuvre within a particular set of spatial dimensions.
5. Herbert Blau, *Reality Principles: From the Absurd to the Virtual* (Ann Arbor: University of Michigan Press, 2011), 156.
6. Kathryn Chiong, 'Nauman's Beckett Walk', *October* 86 (1998): 63–81; Derval Tubridy, 'Samuel Beckett and Performance Art', *Journal of Beckett Studies* 23, no. 1 (2014): 34–53.
7. *CDW*, 92.
8. For example, see Trish McTighe and David Tucker (eds), *Staging Beckett in Ireland and Northern Ireland* (London: Bloomsbury, 2017); the special issue of *Journal of Beckett Studies*, 'The Performance Issue', Jonathan Heron and Nicholas Johnson (eds), *Journal of Beckett Studies* 23, no. 1 (2014); especially: Jonathan Heron and Nicholas Johnson, with Burç İdem Dinçel, Gavin Quinn, Sarah Jane Scaife and Áine Josephine Tyrrell, 'The Samuel Beckett Laboratory 2013', *Journal of Beckett Studies* 23, no. 1 (2014): 73–94; Tubridy, 'Samuel Beckett and Performance Art', 34–53. See also Anna McMullan and Graham Saunders, 'Staging Beckett and Contemporary Theatre and Performance Cultures', *Contemporary Theatre Review* 28, no. 1 (2018): 3–9; Jonathan Heron and Nicholas Johnson, 'Critical Pedagogies and the Theatre Laboratory', *Research in Drama Education: The Journal of Applied Theatre and Performance* 22, no. 2 (2017): 282–7.
9. *DF*, 377.
10. Wolfgang Köhler, *The Mentality of Apes*, trans. Ella Winter (London: Kegan Paul, Trench, Trubner and New York: Harcourt, Brace and Company, 1931), 45–7.

11 *CDW*, 204.
12 Bruno Latour and Steve Wolgar, *Laboratory Life: The Construction of Scientific Facts*, 2nd edn (Princeton, NJ: Princeton University Press, 1986), 244.
13 Ibid., 47.
14 Tim Lawrence, *Samuel Beckett's Critical Aesthetics* (London: Palgrave Macmillan, 2018), 186.
15 Ibid. (my emphasis).
16 Ibid., 187.
17 Bert O. States, '*Catastrophe*: Beckett's Laboratory / Theatre', *Modern Drama* 30, no. 1 (Spring 1987): 14–22, 18.
18 Ibid.
19 Keir Elam, 'Catastrophic Mistakes: Beckett, Havel, The End', *Samuel Beckett Today/Aujourd'hui* 3 (1994): 1–28, 16.
20 Latour and Wolgar, *Laboratory Life*, 285.
21 Émile Zola, 'Émile Zola, *Naturalism in the Theatre*, 1881', in *A Sourcebook on Naturalist Theatre*, trans. Albert Bermel, ed. Christopher Innes (London: Routledge, 2000), 46–52, 49.
22 States, '*Catastrophe*: Beckett's Laboratory / Theatre', 20.
23 Carol Martin, *Theatre of the Real* (Basingstoke: Palgrave Macmillan, 2013), 70.
24 See Robert Mitchell, *Experimental Life: Vitalism in Romantic Science and Literature* (Baltimore: Johns Hopkins University Press, 2013).
25 Ibid., 41.
26 Emmett Stinson, *Satirizing Modernism: Aesthetic Autonomy, Romanticism, and the Avant-Garde* (London: Bloomsbury, 2017), 8.
27 Ibid.
28 Theodor Adorno, 'Trying to Understand *Endgame*', *New German Critique* 26, trans. Michael T. Jones (1982): 119–50, 131.
29 Elin Diamond, *Unmaking Mimesis: Essays on Feminism and Theatre* (London: Routledge, 1997), 38.
30 Erika Fischer-Lichte, *The Transformative Power of Performance: A New Aesthetics* (London: Routledge, 2008), 124.
31 Ibid.
32 Simone Weil, *Gravity and Grace,* trans. Emma Crawford and Mario von der Ruhr (London: Routledge, 2002), 32.
33 Anna McMullan, 'Beckett as Director', in *The Cambridge Companion to Beckett*, ed. John Pilling (Cambridge: Cambridge University Press, 1994), 196–208, 201.
34 Samuel Weber, *Theatricality as Medium* (New York: Fordham University Press, 2004), 291–2.
35 Jacques Derrida, *Writing and Difference*, trans. Alan Bass (London: Routledge & Kegan Paul, 1981), 237.
36 Ibid.

37 This diary has provided some critical material voicing Beckett's dramaturgical ideas at this active point in his theatre imagination. Dougald McMillan and Martha Fehsenfeld, *Beckett in the Theatre: The Author as Practical Playwright and Director, Volume 1: From* Waiting for Godot *to* Krapp's Last Tape (London: John Calder and New York: Riverrun Press, 1988), 204–38.
38 McMullan, 'Beckett as Director', 201 (my emphasis).
39 See Latour and Woolgar, *Laboratory Life*, chapter 6: 'The Creation of Order Out of Disorder', 235–58.
40 Giorgio Agamben, *Potentialities: Collected Essays in Philosophy*, ed. and trans. Daniel Heller-Roazen (Stanford: Stanford University Press, 1999), 78 (emphasis in the original).
41 Letter to Alan Schneider, written on 23 March 1975; in Maurice Harmon, ed., *No Author Better Served: The Correspondence of Samuel Beckett & Alan Schneider* (Cambridge, MA: Harvard University Press, 1998), 324.
42 This production from 2015 is shown in an ARTE France TV feature *Beckett by Brook* (2018) interspersed with interviews with Brook, Estienne, and cast members of the show. The feature is available here: 'Beckett by Brook • Samuel Beckett • Peter Brook & Marie-Hélène Estienne', Vimeo video, 1:00:50, 'Théâtre des Bouffes du Nord', 19 March 2020, https://vimeo.com/398851333.

1 Laboratory acts without words

1 See S. E. Gontarski, 'Birth Astride a Grave: Samuel Beckett's "Act Without Words 1"', *Journal of Beckett Studies* 1 (1976): 37–40.
2 Ruby Cohn, *Just Play: Beckett's Theatre* (Princeton, NJ: Princeton University Press, 1980), 4–5.
3 *DF*, 378.
4 See Dirk Van Hulle and Shane Weller, *Beckett Digital Manuscript Project, Vol. 7: The Making of Samuel Beckett's* Fin de partie / Endgame (Brussels: University Press Antwerp and London: Bloomsbury, 2018); Mark Nixon, 'Beckett's Unpublished Canon', in *The Edinburgh Companion to Samuel Beckett and the Arts*, ed. S. E. Gontarski (Edinburgh: Edinburgh University Press, 2014), 282–305, 291–2.
5 Theodor Adorno, 'Trying to Understand *Endgame*', *New German Critique* 26, trans. Michael T. Jones (1982): 119–50, 136.
6 See Elin Diamond, *Unmaking Mimesis: Essays on Feminism and Theatre* (London: Routledge, 1997), 38; Herbert Blau, *Sails of the Herring Fleet: Essays on Samuel Beckett* (Ann Arbor: University of Michigan Press, 2000), 59.
7 Cohn, *Just Play*, 6.

8 Gontarski, 'Birth Astride a Grave: Samuel Beckett's "Act Without Words 1"', 39.
9 Jonathan Kalb, *Beckett in Performance* (Cambridge: Cambridge University Press, 1991), 144.
10 W. B. Worthen, *Drama: Between Poetry and Performance* (Chichester: Wiley-Blackwell, 2010), 205.
11 See Jacques Guicharnaud, *Modern French Theatre: From Giraudoux to Genet* (New Haven: Yale University Press, 1967), 230.
12 Tim Lawrence, *Samuel Beckett's Critical Aesthetics* (London: Palgrave Macmillan, 2018), 111.
13 Nixon, 'Beckett's Unpublished Canon', 292.
14 See Van Hulle and Weller, *Beckett Digital Manuscript Project, Vol. 7*, 191–4.
15 For example, see Peter Fifield, 'Gaping Mouths and Bulging Bodies: Beckett and Francis Bacon', *Journal of Beckett Studies* 18, nos. 1–2 (2009): 57–71.
16 Gilles Deleuze, *Francis Bacon: The Logic of Sensation*, trans. Daniel W. Smith (London: Bloomsbury, 2017), 110.
17 Ibid., xii. *Le Dépeupleur*, or *The Lost Ones*, is not a novel – hence the '*sic*' – but rather a long short story. See Chapter 7, where I discuss the adaptation of this short story.
18 *CDW*, 203.
19 Ibid., 211.
20 Ibid., 209.
21 Ibid., 399.
22 Ibid., 451.
23 Chris Ackerley, '"Ever Know What Happened?": Shades and Echoes in Samuel Beckett's Television Plays', *Journal of Beckett Studies* 18, nos. 1–2 (2009): 136–64, 151.
24 Anna McMullan, 'Samuel Beckett's "JM Mime": Generic Mutations of a Dramatic Fragment', *Samuel Beckett Today/Aujourd'hui* 16, no. 1 (2006): 333–45, 341.
25 *DF*, 593.
26 Baylee Brits, 'Ritual, Code, and Matheme in Samuel Beckett's *Quad*', *Journal of Modern Literature* 40, no. 4 (2017): 122–33, 124.
27 For Worthen's argument about 'agency' as the most appropriate conception of how a play exists at once as a text and as performance, see Worthen, *Drama*.
28 Ibid., 126.
29 The kinetic calculus of a piece of physical performance I will continue to call choreography. Brits's use of the term as choreographic style here differs from my commitment to choreography as a term for the multiplicity of compositional corporeal modalities the term tends to mean in performance studies.
30 Snippets of Pan Pan Theatre Company's production of *Quad* can be found in the following video, with accompanied lecture extracts: 'Quad', YouTube

video, 2:08, 'Pan Pan Theatre', 5 June 2014, https://www.youtube.com/watch?v=34NNTgvUE7c. An excerpt of Surreal SoReal Theatre's production can be found here: Surreal SoReal Theatre, 'QUAD by Samuel Beckett as a part of Beckett's Shorts, a Surreal SoReal production', YouTube video, 4:16, 'John Lachlan Stewart', 31 October 2014, https://youtu.be/Q7DZgHA6798.

31 S. E. Gontarski, 'Staging Himself, or Beckett's Late Style in the Theatre', *Samuel Beckett Today/Aujourd'hui* 6, no. 1 (1997): 87–97, 88.

32 See Deirdre Bair, *Samuel Beckett: A Biography* (New York: Harcourt Brace Jovanovich, 1978), 306.

33 See McMullan, 'Samuel Beckett's "JM Mime"'.

34 Ibid., 334.

35 Sarah Jane Scaife, 'Practice in Focus: Beckett in the City', in *Staging Beckett in Ireland and Northern Ireland*, ed. Trish McTighe and David Tucker (London: Bloomsbury, 2017), 153–67, 154.

36 See the interview conducted with Scaife by Gabriel Quigley: Gabriel Quigley and Sarah Jane Scaife, 'Howling from the Margins of History: Beckett's Women Speak', *The Beckett Circle* (Spring 2018): n. pag.

37 Ibid.

38 Scaife, 'Practice in Focus: Beckett in the City', 165–6.

39 Available for viewing here: 'The Goad (1965)', YouTube video, 17:51, '16mmlostandfound', 25 May 2013, https://youtu.be/p0hJWSxtIlY.

40 Phillip B. Zarrilli, '"On the Edge of a Breath, Looking": Cultivating the Actor's Bodymind through Asian Martial/Meditation Arts', in *Acting Reconsidered: A Theoretical and Practical Guide,* 2nd edn, ed. Phillip B. Zarrilli (London: Routledge, 2002), 181–99, 197.

41 For the metaphysical orientation of Zarrilli's practice-based research, see Phillip B. Zarilli, 'The Metaphysical Studio', *TDR: The Drama Review* 46, no. 2 (Summer 2002): 157–70.

42 Jonathan Heron and Nicholas Johnson, with Burç Îdem Dinçel, Gavin Quinn, Sarah Jane Scaife, and Áine Josephine Tyrrell, 'The Samuel Beckett Laboratory 2013', *Journal of Beckett Studies* 23, no. 1 (2014): 73–94, 91.

43 Jonathan Heron and Nicholas Johnson, 'Critical Pedagogies and the Theatre Laboratory', *Research in Drama Education: The Journal of Applied Theatre and Performance* 22, no. 2 (2017): 282–7.

44 View a film version of this routine, one of Marceau's best known, here: 'The Cage: Marcel Marceau – French Actor and Mime', YouTube video, 7:58, 'Educational Video Library', 4 October 2017, https://youtu.be/U5JsopY1EpE.

45 *DF*, 377.

46 Samuel Beckett, *The Letters of Samuel Beckett, Vol. 2: 1941–1956*, ed. George Craig, Martha Dow Fehsenfeld, Dan Gunn and Lois More Overbeck (Cambridge: Cambridge University Press, 2011), 556–67.

47 Gaby Hartel, Klaus Völker and Thomas Irmer, 'The Reception of Beckett's Theatre and Television Pieces in West and East Germany', in *The*

International Reception of Samuel Beckett, ed. Mark Nixon and Matthew Feldman (London: Continuum, 2009), 79–96, 85.
48 *CDW*, 209.
49 Ibid., 210.
50 Henri Lefebvre, *The Production of Space*, trans. Donald Nicholson-Smith (Malden, MA: Blackwell Publishing, 1991), 376.
51 Beckett, *The Letters of Samuel Beckett, Vol. 2*, 540.
52 Jonathan Tadashi Naito, 'Writing Silence: Samuel Beckett's Early Mimes', *Samuel Beckett Today/Aujourd'hui* 19, no. 1 (2008): 393–402, 394–5.
53 Ibid., 400.
54 *CDW*, 166, 168.
55 Gilles Deleuze 'The Exhausted', in *Essays Critical and Clinical*, trans. Daniel W. Smith and Michael A. Greco (Minneapolis: University of Minnesota Press, 1997), 152–74.
56 Deleuze, *Francis Bacon*, 31.
57 See Michael Fried, *Absorption and Theatricality: Painting and Beholder in the Age of Diderot* (Berkeley: University of California Press, 1980).
58 Ibid., 173.
59 *CDW*, 203, 205, 206.
60 See Van Hulle and Weller, *Beckett Digital Manuscript Project, Vol. 7*, passim.
61 Naito, 'Writing Silence: Samuel Beckett's Early Mimes', 397 (my emphasis).
62 Theodor Adorno, *Aesthetic Theory*, trans. Robert Hullot-Kentor (London: Continuum, 2002), 119.
63 Martin Puchner, *Stage Fright: Modernism, Anti-Theatricality, and Drama* (Baltimore, MD: Johns Hopkins University Press, 2002), 39.
64 Ibid.
65 Ibid., 170, 172.
66 *CDW*, 39.
67 Ibid.
68 For the curious case of Bert Lahr's involvement in the first American production of *Godot*, see David Bradby, *Beckett:* Waiting for Godot (Cambridge: Cambridge University Press, 2001), 90–5.
69 Ibid., 34.
70 Yoshiki Tajiri, *Samuel Beckett and the Prosthetic Body: The Organs and Senses in Modernism* (London: Palgrave Macmillan, 2007), 37, 42.
71 Andrew Stott, *Comedy*, 2nd edn (London: Routledge, 2014), 75.
72 Normand Berlin, 'Traffic of Our Stage: Why Waiting for Godot?', *The Massachusetts Review* 40, no. 3 (Autumn 1999): 420–34, 424.
73 Mallarme's short text is reproduced in Jacques Derrida, *Disseminations*, trans. Barbara Johnson (London: Athlone Press, 1981), xxii.
74 Ibid., 206.
75 Joseph Anderton, *Beckett's Creatures: Art of Failure after the Holocaust* (London: Bloomsbury, 2016), 228.

76 Simone Weil, *Gravity and Grace,* trans. Emma Crawford and Mario von der Ruhr (London: Routledge, 2002), 11.
77 Samuel Weber, *Theatricality as Medium* (New York: Fordham University Press, 2004), 312 (emphasis in the original).

2 Sensory deprivation

1 Elizabeth Knowlson and James Knowlson (eds), *Beckett Remembering, Remembering Beckett* (London: Bloomsbury, 2006): 169-70.
2 Zoe Ingalls, 'A Rich, Idiosyncratic Journey into the Plays of Samuel Beckett', *The Chronicle of Higher Education* 38, no. 35 (May 1992): B5.
3 Billie Whitelaw, *Billie Whitelaw... Who He?* (London: Hodder and Stoughton, 1995), 117-18.
4 See Chapter 1, 'Laboratory acts without words'.
5 *CDW*, 162.
6 W. B. Worthen, *The Idea of the Actor: Drama and the Ethics of Performance* (Princeton: Princeton University Press, 1984), 205.
7 See Martin Esslin, *Mediations: Essays on Brecht, Beckett, and the Media* (Baton Rouge: Louisiana State University Press, 1980); Katherine Worth, *The Irish Drama of Europe from Yeats to Beckett* (London: Athlone Press, 1978); Katherine Worth, *Samuel Beckett: Life Journeys* (Oxford: Oxford University Press, 1999).
8 Brian Massumi, *Parables for the Virtual* (Durham, NC: Duke University Press, 2002), 106.
9 Anna McMullan, *Performing Embodiment in Samuel Beckett's Drama* (London: Routledge, 2010), 107.
10 See Stanton B. Garner, Jr., *Bodied Spaces: Phenomenology and Performance in Contemporary Drama* (New York: Cornell University Press, 1994); Bert O. States, *Great Reckonings in Little Rooms: On the Phenomenology of the Theatre* (Berkeley: University of California Press, 1987).
11 Marvin Carlson, *The Haunted Stage: The Theatre as Memory Machine* (Ann Arbor: University of Michigan Press, 2003), 15 (my emphasis).
12 Gilles Deleuze, 'The Exhausted', in *Essays Critical and Clinical,* trans. Daniel W. Smith and Michael A. Greco (Minneapolis: University of Minnesota Press, 1997), 158.
13 In addition to the negative concept of exhaustion discussed in relation to Deleuze's essay, other approaches to a negative aesthetic include Elizabeth Klaver, 'Samuel Beckett's *"Ohio Impromptu, Quad,"* and *"What Where"*: How It Is in the Matrix of Text and Television', *Contemporary Literature* 32, no. 3 (1991): 366-82; S. E. Gontarski, *Revisioning Beckett: Samuel Beckett's Decadent Turn* (London: Bloomsbury, 2018), 195-207. Alain Badiou's philosophical discussion of the concept of failure contributes to an aesthetics of negativity by way of Beckett also; see Alain Badiou, *On Beckett,*

trans. Alberto Toscano (Manchester: Clinamen Press, 2003); Andrew Gibson, *Beckett and Badiou* (Oxford: Oxford University Press, 2006).
14 'Fictive cosmos' is an expression that Lehmann uses to distinguish spectacle's virtual field from a narrative, a text-based notion, and accounts for the varied kinds of simulation that feature in postmodern performance. Hans-Thies Lehmann, *Postdramatic Theatre*, trans. Karen Jürs-Munby (London: Routledge, 2006), 31.
15 Steven Connor, *Samuel Beckett: Repetition, Theory, and Text* (Oxford: Basil Blackwell, 1988), 193.
16 Ibid., 196.
17 Peggy Phelan, 'Lessons in Blindness from Samuel Beckett', *Modern Language Association* 119, no. 5 (2004): 1279–88, 1281.
18 S. E. Gontarski, 'Introduction: De-theatricalizing Theatre: The Post-Play Plays', in Samuel Beckett, *The Theatrical Notebooks of Samuel Beckett, Vol. 4: The Shorter Plays*, ed. S. E. Gontarski (London: Faber and New York: Grove Press, 1999), xv–xxix, xv; the point is also made in Gontarski, 'Staging Himself, or Beckett's Late Style in the Theatre', 88.
19 Quoted in C. J. Ackerley and S. E. Gontarski, *The Grove Companion to Samuel Beckett: A Reader's Guide to His Works, Life, and Thought* (New York: Grove Press, 2004), 445.
20 Angela Moorjani, '"Just looking": Ne(i)ther-World Icons, Elsheimer Nocturnes, and Other Simultaneities in Beckett's *Play*', in *Beckett at 100: Revolving It All*, ed. Linda Ben-Zvi and Angela Moorjani (Oxford: Oxford University Press, 2008), 123–38, 124.
21 *CDW*, 376.
22 Lehmann, *Postdramatic Theatre*, passim.
23 Ibid., 32.
24 Quoted in Whitelaw, *Billie Whitelaw… Who He?*, 126.
25 Ibid., 131.
26 *CDW*, 375.
27 Whitelaw, *Billie Whitelaw… Who He?*, 237.
28 McMullan, *Performing Embodiment*, 125.
29 Ibid., 11.
30 Ulrika Maude, 'The Body of Memory: Beckett and Merleau-Ponty', in *Beckett and Philosophy*, ed. Richard Lane (London: Palgrave Macmillan, 2002), 108–22, 120.
31 *CDW*, 376.
32 Whitelaw, *Billie Whitelaw… Who He?*, 125.
33 *CDW*, 377.
34 Whitelaw, *Billie Whitelaw… Who He?*, 122.
35 Ibid., 124.
36 Ibid., 118.
37 Ibid., 127.
38 Ibid., 125.

39 Julie Campbell, '*Echo's Bones* and Beckett's Disembodied Voices', *Samuel Beckett Today/Aujourd'hui* 11 (2001): 454–60, 459.
40 Phelan, 'Lessons in Blindness from Samuel Beckett', 1281.
41 For this study, I consulted the 1989 Walter Asmus production recorded for television, with Christine Collins as V and Billie Whitelaw as May. I also draw from the history of the play's productions accounted for in such places as *The Theatrical Notebooks of Samuel Beckett, Vol. 4: The Shorter Plays* (1999) and *No Author Better Served: The Correspondence of Samuel Beckett & Alan Schneider* (1998). The Walter Asmus production is an amended version of *Footfalls*, the seven steps of the phantom-like May having been expanded to nine after collaborations between director Alan Schneider and Samuel Beckett after the premiere 1984 production determined the preference. The video is no longer available online.
42 *CDW*, 399.
43 Ibid., 401.
44 Massumi, *Parables for the Virtual*, 62.
45 For spectrality, see Sarah Balkin, *Spectral Characters: Genre and Materiality on the Modern Stage* (Ann Arbor: University of Michigan Press, 2019).
46 *CDW*, 403.
47 Ibid.
48 Ibid.
49 Anthony Uhlmann, 'Samuel Beckett and the Occluded Image', in *Beckett After Beckett*, ed. S. E. Gontarski and Anthony Uhlmann (Gainesville: University Press of Florida, 2006), 79–97, 91.
50 Deleuze, 'The Exhausted', 160.
51 *CDW*, 439.
52 Stanton B. Garner, Jr., 'Beckett, Merleau-Ponty, and the Phenomenological Body', *Theatre Journal* 45, no. 4 (December 1993): 443–59, 449.
53 Ibid., 451.
54 *CDW*, 442.
55 Herbert Blau, *The Audience* (Baltimore: John Hopkins University Press, 1990), 366 (my emphasis).
56 Ibid., 362, 363.
57 *CDW*, 434.
58 Samuel Beckett, *Three Novels: Molloy, Malone Dies, The Unnamable* (New York: Grove Press, 2006), 414.

3 Impediment and the symbolist dramaturgical inheritance

1 While there is another dramatic piece by Beckett, *Le Kid* (1931), a parody of Pierre Corneille's *Le Cid*, presented at the Trinity College Modern Language Society's foreign drama event, the work continues to be viewed as juvenilia. See Dougald McMillan and Martha Fehsenfeld, *Beckett in the Theatre: The*

Author as Practical Playwright and Director, Volume 1: From Waiting for Godot *to* Krapp's Last Tape (London: John Calder and New York: Riverrun Press, 1988), 17–25. The play is not reproduced in *CDW*, as a result, but, rather, in Samuel Beckett, *Disjecta: Miscellaneous Writings and a Dramatic Fragment*, ed. Ruby Cohn (New York: Grove Press, 1984), 153–66.

2 Martin Puchner, *Stage Fright: Modernism, Anti-Theatricality, and Drama* (Baltimore: Johns Hopkins University Press, 2002), 14–15.

3 For Puchner, closet drama defines the modernist attitude towards spectacle, an experimental urge preferring the freedom of the page over the restrictions of the real stage. We find this urge bracketed somewhat between Mallarmé's *Livre* and Gertrude Stein's *Four Saints in Three Acts*. See Puchner, Section II: The Modernist Closet Drama, in *Stage Fright*, 59–116.

4 Ruby Cohn, *Just Play: Beckett's Theatre* (Princeton: Princeton University Press, 1980), 162.

5 See ibid., 168–9.

6 McMillan and Fehsenfeld, *Beckett in the Theatre*, 31.

7 *DF*, 323–50.

8 See Deirdre Bair, *Samuel Beckett: A Biography* (New York: Harcourt Brace Jovanovich, 1978), 306.

9 S. E. Gontarski, 'Introduction', in *Eleuthéria: A Play in Three Acts*, trans. Michael Brodsky (New York: Foxrock, 1995), vii–xxii.

10 *DF*, 348.

11 To Duthuit, Beckett says, 'I have seen Blin. He wants, sorry, would like to put on *Godot*. My nationality complicates things, apparently, foreign plays can only be put on at the rate of one for every three French plays. Nice fellow, very Montparnasse. I know him well by sight, great friend of Artaud, on whom he is going to do a Broad, in three volumes. But a bit embarrassed all the same. Not very good either as actor or as director, if I am to judge by the *Sonata* that we saw, along with 17 other people, but great love of theatre.' Samuel Beckett, *The Letters of Samuel Beckett, Vol. 2: 1941–1956*, ed. George Craig, Martha Dow Fehsenfeld, Dan Gunn and Lois More Overbeck (Cambridge: Cambridge University Press, 2011), 182.

12 Cohn, *Just Play*, 163–72.

13 Tim Lawrence, *Samuel Beckett's Critical Aesthetics* (London: Palgrave Macmillan, 2018), 111.

14 Beckett voiced this opinion in a letter to Jacoba van Velde on 13 October 1946. He would begin writing *Eleuthéria* in January 1947. See Beckett, *The Letters of Samuel Beckett, Vol. 2: 1941–1956*, 44.

15 Leonard Cabell Pronko, *Avant-Garde: The Experimental Theatre in France* (Berkeley: University of California Press, 1963).

16 Ibid., 1.

17 Katherine Worth, *The Irish Drama of Europe from Yeats to Beckett* (London: Athlone Press of the University of London, 1978); Katherine Worth, *Samuel Beckett: Life Journeys* (Oxford: Clarendon Press, 1999);

Martin Puchner, *Stage Fright: Modernism, Anti-Theatricality, and Drama* (Baltimore: Johns Hopkins University Press, 2002); Allen Lane, *Symbolism* (London: Penguin Books, 1979); Lawrence, *Samuel Beckett's Critical Aesthetics*.

18 Antonin Artaud, *The Theatre and Its Double*, trans. Victor Corti (London: John Calder, 1985), 28.
19 Samuel Weber, *Theatricality as Medium* (New York: Fordham University Press, 2004), 291–2.
20 Quoted in Marvin Carlson, *Shattering Hamlet's Mirror: Theatre and Reality* (Ann Arbor: University of Michigan Press, 2016), 107.
21 See Puchner 2002, especially chapter II: 'Modernist Closet Drama', 59–116.
22 For Kleist's essay, Heinrich von. 'On the Marionette Theatre', *TDR: The Drama Review* 16, no. 3 (Sep. 1972): 22–6; For Beckett's philosophical interest in the thought of German Romantic Kleist and cognate models of ontology found in Arnold Geulincx's philosophy, see David Tucker, *Samuel Beckett and Arnold Geulincx: Tracing 'a Literary Fantasia'* (London: Continuum, 2012), 170; James Knowlson and John Pilling, *Frescoes of the Skull* (London: John Calder, 1979), 282; Anthony Uhlmann, *Thinking in Literature* (New York: Continuum, 2011), 39–40. Kleist, in short, can be credited as the source of Beckett's effort to realize depsychologized figures defined by the constraint to life's physical laws rather than the willpower that exists within living actors.
23 Puchner, *Stage Fright*, 128.
24 Ibid., 161.
25 Ibid., 162.
26 Edward Gordon Craig, *On the Art of the Theatre* (London: William Heinemann, 1911), 37, 39.
27 Gontarski, 'Introduction', xiii.
28 Herbert Blau, *The Audience* (Baltimore: John Hopkins University Press, 1990), 366.
29 Ulrika Maude, *Beckett, Technology and the Body* (Cambridge: Cambridge University Press, 2009), 2.
30 See Anna McMullan, *Performing Embodiment in Samuel Beckett's Drama* (London: Routledge, 2010).
31 Martin Esslin, *Mediations: Essays on Brecht, Beckett, and the Media* (Baton Rouge: Louisiana State University Press, 1980); Theodor Adorno, 'Trying to Understand Endgame', *New German Critique* 26, trans. Michael T. Jones (1982), 119–50, 136.
32 Puchner, *Stage Fright*, 158–9, 165.
33 Allen Lane, *Symbolism* (London: Penguin Books, 1979), 1.
34 Ibid., 109.
35 Samuel Beckett, 'Peintres de l'empêchement', in *Disjecta*, 136. For this theoretical sensibility, as Beckett in 'Three Dialogues' with Georges Duthuit,

also in *Disjecta*, writes, 'expression is an impossible act' (143). Consider 'Three Dialogues' as an expanded theory of *l'empêchement-oeil*.
36 *CDW*, 138.
37 Daniel Albright, *Beckett and Aesthetics* (Cambridge: Cambridge University Press, 2003), 70–1.
38 See Chapter 1 for the discussion of Jean-Louis Barrault in the role of Willie.
39 *CDW*, 164.
40 *DF*, 56.
41 Worth, *The Irish Drama of Europe from Yeats to Beckett*, 241.
42 Ibid., 3. Quote attributed to anonymous 'symbolist critics'.
43 Ibid., 4–5.
44 M. A. R. Habib, *A History of Literary Criticism: From Plato to the Present* (Maldon: Blackwell Publishing, 2005), 491.
45 Allen Lane, *Symbolism* (London: Penguin Books, 1979), 110.
46 Ibid.
47 Sarah Balkin, *Spectral Characters: Genre and Materiality on the Modern Stage* (Ann Arbor: University of Michigan Press, 2019), 40.
48 Lane, *Symbolism*, 109.
49 Ruby Cohn, *Back to Beckett* (Princeton: Princeton University Press, 1973), 127.
50 See Chapter 1. See also Lane, *Symbolism*, 109.
51 Ibid., 24.
52 Worth, *The Irish Drama of Europe from Yeats to Beckett*, 48.
53 W. B. Yeats, *Plays for an Irish Theatre by W.B. Yeats, with Designs by Gordon Craig* (London: A. H. Bullen, 1911), xiii.
54 Edward Gordon Craig, *On the Art of the Theatre* (London: William Heinemann, 1911), 27.
55 These sketches are found, respectively, in Edward Gordon Craig, *Towards a New Theatre; Forty Designs for Stage Scenes with Critical Notes by the Inventor Edward Gordon Craig* (New York: B. Blom, 1969), 56, frontispiece.
56 Yeats, *Plays for an Irish Theatre by W. B. Yeats*, xiii.
57 *CDW*, 445.
58 Chris Ackerley, 'Perfection Is Not of This World: Samuel Beckett and Mysticism', *Mystics Quarterly* 30, no. 1/2 (March/June 2004): 28–55, 46.
59 For a study of this constellation of influences, see John Calder, *The Theology of Samuel Beckett* (Surrey: Calder Publications, 2012).
60 Yeats, *Plays for an Irish Theatre*, 161.
61 W. B. Yeats, *The Variorum Edition of the Plays of W.B. Yeats*, ed. Russell K. Alspach (London: Macmillan, 1966), 645 (my emphasis).
62 The notion that *Ohio Impromptu* involves an act of miniaturization I draw from S. E. Gontarski's admiring description of the first production at Ohio State University in 1981 directed by Alan Schneider, featuring David Warrilow as Reader and Rand Mitchell as Listener, chronicled in S. E. Gontarski, 'Review: The world première of "Ohio Impromptu", directed by

Alan Schneider at Columbus, Ohio', *Journal of Beckett Studies* 8 (Autumn 1982): 133–6.
63 *DF*, 664.
64 Deni McIntosh McHenry, '"Faust in His Study" Reconsidered: A Record of Jewish Patronage and Mysticism in Mid-Seventeenth-Century Amsterdam', *Yale University Art Gallery Bulletin* (Spring 1989): 9–19.
65 *CDW*, 445.
66 Ibid., 448.
67 Ibid.
68 Worth, *Samuel Beckett*, 22.
69 Dirk Van Hulle, '"Accursed Creator": Beckett, Romanticism, and "the Modern Prometheus"', *Samuel Beckett Today/Aujourd'hui* 18 (2007): 15–29, 22.
70 Yeats, *The Variorum Edition of the Plays of W.B. Yeats*, 1050.
71 *CDW*, 11.
72 *DF*, 378.
73 Worth, *Samuel Beckett*, 28.
74 Ibid., 29.
75 Ibid., 28–9.
76 For the Lüttringhausen Prison episode, see *DF*, 368–70.
77 Ibid., 540–2.
78 Matthew Melia, 'Architecture and Cruelty in the Writings of Genet, Artaud and Beckett: A Discussion of Recent Research', *International Journal of the Humanities* 8, no. 9 (2010): 47.
79 One photograph can be found in Worth, *Samuel Beckett*, illustrations insert; the other can be found accompanying an interview with Anna McMullan in Anna McMullan, 'When Beckett wrote *Waiting for Godot* he really didn't know a lot about theatre', *Telegraph*, 5 January 2013, https://www.telegraph.co.uk/culture/theatre/theatre-features/9780077/When-Beckett-wrote-Waiting-for-Godot-he-really-didnt-know-a-lot-about-theatre.html.
80 See Melia, 'Architecture and Cruelty in the Writings of Genet, Artaud and Beckett: A Discussion of Recent Research'.
81 Cohn, *Back to Beckett*, 131–2 (my emphasis).

4 Dream space, the other laboratory

1 Martin Heidegger, *Zollikon Seminars: Protocols, Conversations, Letters*, ed. Medard Boss, trans. Franz Mayr and Richard Askay (Evanston, IL: Northwestern University Press, 2001), 14.
2 Samuel Beckett, *Echo's Bones*, ed. Mark Nixon (London: Faber, 2014), 5.
3 See, for example, Shane Weller, *Literature, Philosophy, Nihilism: The Uncanniest of Guests* (London: Continuum, 2008); Shane Weller, 'Phenomenologies of the Nothing: Democritus, Heidegger, Beckett', in

Beckett and Phenomenology, ed. Ulrika Maude and Matthew Feldman (London: Continuum, 2009), 39–55.
4 Giorgio Agamben, *Potentialities: Collected Essays in Philosophy*, ed. and trans. Daniel Heller-Roazen (Stanford, CA: Stanford University Press, 1999), 78 (emphasis in the original).
5 Herschel Farbman, *The Other Night: Dreaming, Writing, and Restlessness in Twentieth-Century Literature* (New York: Fordham University Press, 2008), 51.
6 Ibid., 43.
7 Farbman, *The Other Night*, 3; Weller, *Literature, Philosophy, Nihilism*, 33.
8 Samuel Beckett, *Collected Poems: A Critical Edition*, ed. Seán Lawlor and John Pilling (London: Faber, 2012), 200.
9 Quoted in Farbman, *The Other Night*, 38.
10 Sarah Balkin, *Spectral Characters: Genre and Materiality on the Modern Stage* (Ann Arbor: University of Michigan Press, 2019); Enoch Brater, *Beyond Minimalism: Beckett's Late Style in the Theater* (New York: Oxford University Press, 1987); Steven Connor, *Beckett, Modernism and the Material Imagination* (Cambridge: Cambridge University Press, 2014); Mary Luckhurst, 'Giving Up the Ghost: The Actor's Body as Haunted House', in *Theatre and Ghosts: Materiality, Performance, and Modernity*, ed. Mary Luckhurst and Emilie Morin (London: Palgrave Macmillan, 2014), 163–77; Ulrika Maude, 'The Body of Memory: Beckett and Merleau-Ponty', in *Beckett and Philosophy*, ed. Richard Lane (London: Palgrave Macmillan, 2002), 108–22; Paul Sheehan, 'Beckett's Ghosts: Monitoring a Phenomenology of Sleep', in *Beckett and Phenomenology*, ed. Ulrika Maude and Matthew Feldman (London: Continuum, 2009), 158–76; Jean-Michel Rabaté, 'Beckett's Ghosts and Fluxions', *Samuel Beckett Today/Aujourd'hui* 5 (1996): 23–41.
11 Ruby Cohn, 'A Krapp Chronology', *Modern Drama* 49, no. 4 (Winter 2006): 414–24, 417; Samuel Beckett, *The Theatrical Notebooks of Samuel Beckett, Vol. 3: Krapp's Last Tape*, ed. James Knowlson (London: Faber, 1992), 241.
12 *CDW*, 395.
13 Ibid., 465.
14 James Knowlson and John Pilling, *Frescoes of the Skull* (London: John Calder, 1979), 206.
15 Julie Campbell, 'A Voice Comes to One in the Dark. Imagine: Radio, the Listener, and the Dark Comedy of *All That Fall*', in *Beckett and Death*, ed. Steven Barfield, Matthew Feldman and Philip Tew (London: Continuum, 2009), 147–68, 162; C. G. Jung, *Analytical Psychology: Its Theory and Practice, The Tavistock Lectures* (London: Routledge & Kegan Paul, 1976), 107.
16 Campbell, 'A Voice Comes to One in the Dark', 155.
17 *CDW*, 93, 92, 425.

18 Ibid., 435, 436, 438, 444.
19 Eddie Paterson, *The Contemporary American Monologue: Performance and Politics* (London: Bloomsbury, 2015), 34–7, 36.
20 *CDW*, 387.
21 Ibid., 136.
22 Ibid., 160.
23 *CDW*, 166. This moment in the play is discussed in Chapter 1, 'Laboratory acts without words'.
24 Trish McTighe, *The Haptic Aesthetic in Samuel Beckett's Drama* (London: Palgrave Macmillan, 2013), 154.
25 Watch Beckett's *Nacht und Träume* in a 1982 production by Süddeutscher Rundfunk here: https://youtu.be/Ewa1SugylEE.
26 *CDW*, 465.
27 Ibid., 466.
28 *DF*, 599–600.
29 Martin Heidegger, *Being and Time*, 7th edn, trans. John Macquarie and Edmund Robinson (Oxford: Basil Blackwell, 1973), 248 (my emphasis).
30 Agamben, *Potentialities*, 78.
31 *CDW*, 395.
32 Ibid., 388.
33 Ibid., 395.
34 Agamben, *Potentialities*, 77.
35 Samuel Beckett, *Nohow On: Company, Ill Seen Ill Said, Worstward Ho* (New York: Grove Press, 1996), 113.

5 Catastrophe and the politics of spectacle

1 Václav Havel, 'The power of the powerless', in *The Power of the Powerless: Citizens Against the State in Central Eastern Europe*, trans. Paul Wilson, ed. John Keane (New York: Routledge, 2009), 10–59, 29–30.
2 Herbert Marcuse, *Art and Liberation: Collected Papers of Herbert Marcuse, Vol. 4*, ed. Douglas Kellner (London: Routledge, 2007), 201.
3 Samuel Beckett, *Collected Poems: A Critical Edition*, ed. Seán Lawlor and John Pilling (London: Faber, 2012), 197–9, 199.
4 Marcuse, *Art and Liberation*, 170.
5 Havel, *The Power of the Powerless*, 10.
6 Translated as 'nowhere' in the reproduction of this *mirlitonnade* fragment in Marcuse, *Art and Liberation*, I favour 'no place' as it sounds more in the style of Beckett's late prose. For this fragment and the Edith Fourier translation, see Marcuse, *Art and Liberation*, 200. For the poem fragment in its place in the full *mirlitonnades*, see Samuel Beckett, *Collected Poems: A Critical Edition*, ed. Seán Lawlor and John Pilling (London: Faber, 2012), 210–20, 216.

7 Jonathan Crary, *24/7: Late Capitalism and the Ends of Sleep* (London: Verso, 2014), 70.
8 Giorgio Agamben, *Infancy and History: On the Destruction of Experience*, trans. Liz Heron (London: Verso, 2007).
9 See Keir Elam, 'Catastrophic Mistakes: Beckett, Havel, the End', *Samuel Beckett Today/Aujourd'hui* 3 (1994): 1–28.
10 Bert O. States, '*Catastrophe*: Beckett's Laboratory / Theatre', *Modern Drama* 30, no. 1 (Spring 1987): 14–22.
11 Elam, 'Catastrophic Mistakes', 13.
12 *CDW*, 461.
13 Anna McMullan, *Theatre on Trial: Samuel Beckett's Later Drama* (London: Routledge, 1993), 25.
14 *CDW*, 460.
15 Elam, 'Catastrophic Mistakes', 2.
16 *CDW*, 461.
17 Jo Glanville, '"Godot Is Here": How Samuel Beckett and Vaclav Havel Changed History', *Guardian*, 15 September 2009, https://www.theguardian.com/culture/2009/sep/15/vaclev-havel-samuel-beckett-catastrophe.
18 Emilie Morin, *Beckett's Political Imagination* (Cambridge: Cambridge University Press, 2017), 249.
19 Marcuse, *Art and Liberation*, 127.
20 Ibid.
21 Theodor Adorno, *Aesthetic Theory*, trans. Robert Hullot-Kentor (London: Continuum, 2002), 31.
22 Marcuse, *Art and Liberation*, 201.
23 Ibid., 202.
24 *CDW*, 461.
25 Havel, *The Power of the Powerless*, 23.
26 Herbert Blau, *Reality Principles: From the Absurd to the Virtual* (Ann Arbor: University of Michigan Press, 2011), 247.
27 Giorgio Agamben, *Profanations* (New York: Zone Books, 2007), 50.
28 Ibid., 41, 50.
29 For an English translation of the letter in which he makes this influential pronouncement, see Arthur Rimbaud, Rimbaud to Georges Izambard, 13 May 1871, in the *Complete Works*, trans. Paul Schmidt (New York: HarperCollins, 2008), 113–14.
30 Agamben, *Profanations*, 50–1.
31 Eddie Paterson, *The Contemporary American Monologue: Performance and Politics* (London: Bloomsbury, 2015), 37.
32 Havel, *The Power of the Powerless*, 23.
33 Marcuse, *Art and Liberation*, 125.
34 Ibid., 124.
35 Ibid., 129.
36 In Beckett, *Collected Poems*, 216. See also Marcuse, *Art and Liberation*, 200.

37 Ibid.
38 Agamben, *Infancy and History*, 6.
39 Ibid., 155.
40 Ibid. (emphasis in the original).
41 Ibid., 58.
42 Marvin Carlson, *The Haunted Stage: The Theatre as Memory Machine* (Ann Arbor: University of Michigan Press, 2003), 79.

6 Hypnosis: A theory of Beckett spectatorship

1 *CDW*, 399, 401.
2 Ibid., 399.
3 Ibid.
4 Although not written to be performed as a trilogy, the tradition of performing the three plays together (since Billie Whitelaw's touring performances from the late 1980s onwards) has established them as a kind of theatrical suite. The complementarity of these plays in the way that Whitelaw presented them – a complementarity that Dwan has extended – should be considered part of their enduring dramaturgical interest in contemporary theatre. In 2014, I saw the Royal Court Theatre production, entitled *Not I / Footfalls / Rockaby: Beckett Trilogy*, which premiered in May 2013 and was directed by Walter Asmus, with Lisa Dwan playing all roles (including the recorded parts of V in both *Footfalls* and *Rockaby*). The show subsequently moved to the Duchess Theatre before embarking on an international tour.
5 See W. B. Worthen, *Drama: Between Poetry and Performance* (Chichester: Wiley-Blackwell, 2010).
6 Brian Massumi, *Politics of Affect* (Cambridge: Polity, 2015), 47.
7 See Léon Chertok and Isabelle Stengers, *A Critique of Psychoanalytic Reason: Hypnosis as a Scientific Problem from Lavoisier to Lacan*, trans. Martha Noel Evans (Stanford: Stanford University Press, 1992), *passim*.
8 See Samuel Beckett, *Proust* (New York: Grove Press, 1970).
9 Ibid., 53 (my emphasis).
10 Ibid., 7.
11 Ibid., 53.
12 Chertok and Stengers, *A Critique of Psychoanalytic Reason*, 86 (my emphasis).
13 Shane Weller, *Beckett, Literature, and the Ethics of Alterity* (London: Palgrave Macmillan, 2006), 183.
14 Elin Diamond, *Unmaking Mimesis: Essays on Feminism and Theatre* (London and New York: Routledge, 1997), 38.
15 Ibid.

16 Josef Breuer and Sigmund Freud, *Studies on Hysteria: The Standard Edition of the Complete Psychological Works of Sigmund Freud*, Vol. 2, trans. and ed. James Strachey with Anna Freud (London: Hogarth, 1981), 3.
17 Ibid., 39 (emphasis in the original).
18 Jonathan Crary, *Suspensions of Perception: Attention, Spectacle, and Modern Culture* (Cambridge, MA: MIT Press, 2001), 65.
19 Here, I am drawing from diverse materials besides the psychoanalytic corpus, including most notably: Chertok and Stengers, *A Critique of Psychoanalytic Reason*; Crary, *Suspensions of Perception*; Brian Massumi, *Parables for the Virtual* (Durham, NC: Duke University Press, 2002); Graham F. Wagstaff, 'On the Centrality of the Concept of an Altered State to Definitions of Hypnosis', *Journal of Mind-Body Regulation* 2, no. 2 (2014): 90–108.
20 Breuer and Freud, *Studies on Hysteria*; S. E. Gontarski, 'The Body in the Body of Beckett's Theatre', *Samuel Beckett Today/Aujourd'hui* 11 (2002): 169–77; S. E. Gontarski, 'Introduction: Towards a Minoritarian Criticism – The Questions We Ask', in *The Edinburgh Companion to Samuel Beckett and the Arts*, ed. S. E. Gontarski (Edinburgh: Edinburgh University Press, 2014), 1–13; Ulrika Maude, 'Convulsive Aesthetics: Beckett, Chaplin and Charcot', in *The Edinburgh Companion to Samuel Beckett and the Arts*, ed. S. E. Gontarski (Edinburgh: Edinburgh University Press, 2014), 44–53; Felicia McCarren, 'The "Symptomatic Act" circa 1900: Hysteria, Hypnosis, Electricity, Dance', *Critical Inquiry* 21, no. 4 (1995): 748–74; Weller, *Beckett, Literature, and the Ethics of Alterity*.
21 *DF*, 615.
22 Wagstaff, 'On the Centrality of the Concept of an Altered State to Definitions of Hypnosis', 91.
23 For this parallelism of sleep and death explored in Beckett's theatre, see Chapter 4, 'Dream space, the other laboratory'.
24 *DF*, 582.
25 Ovid, *Metamorphoses*, trans. A. D. Melville (Oxford: Oxford University Press, 1986), 267.
26 *CDW*, 434.
27 Anthony Uhlmann, 'Samuel Beckett and the Occluded Image', in *Beckett After Beckett*, ed. S. E. Gontarski and Anthony Uhlmann (Gainesville: University Press of Florida, 2006), 79–97, 91.
28 Chertok and Stengers, *A Critique of Psychoanalytic Reason*, 1–10.
29 Crary, *Suspensions of Perception*, 65.
30 Ibid., 42 (emphasis in the original).
31 Billie Whitelaw, *Billie Whitelaw... Who He?* (London: Hodder and Stoughton, 1995), 118.
32 Asmus and Dwan's production followed a tradition, accepted since 1975, of cutting the play's cloaked character, the Auditor. This alteration is due, in part, to the success of the BBC version of the play and to later modifications,

made by Beckett, stemming from his difficulties with the Auditor in a French production starring Madeleine Renaud. See *DF*, 545.
33 *CDW*, 381.
34 See Maude, 'Convulsive Aesthetics: Beckett, Chaplin and Charcot'.
35 Ibid., 51.
36 *CDW*, 377.
37 Ibid., 376.
38 Gontarski, 'Introduction', 10.
39 Mary Bryden, *Women in Samuel Beckett's Prose and Drama: Her Own Other* (Basingstoke: Palgrave Macmillan, 1993), 134.
40 Ibid., 133–4 (my emphasis).
41 Diamond, *Unmaking Mimesis*, 13.
42 Ibid.
43 McCarren, 'The "Symptomatic Act" circa 1900', 764.
44 Ibid., 766.
45 Ibid.
46 See *DF*, 583, 588.
47 Samuel Beckett, *Nohow On: Company, Ill Seen Ill Said, Worstward Ho* (New York: Grove Press, 1996), 54.
48 Ibid., 86; *CDW*, 442.
49 Adam Piette, 'Beckett, Affect and the Face', *Textual Practice* 25, no. 2 (2011): 281–95, 289.
50 *DF*, 588.
51 Piette, 'Beckett, Affect and the Face', 286.
52 Ibid., 295.
53 Once entitled '*Not I*: Lisa Dwan Explains Beckett's Play Backstage', a YouTube video of 29 June 2013, the video is unfortunately no longer accessible online.
54 Paul Taylor, 'Beckett Trilogy: Not I/Footfalls/Rockaby, Theatre Review – "An Unforgettable Show"', *Independent*, 14 January 2014, https://www.independent.co.uk/arts-entertainment/theatre-dance/reviews/beckett-trilogy-not-ifootfallsrockaby-theatre-review-an-unforgettable-show-9058659.html.
55 Lisa Dwan, 'Beckett's *Not I*: How I Became the Ultimate Motormouth', *Guardian*, 8 May 2013, https://www.theguardian.com/culture/2013/may/08/beckett-not-i-lisa-dwan.
56 '*Not I*: Lisa Dwan Explains Beckett's Play Backstage'.
57 Ibid.
58 Dwan, 'Beckett's *Not I*: How I Became the Ultimate Motormouth'.
59 *DF*, 522.
60 Paul Rae, *Theatre & Human Rights* (London: Palgrave Macmillan, 2009), 62.
61 Gontarski, 'The Body in the Body of Beckett's Theatre', 170.
62 Chertok and Stengers, *A Critique of Psychoanalytic Reason*, 277 (emphasis omitted).

63 Gontarski, 'Introduction', 10.

7 *Adaphatrôce*, or the contentious fringes of Beckett's dramaturgy

1 Jonathan Kalb, *Beckett in Performance* (Cambridge: Cambridge University Press, 1991), 132.
2 Ruby Cohn, *Just Play: Beckett's Theatre* (Princeton: Princeton University Press, 1980), 229.
3 Samuel Beckett, *The Complete Short Prose* (New York: Grove Press, 1995), 202.
4 Ibid., 205.
5 S. E. Gontarski, *Beckett Matters: Essays on Beckett's Late Modernism* (Edinburgh: Edinburgh University Press, 2017), *passim*, 64.
6 See *DF*, 481.
7 Clas Zilliacus, *Beckett and Broadcasting* (Åbo: Åbo Akademi, 1976), n. pag.
8 Kalb, *Beckett in Performance*, 142.
9 The image of the figurines is vividly reproduced in a photograph preserved in Kalb's book, *Beckett in Performance*, 141.
10 Lois Oppenheim, *The Painted Word: Samuel Beckett's Dialogue with Art* (Ann Arbor: University of Michigan Press, 2000), 168.
11 For Kantor's concept of a theatre of death, see Tadeusz Kantor, *A Journey through Other Spaces: Essays and Manifestos, 1944–1990* (Berkeley: University of California Press, 1993).
12 Iris Smith Fischer, *Mabou Mines: Making Avant-Garde Theatre in the 1970s* (Ann Arbor: University of Michigan Press, 2012), 100–1.
13 See ibid., 99–119. See also, Laurie Lassiter, 'David Warrilow: Creating Symbol and Cypher', *TDR: The Drama Review* 29, no. 4 (Winter 1985): 3–12.
14 See *DF*, 607–8. See also, Mel Gussow, 'Stage: Disputed 'Endgame' in Debut.' *New York Times*, 20 December 1984, http://www.nytimes.com/1984/12/20/arts/stage-disputed-endgame-in-debut.html?mcubz=0.
15 *DF*, 476.
16 Sozita Goudouna, *Beckett's* Breath *and the Visual Arts* (Edinburgh: Edinburgh University Press, 2018), 55.
17 *CDW*, 371.
18 Samuel Beckett, *Three Novels: Molloy, Malone Dies, The Unnamable* (New York: Grove Press, 2006), 249.
19 The correspondence found with the term 'rattle' also comes from Ricks; Christopher Ricks, *Beckett's Dying Words: The Clarendon Lectures, 1990* (Oxford: Clarendon Press, 1993), 111–12.
20 Thomas H. Ford, *Wordsworth and the Poetics of Air* (Cambridge: Cambridge University Press, 2018), 212.

21 Daniel Katz, *Saying I No More: Subjectivity and Consciousness in the Prose of Samuel Beckett* (Evanston, IL: Northwestern University Press, 1999), 182.
22 Ibid., 26.
23 S. E. Gontarski, *Revisioning Beckett: Samuel Beckett's Decadent Turn* (London: Bloomsbury, 2018), 201.
24 Luke Thurston, 'Outselves: Beckett, Bion and Beyond', *Journal of Modern Literature* 32, no. 3 (2009): 121–43, 128.
25 Martin Puchner, *Stage Fright: Modernism, Anti-Theatricality, and Drama* (Baltimore: Johns Hopkins University Press, 2002), 172.
26 Peter Brook, *The Empty Space* (London: Penguin, 1990), 11.
27 Puchner, *Stage Fright*, 142–3.
28 *Peter Brook: The Tightrope* (2014), dir. Simon Brook, France: Brook Productions / Cinemaundici / ARTE France.
29 A recording of the full production is distributed in parts within the following ARTE France TV feature: 'Beckett by Brook • Samuel Beckett • Peter Brook & Marie-Hélène Estienne', Vimeo video, 1:00:50, 'Théâtre des Bouffes du Nord', 19 March 2020, https://vimeo.com/398851333.
30 See Alexandra Poulain, 'Fragments au Bouffes du Nord', *The Beckett Circle / Le Cercle de Beckett: Newsletter of the Samuel Beckett Society* 30, no. 1 (Spring 2007): 7–8.
31 W. B. Worthen, *Drama: Between Poetry and Performance* (Chichester: Wiley-Blackwell, 2010), 211.
32 *CDW*, 227
33 Quoted in *DF*, 556.
34 Beckett, *The Complete Short Prose*, 258.
35 Beckett, *Three Novels*, 334–5.
36 Samuel Beckett, *Disjecta: Miscellaneous Writings and a Dramatic Fragment* (New York: Grove Press, 1984), 33.
37 See the Schiller Manuscript, '*Tritte (Footfalls)*', in Samuel Beckett, *The Theatrical Notebooks of Samuel Beckett, Vol. 4: The Shorter Plays*, ed. S. E. Gontarski (London: Faber and New York: Grove Press, 1999), 313–66. The Billie Whitelaw production is discussed in my Chapter 2.
38 *DF*, 554.
39 For an account of the intersection in Berlin, see ibid., 555–6. For a discussion of Neumann's adaptations of Beckett prose with Mabou Mines and an interview with the performer, see Kalb, *Beckett in Performance*, 120–6, 206–11.
40 An excellent rendering can be found in full, fashioned in a sort of minimalist, post-Symbolist mise en scène in a film by Barrie Gavin from 1980, featuring soprano Sarah Leonard with the Frankfurt Radio Symphony Orchestra and conducted by Zoltan Peskó, spread across five clips starting here: 'Morton Feldman and Samuel Beckett – Neither – Opera. First 10 minutes', YouTube video, 9:27, 'Andrew Toovey', 1 June 2012, https://youtu.be/0exs9F-888s.

41 Catherine Laws, 'Beckett – Feldman – Johns', in *Beckett at 100: Revolving It All*, ed. Linda Ben-Zvi and Angela Moorjani (Oxford: Oxford University Press, 2008), 230–45, 231, 234.

42 Michael Coffey, *Samuel Beckett Is Closed* (New York: Foxrock Books, 2018), 144.

43 An extended, continuous excerpt from this revered theatrical event can be found in the adaptation of the same name for RTÉ Television from 1966, viewable here: 'Beginning to End – Samuel Beckett', YouTube video, 48:23, 'Kid Curry', 15 February 2011, https://www.youtube.com/watch?v=D7zXy57O7bc.

44 Jordan R. Young, *The Beckett Actor: Jack MacGowran, Beginning to End* (Beverly Hills: Moonstone Press, 1987), 124.

45 Ibid., 78–81, 104–5, 129–38.

46 For the 'HUMINID' section of *ACTOR #1*, See 'HUMINID – A Two Dogs Company / Kris Verdonck', YouTube video, 1:39, 'atwodogscompany', March 18, 2011, https://youtu.be/3VHvC2Ah-YU. 'Lessness' is a more musical, but similarly philosophical, work of prose poetry attempting to mark out the figural dimensions of an enigmatic, embryonic pseudo-being anterior to the material realm; see Beckett, *The Complete Short Prose*, 194–6.

47 Mary Bryden claims in 'Beckett and the Sound of Silence' that Beckett once used this evocative concept of the static fugue to characterize the form of *Quad*, a concept of what she explains earlier in the essay as a 'back-and-forth movement' which 'may be between two poles, or it may be between movement and immobility'; *Quad*'s interdependent elements, she surmises, 'contain the threat, or possibility, of their own extinction'. Mary Bryden, 'Beckett and the Sound of Silence', in *Samuel Beckett and Music*, ed. Mary Bryden (Oxford: Clarendon Press, 1998), 21–46, 36.

48 Peter Eckersall, Helena Grehan and Edward Scheer, *New Media Dramaturgy: Performance, Media and New-Materialism* (London: Palgrave Macmillan, 2017), 28.

49 Ibid., 38

50 See Marvin Carlson, *The Haunted Stage: The Theatre as Memory Machine* (Ann Arbor: University of Michigan Press, 2003).

51 W. B. Worthen, *The Idea of the Actor: Drama and the Ethics of Performance* (Princeton: Princeton University Press, 1984), 205.

52 Herbert Blau, *Reality Principles: From the Absurd to the Virtual* (Ann Arbor: University of Michigan Press, 2011), 247.

53 Adam Alston and Martin Welston, 'Introduction: The Dark Draws In', in *Theatre in the Dark: Shadow, Gloom and Blackout in Contemporary Theatre*, ed. Adam Alston and Martin Welston (London: Bloomsbury, 2019), 1–34, 2.

54 For an account of Pan Pan Theatre's productions' contribution to the question of adapting Beckett for live and intermedial performance among many other related experiments, see Nicholas E. Johnson, '"The Neatness of Identifications": Transgressing Beckett's Genres in Ireland and Northern

Ireland, 2000–2015', in *Staging Beckett in Ireland and Northern Ireland*, ed. Trish McTighe and David Tucker (London: Bloomsbury, 2017), 185–204.
55 Kathryn Chiong, 'Nauman's Beckett Walk', *October* 86 (1998): 74.
56 Simone Weil, *Gravity and Grace*, trans. Emma Crawford and Mario von der Ruhr (London: Routledge, 2002), 181.
57 As discussed in Chapter 3, Dirk Van Hulle presents the infinitesimal as Beckett's post-Romantic notion of artistic creation, an alternative to Romanticism's devotion to the concept of infinitude. See Dirk Van Hulle, '"Accursed Creator": Beckett, Romanticism, and "the Modern Prometheus"', *Samuel Beckett Today/Aujourd'hui* 18 (2007): 15–29, 22.
58 Herbert Blau, *The Audience* (Baltimore: John Hopkins University Press, 1990), 366; Andrew Gibson, *Beckett and Badiou* (Oxford: Oxford University Press, 2006), 235; Steven Connor, *Beckett, Modernism and the Material Imagination* (Cambridge: Cambridge University Press, 2014).
59 Dougald McMillan and Martha Fehsenfeld, *Beckett in the Theatre: The Author as Practical Playwright and Director, Volume 1: From* Waiting for Godot *to* Krapp's Last Tape (London: John Calder and New York: Riverrun Press, 1988), 257.
60 *CDW*, 223.
61 Cluchey: *Krapp's Last Tape*, San Quentin Drama Workshop / Visual Press, 'Beckett Directs Beckett' series, performed by Cluchey, directed by Walter Asmus, designed by Bud Thorpe, produced in 1988. Available online: http://www.youtube.com/watch?v=af5NohyiQrA. Magee: *Krapp's Last Tape*, directed by Donald McWhinnie, BBC Television, 25 October 1972. Available online: http://www.youtube.com/watch?v=uphqyjAkYIU& list=PLAA5D928 4539A095A. For a comprehensive study of *Krapp's Last Tape's* productions and revisions during Beckett's lifetime, see McMillan and Fehsenfeld, *Beckett in the Theatre*, 241–311; Ruby Cohn, 'A Krapp Chronology', *Modern Drama* 49, no. 4 (2006): 514–24.
62 Parabasis in its definition by Giorgio Agamben is discussed in Chapter 5.
63 William E. Gruber, *Missing Persons: Character and Characterization in Modern Drama* (Athens: University of Georgia Press, 1994), 88.

Bibliography

Ackerley, Chris. '"Ever Know What Happened?": Shades and Echoes in Samuel Beckett's Television Plays'. *Journal of Beckett Studies* 18, nos. 1-2 (2009): 136-64.

Ackerley, Chris. 'Perfection Is Not of This World: Samuel Beckett and Mysticism'. *Mystics Quarterly* 30, nos. 1-2 (March/June 2004): 28-55.

Ackerley, C. J., and S. E. Gontarski. *The Grove Companion to Samuel Beckett: A Reader's Guide to His Works, Life, and Thought*. New York: Grove Press, 2004.

Adorno, Theodor. *Aesthetic Theory*. Translated by Robert Hullot-Kentor. London: Continuum, 2002.

Adorno, Theodor. 'Trying to Understand *Endgame*'. *New German Critique* 26, translated by Michael T. Jones (Spring/Summer 1982): 119-50.

Agamben, Giorgio. *Infancy and History: On the Destruction of Experience*. Translated by Liz Heron. London: Verso, 2007.

Agamben, Giorgio. *Potentialities: Collected Essays in Philosophy*. Edited and translated by Daniel Heller-Roazen. Stanford: Stanford University Press, 1999.

Agamben, Giorgio. *Profanations*. New York: Zone Books, 2007.

Albright, Daniel. *Beckett and Aesthetics*. Cambridge: Cambridge University Press, 2003.

Alston, Adam, and Martin Welston. 'Introduction: The Dark Draws In'. In *Theatre in the Dark: Shadow, Gloom and Blackout in Contemporary Theatre*, edited by Adam Alston and Martin Welston, 1-34. London: Bloomsbury, 2019.

Anderton, Joseph. *Beckett's Creatures: Art of Failure after the Holocaust*. London: Bloomsbury, 2016.

Artaud, Antonin. *The Theatre and Its Double*. Translated by Victor Corti. London: John Calder, 1985.

Badiou, Alain. *On Beckett*. Translated by Alberto Toscano. Manchester: Clinamen Press, 2003.

Bair, Deirdre. *Samuel Beckett: A Biography*. New York: Harcourt Brace Jovanovich, 1978.

Balkin, Sarah. *Spectral Characters: Genre and Materiality on the Modern Stage*. Ann Arbor: University of Michigan Press, 2019.

Beckett, Samuel. *Collected Poems: A Critical Edition*. Edited by Seán Lawlor and John Pilling. London: Faber, 2012.

Beckett, Samuel. *The Complete Short Prose*. New York: Grove Press, 1995.

Beckett, Samuel. *Disjecta: Miscellaneous Writings and a Dramatic Fragment*. Edited by Ruby Cohn. New York: Grove Press, 1984.

Beckett, Samuel. *Echo's Bones*. Edited by Mark Nixon. London: Faber, 2014.

Beckett, Samuel. *Eleuthéria: A Play in Three Acts*. Translated by Michael Brodsky. New York: Foxrock, 1995.
Beckett, Samuel. 'Facsimile of Beckett's Production Notebook for Das letzte Band, Schiller-Theater Werkstatt, Berlin 1969'. Beckett archive, University of Reading, RUL 1396/4/16.
Beckett, Samuel. *The Letters of Samuel Beckett, Vol. 2: 1941–1956*. Edited by George Craig, Martha Dow Fehsenfeld, Dan Gunn and Lois More Overbeck. Cambridge: Cambridge University Press, 2011.
Beckett, Samuel. *Mercier and Camier*. London: John Calder, 1999.
Beckett, Samuel. *Nohow On: Company, Ill Seen Ill Said, Worstward Ho*. New York: Grove Press, 1996.
Beckett, Samuel. *Proust*. New York: Grove Press, 1970.
Beckett, Samuel. *The Theatrical Notebooks of Samuel Beckett: Vol. 2: Endgame*. Edited by S. E. Gontarski. London: Faber, 1992.
Beckett, Samuel. *The Theatrical Notebooks of Samuel Beckett, Vol. 3: Krapp's Last Tape*. Edited by James Knowlson. London: Faber, 1992.
Beckett, Samuel. *The Theatrical Notebooks of Samuel Beckett, Vol. 4: The Shorter Plays*. Edited by S. E. Gontarski. New York: Faber, Grove Press, 1999.
Beckett, Samuel. *The Theatrical Notebooks of Samuel Beckett, Vol. 1: Waiting for Godot*. Edited by Dougald McMillan and James Knowlson. London: Faber, 1993.
Beckett, Samuel. *Three Novels: Molloy, Malone Dies, The Unnamable*. New York: Grove Press, 2006.
Berlin, Normand. 'Traffic of Our Stage: Why Waiting for Godot?'. *The Massachusetts Review* 40, no. 3 (Autumn 1999): 420–34.
Blau, Herbert. *The Audience*. Baltimore: John Hopkins University Press, 1990.
Blau, Herbert. *Reality Principles: From the Absurd to the Virtual*. Ann Arbor: University of Michigan Press, 2011.
Blau, Herbert. *Sails of the Herring Fleet: Essays on Samuel Beckett*. Ann Arbor: University of Michigan Press, 2000.
Blau, Herbert. *Take Up the Bodies: Theatre at the Vanishing Point*. Urbana: University of Illinois Press, 1982.
Bradby, David. *Beckett: Waiting for Godot*. Cambridge: Cambridge University Press, 2001.
Brater, Enoch. *Beyond Minimalism: Beckett's Late Style in the Theater*. New York: Oxford University Press, 1987.
Breuer, Josef, and Sigmund Freud. *Studies on Hysteria: The Standard Edition of the Complete Psychological Works of Sigmund Freud, Vol. 2*. Translated and edited by James Strachey with Anna Freud. London: Hogarth Press, 1981.
Brits, Baylee. 'Ritual, Code, and Matheme in Samuel Beckett's Quad'. *Journal of Modern Literature* 40, no. 4 (2017): 122–33.
Brook, Peter. *The Empty Space*. London: Penguin, 1990.
Bryden, Mary. 'Beckett and the Sound of Silence'. In *Samuel Beckett and Music*, edited by Mary Bryden, 21–46. Oxford: Clarendon Press, 1998.

Bryden, Mary. *Women in Samuel Beckett's Prose and Drama: Her Own Other*. Basingstoke: Palgrave Macmillan, 1993.
Bryden, Mary, ed. *Samuel Beckett and Music*. Oxford: Oxford University Press, 1998.
Calder, John. *The Theology of Samuel Beckett*. Surrey: Calder Publications, 2012.
Campbell, Julie. '*Echo's Bones* and Beckett's Disembodied Voices'. *Samuel Beckett Today/Aujourd'hui* 11 (2001): 454–60.
Campbell, Julie. 'A Voice Comes to One in the Dark. Imagine: Radio, the Listener, and the Dark Comedy of *All That Fall*'. In *Beckett and Death*, edited by Steven Barfield, Matthew Feldman and Philip Tew, 147–68. London: Continuum, 2009.
Carlson, Marvin. *The Haunted Stage: The Theatre as Memory Machine*. Ann Arbor: University of Michigan Press, 2003.
Carlson, Marvin. *Shattering Hamlet's Mirror: Theatre and Reality*. Ann Arbor: University of Michigan Press, 2016.
Chertok, Léon, and Isabelle Stengers. *A Critique of Psychoanalytic Reason: Hypnosis as a Scientific Problem from Lavoisier to Lacan*. Translated by Martha Noel Evans. Stanford: Stanford University Press, 1992.
Chiong, Kathryn. 'Nauman's Beckett Walk'. *October* 86 (1998): 63–81.
Coffey, Michael. *Samuel Beckett Is Closed*. New York: Foxrock Books, 2018.
Cohn, Ruby. *Back to Beckett*. Princeton: Princeton University Press, 1973.
Cohn, Ruby. *A Beckett Canon*. Ann Arbor: University of Michigan Press, 2001.
Cohn, Ruby. *Just Play: Beckett's Theatre*. Princeton: Princeton University Press, 1980.
Cohn, Ruby. 'A Krapp Chronology'. *Modern Drama* 49, no. 4 (Winter 2006): 514–24.
Connor, Steven. *Beckett, Modernism and the Material Imagination*. Cambridge: Cambridge University Press, 2014.
Connor, Steven. *Samuel Beckett: Repetition, Theory, and Text*. Oxford: Basil Blackwell, 1988.
Craig, Edward Gordon. *On the Art of the Theatre*. London: William Heinemann, 1911.
Craig, Edward Gordon. *Towards a New Theatre; Forty Designs for Stage Scenes with Critical Notes by the Inventor Edward Gordon Craig*. New York: B. Blom, 1969.
Crary, Jonathan. *24/7: Late Capitalism and the Ends of Sleep*. London: Verso, 2014.
Crary, Jonathan. *Suspensions of Perception: Attention, Spectacle, and Modern Culture*. Cambridge, MA: MIT Press, 2001.
Deleuze, Gilles. 'The Exhausted'. In *Essays Critical and Clinical*, translated by Daniel W. Smith and Michael A. Greco, 152–74. Minneapolis: University of Minnesota Press, 1997.

Deleuze, Gilles. *Francis Bacon: The Logic of Sensation*. Translated by Daniel W. Smith. London: Bloomsbury, 2017.

Derrida, Jacques. *Disseminations*. Translated by Barbara Johnson. London: Athlone Press, 1981.

Derrida, Jacques. *Writing and Difference*. Translated by Alan Bass. London: Routledge & Kegan Paul, 1981.

Diamond, Elin. *Unmaking Mimesis: Essays on Feminism and Theatre*. London: Routledge, 1997.

Dwan, Lisa. 'Beckett's Not I: How I Became the Ultimate Motormouth'. *Guardian*, 9 May 2013. https://www.theguardian.com/culture/2013/may/08/beckett-not-i-lisa-dwan.

Eckersall, Peter, Helena Grehan and Edward Scheer. *New Media Dramaturgy: Performance, Media and New-Materialism*. London: Palgrave Macmillan, 2017.

Elam, Keir. 'Catastrophic Mistakes: Beckett, Havel, the End'. *Samuel Beckett Today/Aujourd'hui* 3 (1994): 1–28.

Esslin, Martin. *Mediations: Essays on Brecht, Beckett, and the Media*. Baton Rouge: Louisiana State University Press, 1980.

Farbman, Herschel. *The Other Night: Dreaming, Writing, and Restlessness in Twentieth-Century Literature*. New York: Fordham University Press, 2008.

Fifield, Peter. 'Gaping Mouths and Bulging Bodies: Beckett and Francis Bacon'. *Journal of Beckett Studies* 18, nos. 1–2 (2009): 57–71.

Fischer, Iris Smith. *Mabou Mines: Making Avant-Garde Theatre in the 1970s*. Ann Arbor: University of Michigan Press, 2012.

Fischer-Lichte, Erika. *The Transformative Power of Performance: A New Aesthetics*. London: Routledge, 2008.

Ford, Thomas H. *Wordsworth and the Poetics of Air*. Cambridge: Cambridge University Press, 2018.

Fried, Michael. *Absorption and Theatricality: Painting and Beholder in the Age of Diderot*. Berkeley: University of California Press, 1980.

Garner Jr., Stanton B. 'Beckett, Merleau-Ponty, and the Phenomenological Body'. *Theatre Journal* 45, no. 4 (December 1993): 443–59.

Garner Jr., Stanton B. *Bodied Spaces: Phenomenology and Performance in Contemporary Drama*. New York: Cornell University Press, 1994.

Gibson, Andrew. *Beckett and Badiou*. Oxford: Oxford University Press, 2006.

Glanville, Jo. '"Godot Is Here": How Samuel Beckett and Vaclav Havel Changed History'. *Guardian*, 15 September 2009. https://www.theguardian.com/culture/2009/sep/15/vaclev-havel-samuel-beckett-catastrophe.

Gontarski, S. E. *Beckett Matters: Essays on Beckett's Late Modernism*. Edinburgh: Edinburgh University Press, 2017.

Gontarski, S. E. 'Birth Astride a Grave: Samuel Beckett's "Act Without Words 1"'. *Journal of Beckett Studies* 1 (1976): 37–40.

Gontarski, S. E. 'The Body in the Body of Beckett's Theatre'. *Samuel Beckett Today/Aujourd'hui* 11 (2002): 169–77.

Gontarski, S. E. 'Introduction: De-theatricalizing Theatre: The Post-*Play* Plays'. In Samuel Beckett, *The Theatrical Notebooks of Samuel Beckett, Vol. 4: The Shorter Plays*, edited by S.E. Gontarski, xv–xxix. London: Faber and New York: Grove Press, 1999.

Gontarski, S. E. 'Introduction'. In *Eleuthéria: A Play in Three Acts*, translated by Michael Brodsky, vii–xxii. New York: Foxrock, 1995.

Gontarski, S. E. 'Introduction: Towards a Minoritarian Criticism – The Questions We Ask'. In *The Edinburgh Companion to Samuel Beckett and the Arts*, edited by S. E. Gontarski, 1–13. Edinburgh: Edinburgh University Press, 2014.

Gontarski, S. E. 'Review: The World Première of "Ohio Impromptu", Directed by Alan Schneider at Columbus, Ohio'. *Journal of Beckett Studies* 8 (Autumn 1982): 133–36.

Gontarski, S. E. *Revisioning Beckett: Samuel Beckett's Decadent Turn*. London: Bloomsbury, 2018.

Gontarski, S. E. 'Staging Himself, or Beckett's Late Style in the Theatre'. *Samuel Beckett Today/Aujourd'hui* 6, no. 1 (1997): 87–97.

Goudouna, Sozita. *Beckett's* Breath *and the Visual Arts*. Edinburgh: Edinburgh University Press, 2018.

Gruber, William E. *Missing Persons: Character and Characterization in Modern Drama*. Athens: University of Georgia Press, 1994.

Guicharnaud, Jacques. *Modern French Theatre: From Giraudoux to Genet*. New Haven: Yale University Press, 1967.

Gussow, Mel. 'Stage: Disputed "Endgame" in Debut.' *New York Times*. 20 December 1984. http://www.nytimes.com/1984/12/20/arts/stage-disputed-endgame-in-debut.html?mcubz=0.

Habib, M. A. R. *A History of Literary Criticism: From Plato to the Present*. Maldon: Blackwell Publishing, 2005.

Harmon, Maurice (ed.). *No Author Better Served: The Correspondence of Samuel Beckett & Alan Schneider*. Cambridge, MA: Harvard University Press, 1998.

Hartel, Gaby, Klaus Völker and Thomas Irmer. 'The Reception of Beckett's Theatre and Television Pieces in West and East Germany'. In *The International Reception of Samuel Beckett*, edited by Mark Nixon and Matthew Feldman, 79–96. London: Continuum, 2009.

Havel, Václav. 'The Power of the Powerless'. Translated by Paul Wilson. In *The Power of the Powerless: Citizens Against the State in Central Eastern Europe*, edited by John Keane, 10–59. New York: Routledge, 2009.

Heidegger, Martin. *Being and Time*, 7th edn. Translated by John Macquarie and Edmund Robinson. Oxford: Basil Blackwell, 1973.

Heidegger, Martin. *Zollikon Seminars: Protocols, Conversations, Letters*. Edited by Medard Boss. Translated by Franz Mayr and Richard Askay. Evanston, IL: Northwestern University Press, 2001.

Heron, Jonathan, and Nicholas Johnson. 'Critical Pedagogies and the Theatre Laboratory'. *Research in Drama Education: The Journal of Applied Theatre and Performance* 22, no. 2 (2017): 282–7.

Heron, Jonathan, and Nicholas Johnson (eds). 'The Performance Issue'. *Journal of Beckett Studies* 23, no. 1 (2014).

Heron, Jonathan, and Nicholas Johnson, with Burç İdem Dinçel, Gavin Quinn, Sarah Jane Scaife and Áine Josephine Tyrrell. 'The Samuel Beckett Laboratory 2013.' *Journal of Beckett Studies* 23, no. 1 (2014): 73–94.

Hulle, Dirk Van, and Shane Weller. *Beckett Digital Manuscript Project, Vol. 7: The Making of Samuel Beckett's* Fin de partie / Endgame. Brussels: University Press Antwerp and London: Bloomsbury, 2018.

Hulle, Dirk Van. '"Accursed Creator": Beckett, Romanticism, and "the Modern Prometheus"'. *Samuel Beckett Today/Aujourd'hui* 18 (2007): 15–29.

Ingalls, Zoe. 'A Rich, Idiosyncratic Journey into the Plays of Samuel Beckett'. *Chronicle of Higher Education* 38, no. 35 (May 1992): B5.

Johnson, Nicholas E. '"The Neatness of Identifications": Transgressing Beckett's Genres in Ireland and Northern Ireland, 2000–2015'. In *Staging Beckett in Ireland and Northern Ireland*, edited by Trish McTighe and David Tucker, 185–204. London: Bloomsbury, 2017.

Jung, C. G. *Analytical Psychology: Its Theory and Practice, The Tavistock Lectures*. London: Routledge & Kegan Paul, 1976.

Kalb, Jonathan. *Beckett in Performance*. New York: Cambridge University Press, 1991.

Kantor, Tadeusz. *A Journey through Other Spaces: Essays and Manifestos, 1944–1990*. Berkeley: University of California Press, 1993.

Katz, Daniel. *Saying I No More: Subjectivity and Consciousness in the Prose of Samuel Beckett*. Evanston, IL: Northwestern University Press, 1999.

Klaver, Elizabeth. 'Samuel Beckett's *Ohio Impromptu*, *Quad*, and *What Where*: How It Is in the Matrix of Text and Television'. *Contemporary Literature* 32, no. 3 (Autumn 1991): 366–82.

Kleist, Heinrich von. 'On the Marionette Theatre'. *TDR: The Drama Review* 16, no. 3 (September 1972): 22–6.

Knowlson, Elizabeth, and James Knowlson (eds). *Beckett Remembering, Remembering Beckett*. London: Bloomsbury, 2006.

Knowlson, James. *Damned to Fame: The Life of Samuel Beckett*. London: Bloomsbury, 1996.

Knowlson, James, and John Haynes. *Images of Beckett*. Cambridge: Cambridge University Press, 2003.

Knowlson, James, and John Pilling. *Frescoes of the Skull*. London: John Calder, 1979.

Köhler, Wolfgang. *The Mentality of Apes*. Translated by Ella Winter. London: Kegan Paul, Trench, Trubner, 1931.
Lane, Allen. *Symbolism*. London: Penguin Books, 1979.
Lassiter, Laurie. 'David Warrilow: Creating Symbol and Cypher'. *TDR: The Drama Review* 29, no. 4 (Winter 1985): 3–12.
Latour, Bruno, and Steve Wolgar. *Laboratory Life: The Construction of Scientific Facts*, 2nd edn. Princeton: Princeton University Press, 1986.
Lawrence, Tim. *Samuel Beckett's Critical Aesthetics*. London: Palgrave Macmillan, 2018.
Laws, Catherine. 'Beckett – Feldman – Johns'. In *Beckett at 100: Revolving It All*, edited by Linda Ben-Zvi and Angela Moorjani, 230–45. Oxford: Oxford University Press, 2008.
Lefebvre, Henri. *The Production of Space*. Translated by Donald Nicholson-Smith. Malden, MA: Blackwell Publishing, 1991.
Lehmann, Hans-Thies. *Postdramatic Theatre*. Translated by Karen Jürs-Munby. London: Routledge, 2006.
Luckhurst, Mary. 'Giving Up the Ghost: The Actor's Body as Haunted House'. In *Theatre and Ghosts: Materiality, Performance, and Modernity*, edited by Mary Luckhurst and Emilie Morin, 163–77. London: Palgrave Macmillan, 2014.
Marcuse, Herbert. *Art and Liberation: Collected Papers of Herbert Marcuse, Vol. 4*. Edited by Douglas Kellner. London: Routledge, 2007.
Martin, Carol. *Theatre of the Real*. Basingstoke: Palgrave Macmillan, 2013.
Massumi, Brian. *Parables for the Virtual*. Durham: Duke University Press, 2002.
Massumi, Brian. *Politics of Affect*. Cambridge: Polity, 2015.
Maude, Ulrika. *Beckett, Technology and the Body*. Cambridge: Cambridge University Press, 2009.
Maude, Ulrika. 'The Body of Memory: Beckett and Merleau-Ponty'. In *Beckett and Philosophy*, edited by Richard Lane, 108–22. London: Palgrave Macmillan, 2002.
Maude, Ulrika. 'Convulsive Aesthetics: Beckett, Chaplin and Charcot'. In *The Edinburgh Companion to Samuel Beckett and the Arts*, edited by S. E. Gontarski, 44–53. Edinburgh: Edinburgh University Press, 2014.
McCarren, Felicia. 'The "Symptomatic Act" circa 1900: Hysteria, Hypnosis, Electricity, Dance'. *Critical Inquiry* 21, no. 4 (1995): 748–74.
McHenry, Deni McIntosh. ' "Faust in His Study" Reconsidered: A Record of Jewish Patronage and Mysticism in Mid-Seventeenth-Century Amsterdam'. *Yale University Art Gallery Bulletin* (Spring 1989): 9–19.
McMillan, Dougald, and Martha Fehsenfeld, *Beckett in the Theatre: The Author as Practical Playwright and Director, Volume 1: From* Waiting for Godot *to* Krapp's Last Tape. London: John Calder and New York: Riverrun Press, 1988.
McMullan, Anna. 'Beckett as Director: The Art of Mastering Failure'. In *The Cambridge Companion to Beckett*, edited by John Pilling, 196–208. Cambridge: Cambridge University Press, 1994.

McMullan, Anna. *Performing Embodiment in Samuel Beckett's Drama*. London: Routledge, 2010.

McMullan, Anna. 'Samuel Beckett's "JM Mime": Generic Mutations of a Dramatic Fragment'. *Samuel Beckett Today/Aujourd'hui* 16, no. 1 (2006): 333–45.

McMullan, Anna. *Theatre on Trial: Samuel Beckett's Later Drama*. New York: Routledge, 1993.

McMullan, Anna. 'When Beckett Wrote *Waiting for Godot* He Really Didn't Know a Lot about Theatre'. *Telegraph*, 5 January, 2013. https://www.telegraph.co.uk/culture/theatre/theatre-features/9780077/When-Beckett-wrote-Waiting-for-Godot-he-really-didnt-know-a-lot-about-theatre.html.

McMullan, Anna, and Graham Saunders. 'Staging Beckett and Contemporary Theatre and Performance Cultures'. *Contemporary Theatre Review* 28, no. 1 (2018): 3–9.

McTighe, Trish. *The Haptic Aesthetic in Samuel Beckett's Drama*. London: Palgrave Macmillan, 2013.

McTighe, Trish, and David Tucker (eds). *Staging Beckett in Ireland and Northern Ireland*. London: Bloomsbury, 2017.

Melia, Matthew. 'Architecture and Cruelty in the Writings of Genet, Artaud and Beckett: A Discussion of Recent Research'. *International Journal of the Humanities* 8, no. 9 (2010): 39–48.

Mitchell, Robert. *Experimental Life: Vitalism in Romantic Science and Literature*. Baltimore: Johns Hopkins University Press, 2013.

Moorjani, Angela. '"Just looking": Ne(i)ther-World Icons, Elsheimer Nocturnes, and Other Simultaneities in Beckett's *Play*'. In *Beckett at 100: Revolving It All*, edited by Linda Ben-Zvi and Angela Moorjani, 123–38. Oxford: Oxford University Press, 2008.

Morin, Emilie. *Beckett's Political Imagination*. Cambridge: Cambridge University Press, 2017.

Naito, Jonathan Tadashi. 'Writing Silence: Samuel Beckett's Early Mimes', *Samuel Beckett Today/Aujourd'hui* 19, no. 1 (2008): 393–402.

Nixon, Mark. 'Beckett's Unpublished Canon'. In *The Edinburgh Companion to Samuel Beckett and the Arts*, edited by S. E. Gontarski, 282–305. Edinburgh: Edinburgh University Press, 2014.

Oppenheim, Lois. *The Painted Word: Samuel Beckett's Dialogue with Art*. Ann Arbor: University of Michigan Press, 2000.

Ovid. *Metamorphoses*. Translated by A. D. Melville. Oxford: Oxford University Press, 1986.

Paterson, Eddie. *The Contemporary American Monologue: Performance and Politics*. London: Bloomsbury, 2015.

Phelan, Peggy. 'Lessons in Blindness from Samuel Beckett'. *Modern Language Association* 119, no. 5 (2004): 1279–88.

Piette, Adam. 'Beckett, Affect and the Face'. *Textual Practice* 25, no. 2 (2011): 281–95.

Poulain, Alexandra. 'Fragments au Bouffes du Nord'. *The Beckett Circle / Le Cercle de Beckett: Newsletter of the Samuel Beckett Society* 30, no. 1 (Spring 2007): 7–8.

Pronko, Leonard Cabell. *Avant-Garde: The Experimental Theatre in France*. Berkeley: University of California Press, 1963.

Puchner, Martin. *Stage Fright: Modernism, Anti-Theatricality, and Drama*. Baltimore: Johns Hopkins University Press, 2002.

Quigley, Gabriel, and Sarah Jane Scaife. 'Howling from the Margins of History: Beckett's Women Speak'. *The Beckett Circle* (Spring 2018): n. pag.

Rabaté, Jean-Michel. 'Beckett's Ghosts and Fluxions'. *Samuel Beckett Today/Aujourd'hui* 5 (1996): 23–41.

Rae, Paul. *Theatre & Human Rights*. Basingstoke: Palgrave Macmillan, 2009.

Ricks, Christopher. *Beckett's Dying Words: The Clarendon Lectures, 1990*. Oxford: Clarendon Press, 1993.

Rimbaud, Arthur. Rimbaud to Georges Izambard, 13 May 1871. In *Complete Works*, translated by Paul Schmidt, 113–14. New York: HarperCollins, 2008.

Scaife, Sarah Jane. 'Practice in Focus: Beckett in the City'. In *Staging Beckett in Ireland and Northern Ireland*, edited by Trish McTighe and David Tucker, 153–67. London: Bloomsbury, 2017.

Sheehan, Paul (2009) 'Beckett's Ghosts: Monitoring a Phenomenology of Sleep'. In *Beckett and Phenomenology*, edited by Ulrika Maude and Matthew Feldman, 158–76. London: Continuum.

States, Bert O. '*Catastrophe*: Beckett's Laboratory / Theatre'. *Modern Drama* 30, no. 1 (Spring 1987): 14–22.

States, Bert O. *Great Reckonings in Little Rooms: On the Phenomenology of the Theatre*. Berkeley: University of California Press, 1987.

Stinson, Emmett. *Satirizing Modernism: Aesthetic Autonomy, Romanticism, and the Avant-Garde*. London: Bloomsbury, 2017.

Stott, Andrew. *Comedy*, 2nd edn. London: Routledge, 2014.

Tajiri, Yoshiki. *Samuel Beckett and the Prosthetic Body: The Organs and Senses in Modernism*. London: Palgrave Macmillan, 2007.

Taylor, Paul. 'Beckett Trilogy: *Not I/Footfalls/Rockaby*, Theatre Review – "An Unforgettable Show"'. *Independent*, 14 January 2014. http://www.independent.co.uk/artsentertainment/theatre-dance/reviews/beckett-trilogy-not-ifootfallsrockaby-theatre-review-an-unforgettable-show-9058659.html.

Thurston, Luke. 'Outselves: Beckett, Bion and Beyond'. *Journal of Modern Literature* 32, no. 3 (2009): 121–43.

Tubridy, Derval. 'Samuel Beckett and Performance Art'. *Journal of Beckett Studies* 23, no. 1 (2014): 34–53.

Tucker, David. *Samuel Beckett and Arnold Geulincx: Tracing 'a Literary Fantasia'*. London: Continuum, 2012.

Uhlmann, Anthony. *Beckett and Poststructuralism*. Cambridge: Cambridge University Press, 2009.

Uhlmann, Anthony. 'Samuel Beckett and the Occluded Image'. In *Beckett After Beckett*, edited by S. E. Gontarski and Anthony Uhlmann, 79–97. Gainesville: University Press of Florida, 2006.

Uhlmann, Anthony. *Thinking in Literature*. New York: Continuum, 2011.

Wagstaff, Graham F. 'On the Centrality of the Concept of an Altered State to Definitions of Hypnosis'. *Journal of Mind-Body Regulation* 2, no. 2 (2014): 90–108.

Wakeling, Corey. '"Only Her Mouth Could Move": Sensory Deprivation and the Billie Whitelaw Plays'. *TDR: The Drama Review* 59, no. 3 (2015): 91–107.

Wakeling, Corey. 'Sleeplessness in Sleep: Beckett's Gestures of Dream'. *Performance Research* 21, no. 1 (2016): 42–8.

Wakeling, Corey. 'Samuel Beckett's Hypnotic Theatre'. *Modern Drama* 60, no. 3 (2017): 342–63

Weber, Samuel. *Theatricality as Medium*. New York: Fordham University Press, 2004.

Weil, Simone. *Gravity and Grace*. Translated by Emma Crawford and Mario von der Ruhr. London: Routledge, 2002.

Weiss, Katherine. 'Perceiving Bodies in Beckett's *Play*'. *Samuel Beckett Today/Aujourd'hui* 11 (2001): 186–93.

Weller, Shane. *Beckett, Literature, and the Ethics of Alterity*. Basingstoke: Palgrave Macmillan, 2006.

Weller, Shane. *Literature, Philosophy, Nihilism: The Uncanniest of Guests*. London: Continuum, 2008.

Weller, Shane. 'Phenomenologies of the Nothing: Democritus, Heidegger, Beckett'. In *Beckett and Phenomenology*, edited by Ulrika Maude and Matthew Feldman, 39–55. London: Continuum, 2009.

Whitelaw, Billie. *Billie Whitelaw… Who He?* London: Hodder and Stoughton, 1995.

Worth, Katherine. *The Irish Drama of Europe from Yeats to Beckett*. London: Athlone Press, 1978.

Worth, Katherine. *Samuel Beckett: Life Journeys*. Oxford: Oxford University Press, 1999.

Worthen, W. B. *Drama: Between Poetry and Performance*. Chichester: Wiley-Blackwell, 2010.

Worthen, W. B. *The Idea of the Actor: Drama and the Ethics of Performance*. Princeton: Princeton University Press, 1984.

Yeats, W. B. *Plays for an Irish Theatre by W.B. Yeats, with Designs by Gordon Craig*. London: A. H. Bullen, 1911.

Yeats, W. B. *The Variorum Edition of the Plays of W. B. Yeats*. Edited by Russell K. Alspach. London: Macmillan, 1966.

Young, Jordan R. *The Beckett Actor: Jack MacGowran, Beginning to End*. Beverly Hills: Moonstone Press, 1987.

Zarrilli, Phillip B. '"On the Edge of a Breath, Looking": Cultivating the Actor's Bodymind through Asian Martial/Meditation Arts'. In *Acting*

Reconsidered: A Theoretical and Practical Guide, 2nd edn, edited by Phillip B. Zarrilli, 181–99. London: Routledge, 2002.

Zarilli, Phillip B. 'The Metaphysical Studio'. *TDR: The Drama Review* 46, no. 2 (Summer 2002): 157–70.

Zilliacus, Clas. *Beckett and Broadcasting*. Åbo: Åbo Akademi, 1976.

Zola, Émile. 'Émile Zola, *Naturalism in the Theatre*, 1881'. Translated by Albert Bermel. In *A Sourcebook on Naturalist Theatre*, edited by Christopher Innes, 46–52. London: Routledge, 2000.

Index

A Piece of Monologue 1, 101, 163
abstraction 11–14, 16, 28, 29, 92,
 122, 128
Ackerley, Chris 32, 88
Act Without Words I 1, 4, 5, 6, 7, 23–5,
 28, 34–6, 38, 41, 42, 45, 47–8, 64,
 65, 67, 82, 118, 140
 See also acts without words
Act Without Words II 1, 5, 23, 24, 25,
 28, 30, 34, 35, 38, 42, 45, 64, 101,
 102, 158, 159, 160
 See also acts without words
acts without words 18, 27, 164, 167, 168
 See also *Act Without Words I*; *Act
 Without Words II*
Adamov, Arthur 27, 37, 75
adaphatrôce 20, 147, 149
adaptation 20, 21, 26, 34, 35, 45, 56
 Godot for television 44–5
 prose to stage 147–68
 See also adaphatrôce
Adorno, Theodor 5, 14, 15, 25, 43–5,
 48, 82, 116–17, 170 n.28, 171 n.5,
 174 n.62, 179 n.31, 184 n.21
aesthetics 11, 14, 16, 19, 28, 29, 34,
 44, 52–4, 56, 58, 61, 77, 80–1,
 175 n.13
'affective athleticism' 14
 See also 'negative athleticism'
Agamben, Giorgio 19
 gesture 98, 105, 106–7
 parabasis 119, 120–1, 167, 168,
 191 n.62
 theory of infancy 112, 121–3
agency (human, performer) 2, 18, 38,
 41, 68, 70, 89, 139
 See also constraint; sensory
 deprivation
agency (playscript) 33, 34, 126, 127,
 172 n.27

Akalaitis, JoAnne 151–2
All That Fall 25, 101, 149
animal behaviour 6, 43, 134
Anna O. (Bertha Pappenheim)
 129–30, 137
anti-realist tendencies *see* non-
 naturalistic dramaturgy
anti-theatricality 41, 43, 44, 74, 80, 82,
 122, 157–8, 160
apes 6–8, 43
Artaud, Antonin 14, 17, 19, 27, 31, 74,
 75, 76, 78, 93, 94, 153, 178 n.11
 See also 'affective athleticism'
Asmus, Walter 20, 51, 64, 67, 92, 125,
 130–1, 136, 141–2, 144, 177 n.41,
 185 n.4, 186 n.32, 191 n.61
authorial intent *see* authorship
authorship 3, 16, 20, 21, 80
autonomy 3, 11, 12, 13, 16, 17, 43, 65,
 117, 121, 127, 133, 134–5, 139
avant-gardism 17, 19, 23, 26, 31, 37,
 39, 44, 47, 73–8, 85, 147, 149
 Godot and 91–4

Bacon, Francis 28–9, 40
Bair, Deirdre 2, 75
Balkin, Sarah 66, 84, 100
Baudelaire, Charles 85
Bauer, Hans 37–8
Beckett
 'Dante…Bruno. Vico…Joyce' 162
 'J.M. Mime' 34, 164
 'Long After Chamfort' 99, 109
 'Mime du rêveur' 27, 28
 'pas à pas' 109, 116, 121–2
Berlin, Normand 46
Bion, Wilfred 155
Blanchot, Maurice 98
Blau, Herbert 3, 4, 26, 70, 81, 93,
 118–19, 151, 166, 167

See also San Francisco Actor's
   Workshop
Blin, Roger 27, 39, 75, 94, 178 n.11
Bloch, Ernst 117
body *see* physicality
Bourdieu, Pierre 12, 13
Bray, Barbara 116
Breath 1, 55, 148, 153–5
Brecht, Bertolt 2, 9, 14, 151, 160
Brechtian *see* Brecht, Bertolt
Breuer, Josef 20, 129–30
Breuer, Lee 148, 150, 151
Brits, Baylee 33, 172 n.29
Brook, Peter 21, 26, 156–7, 159, 161
   anti-theatricalism 157–8
   the empty space 158, 159, 160
   See also Fragments (Peter Brook
      production)
Bryden, Mary 137–8, 190 n.47

cage 7, 8, 23, 37
   See also enclosure
Cage, John 15, 166
calculation 1, 18, 28, 29, 31, 32, 33, 36,
   66, 68, 69, 147, 162, 165, 172 n.29
Campbell, Julie 62, 101
Carlson, Marvin 53, 64, 78, 122–3,
   127, 165
Cartesian thought 24, 134, 156
Catastrophe 8, 9, 19, 39, 99, 109–23
   the body in 67, 99, 106, 117, 122
   spectacle 19, 99, 111, 112, 113, 116,
      118–21, 122–3
   'theatre-as-laboratory' 8
   tragedy and 1, 8, 112, 113
   Václav Havel connection 19, 109–
      11, 113, 114–15, 118, 120, 123
Chamfort, Nicholas-Sébastien Roch
   99, 109, 121
Chaplin, Charlie 4, 44, 135
Charcot, Jean-Martin 20, 129, 130,
   132, 136, 138–40
Chekhov, Anton 62, 63
Chertok, Léon 127, 145
Chiong, Kathryn 4, 167

choreography 3, 4, 18, 26, 27, 28, 31,
   32, 34, 35, 36, 41, 44, 46–7, 48,
   51, 63, 105, 161, 162, 166, 167,
   169 n.4, 172 n.29
closet drama 47, 73–4, 78, 81, 89, 158,
   178 n.3
clothing *see* costume
Clov 4, 18, 27–8, 41, 42, 43, 44, 46
clown 1, 4, 37–9, 41, 42, 43, 48, 160
   See also pantomime
Cluchey, Rick 93, 168
Coffey, Michael 163
Cohn, Ruby 24, 26, 74, 75, 85, 91,
   94–5, 147
Collins, Christine 64, 177 n.41
Come and Go 1, 55, 158, 160, 166
comedy *see* comic elements
comic elements 23–5, 26, 44–6, 97,
   119–20, 135, 158
   See also slapstick (comedy)
confinement *see* enclosure
Connor, Steven 54, 100, 167
consciousness 19, 53, 97, 99–100,
   102, 103, 105, 119, 120, 128,
   132–4, 137
constraint 16, 19, 23–4, 26, 33, 49, 52,
   54–5, 61, 65, 68, 77, 179 n.22
contingency 5, 11, 12, 20, 21, 30, 48,
   62, 64, 66, 68, 76, 77, 80, 85, 104,
   126, 152, 156, 167
Copeau, Jacques 39
Corneille, Pierre 177–8 n.1
corporeal mime 38, 39
   See also pantomime
costume 32, 38, 59, 67, 101, 159, 160
Crary, Jonathan 112, 131, 135
Cronyn, Hume 50

dance 3, 18, 34, 37, 44–5, 63, 157
Dante Alighieri 88, 97, 147, 150, 162
Debord, Guy 112
Deburau, Jean-Baptiste Gaspard 38–9
Decroux, Étienne 38, 39
dehumanization 111, 113, 115, 116,
   117–18, 123

Deleuze, Gilles 28–9, 40, 53, 69, 167, 175 n.13
Le Dépeupleur see *The Lost Ones* (short story)
Derrida, Jacques 17, 47, 48, 170 n.35, 174 n.73
Descartes, René *see* Cartesian thought
Deschevaux-Dumesnil, Suzanne 75
desubjectivization *see* dehumanization
Devine, George 42, 50
diagram 4, 5, 18, 23, 26, 28–37, 41, 42, 44, 55, 64–5, 68–9, 126, 160, 162, 165–7
Diamond, Elin 14, 15, 16, 26, 130, 138, 139
diminution *see* miniaturization
'drama of sight' 54, 62, 64, 66, 70
Dream of Fair to Middling Women 97
Duchess Theatre 125, 185 n.4
Duckworth, Colin 2
duration 1, 3, 30, 33, 57, 68–9, 89, 93, 113, 153–4
Dwan, Lisa 125–6, 130, 136, 141–4, 185 n.4, 186 n.32

Echo's Bones (short story) 97
Eckersall, Peter 165
Eh Joe 50–1, 63, 70, 101, 103
Elam, Keir 9, 112, 114
Eleuthéria 19, 27, 34, 73–7, 87, 178 n.14
Embers 63
En attendant Godot see *Waiting for Godot*
enclosure 4, 6, 7, 8, 23, 24, 32, 61, 64, 66, 67, 68, 92, 95, 97–8, 130, 147, 150, 167
Endgame 17–18, 29, 34, 37–8, 39, 42, 61, 101, 164
   Act Without Words I and 42
   Theodor Adorno about 14, 43, 44, 82
   choreography 18, 27–8, 167
   drafts 27–8
   mime 4, 25, 27–8, 43–4

   See also Clov; clown
Endspiel see *Endgame*
Enough 34
epic theatre 14, 76
ethology *see* animal behaviour
être manqué 155–6, 166
exhaustion 53, 62, 69, 159, 167, 175 n.13
experimental art 2–3, 16, 26
expropriation 17, 119

Farbman, Herschel 98
Faust (character) 89, 90
Fehsenfeld, Martha 168, 171 n.37
Feldman, Morton 161, 162, 163, 166
Film 4
film and television *see* screen
Fin de partie see *Endgame*
Fischer, Irish Smith 151–2
Fischer-Lichte, Erika 15, 16
fool (role, type) 43, 88, 164
Footfalls 1, 18, 20, 31, 34, 51, 63–7, 101, 125, 131, 143, 144, 167
   Billie Whitelaw performing 18, 50, 58, 63–4, 66, 67
   choreography of footsteps 121–2, 162, 177 n.41
   disembodiment in 101
   Lisa Dwan performing 125, 185 n.4
   psychoanalysis 130, 131, 140
Fragments (Peter Brook production), 21, 156–7, 158
Freud, Sigmund 20, 99, 129–30, 135
Fried, Michael 40–1
Friedrich, Caspar David 91
fugue 5, 105, 165–6, 168, 190 n.47

Garner Jr., Stanton B. 53, 69
Genet, Jean 93, 94
Geulincx, Arnold 24, 68, 134, 179 n.22
The Goad 35
Gontarski, S. E. 24, 26, 33, 54–5, 75, 145, 147, 155, 180–1 n.62
Gray, Spalding 13–14
Greenberg, Clement 11, 12, 13, 14

Grehan, Helena 165
Grotowski, Jerzy 2, 51–2, 152
Guicharnaud, Jacques 27

Habib, M. A. R. 84
Haerdter, Michael 17
Hall, Peter 92
Hamlet 62, 86, 123
happenings 3, 36
Happy Days 1, 39, 40, 51, 83, 105, 106
  final tableau 40–1, 43, 104
  gesture in 99, 100, 103–4
  Jean-Louis Barrault as Willie 39–40, 41, 43–4, 48, 180 n.38
  pantomime and 40–2, 44
  scenography 83
  sleeplessness in 102, 103
  suspended animation 40
haunted spectacle *see* haunting
haunting 19, 49, 52–3, 58, 63–4, 66, 71, 103, 110–12, 122–3, 127, 141, 165
  See also spectrality
Havel, Václav *see* *Catastrophe*, Václav Havel connection
Haynes, John 33
Hendry, Robbie 67
Herbert, Jocelyn 57
Herm, Klaus 51
Heron, Jonathan 36–7
hope 109, 110, 111, 115–17, 121, 123
Houben, Jos 158–9, 160
humanism 38, 47, 110, 145
Human Wishes 73–4
Hunter, Kathryn 158–9, 160, 161–4, 165–6
hypnosis 20, 133, 134–5
  affect and 127, 129, 134–5
  clinical applications 129, 130, 132, 136, 138–40
  memory and 127–8, 129, 133
  stage 132
  as a technology of attention 131, 135

therapeutic application 20, 126, 127, 129, 132, 135, 140
  See also hypnotic theatre
hypnotic theatre 20, 125–8, 130, 131–45
hypnotic therapy *see* hypnosis

Ibsen, Henrik 75, 84–5
Ill Seen Ill Said 140–1
imitation *see* mimesis
immersion *see* immersive dramaturgy
immersive dramaturgy 20, 35, 58, 125–6, 127–8, 131, 133, 144, 148–50
impossibility 8, 15, 18, 23, 61, 62, 77, 78, 98, 100, 104, 111, 119, 150, 180 n.35
incarceration *see* enclosure
indeterminacy 2, 13, 19, 76, 168
Ingalls, Zoe 49
installation (art) 3, 17, 36, 153–4, 165
intentionality 12, 13, 15, 95, 127, 148, 151, 167
  See also authorship
intermediality 3, 34, 76, 153, 191 n.54
Ionesco, Eugène 27, 37

Jarry, Alfred 74, 78
Johnson, Nicholas 36–7
Johnson, Samuel (Dr Johnson) 74, 112
Joyce, Paul 35
Jung, Carl 101, 155

Kafka, Franz 40, 122, 161
Kalb, Jonathan 26, 147, 149–50, 151, 188 n.9
Kantor, Tadeusz 13, 151, 188 n.11
Katz, Daniel 155
Keaton, Buster 4, 44
Knowlson, James 6, 25, 32, 33, 53, 55, 75, 100, 105, 115, 131, 141, 143
  anecdote about Beckett and *Catastrophe* 115
  on Beckett and the visual arts 89, 91, 105, 133, 149

Köhler, Wolfgang 6–8, 140
Krapp's Last Tape 61, 100, 103, 168

Lawlor, Tom 92
Laws, Catherine 163
l'empêchement-oeil 82–3, 150
Lahr, Bert 45, 174 n.68
Lane, Allen 82, 83–5
Latour, Bruno 7, 9, 18
Lawrence, Tim 8, 76, 77
le Brocquy, Louis 92
Lear (*King Lear*) 10, 164
Lefebvre, Henri 38
Lehmann, Hans-Thies 56, 176 n.14
Les Enfants du paradis (*Children of Paradise*) (1945 film) 39–40
Levinas, Emmanuel 141
Lewis, Jim 33
light (dramaturgy) 10, 19, 25, 29, 32, 38, 61, 63, 68, 70–1, 81, 94, 97, 99, 101, 103, 104, 113, 118, 120, 125, 140, 159, 163–4, 165, 168
    See also Ohio Impromptu, Manichean elements; *Play*, lighting
live body *see* liveness
live materiality *see* liveness
live performance *see* liveness
liveness
    actor's presence and 14, 19, 48, 50, 51, 63–6, 67–70, 81–2, 106, 107, 123, 139, 165
    corporeality and 70
    dramaturgy and 5, 11, 14, 17, 20, 30, 34, 49–53, 55, 56, 61–2, 64–7, 68, 70, 74, 77, 100, 103, 120, 123, 126–7, 150, 153–4, 159, 166, 168
    Herbert Blau's concept of 70, 81, 118
    spectatorship and 95, 106, 123, 126, 127, 168
    subjectivity and 62, 114
The Lost Ones (Mabou Mines production) 20, 147–53, 161, 163, 167

The Lost Ones (short story) 29, 147–9, 172 n.17
Lugné-Poë, Aurélien 84

Mabou Mines 20, 26, 147–53, 161, 163, 167, 189 n.39
    See also The Lost Ones (Mabou Mines production)
MacGowran, Jack 34, 51, 164
Maeterlinck, Maurice 82, 87, 91
Magee, Patrick 168, 191 n.61
Magni, Marcello 158–9
Mallarmé, Stephane
    concept of mime 47, 48, 85, 174 n.73
    La Livre 74, 83, 178 n.3
    symbolism 79, 82, 85, 88, 95
Malone Dies 154–5
manifesto 2, 75, 86
Marceau, Marcel 37, 38, 39, 173 n.44
Marcuse, Herbert 19, 109–11, 116–17, 119, 121, 123
Marinetti, Filippo 78
marionette 78–9, 82, 115
    See also Yeats, William Butler, Edward Gordon Craig
Martin, Alston 167
Martin, Carol 10–11
Martin, Jean 167–8
Marx Brothers 44, 46
Massumi, Brian 52, 65, 127
mathematics 33, 36
Maude, Ulrika 58–9, 81, 100, 137
McCarren, Felicia 139–40
McGovern, Barry 36, 92
McHenry, Deni Mcintosh 89
McMillan, Dougald 168, 171 n.37
McMullan, Anna 16, 18, 32, 34, 52–3, 58, 81, 181 n.79
McTighe, Trish 104
Melia, Matthew 93
Melville, Herman 161
Mendel, Deryk 37
Mercier et Camier (*Mercier and Camier*) 76

Meredith, Burgess 45
Merleau-Ponty, Maurice 53, 58–9
Mesmer, Franz 20, 134, 138, 139
metatheatricality 13, 19, 23, 24, 25, 43, 44, 76, 85, 87, 91, 95, 112, 118
method acting 2, 49, 51
Meyerhold, Vsevolod 14
mime *see* pantomime
mimesis 28, 38, 39, 41, 42, 47, 48, 66, 78, 79, 94, 95, 111, 116, 117, 123, 130, 138, 141, 156, 157, 158, 159, 166
mimicry *see* mimesis
the miniature *see* miniaturization
miniaturization 19, 88–90, 93, 147–8, 165, 180–1 n.62
mirlitonnades 116, 121, 183–4 n.6
See also 'Long After Chamfort'; 'pas à pas'
mise en scène 34, 92, 105, 140, 189 n.40
Mitchell, Pamela 38
Mitchell, Rand 181 n.62
Mitchell, Robert 11, 12, 14, 15, 16
modernism 12, 13, 14, 15, 16, 42, 43
  autonomy and 11, 12, 13, 14, 16
  Beckett as a modernist 2, 25, 116
  concept of 11, 12, 13, 14, 15, 16, 26, 39, 42, 43, 45, 47, 74, 116, 158, 161
  modernist theatre 14, 43, 47, 48, 74, 158
monologist *see* monologue
monologue 1, 49, 52, 55–6, 59, 61–9, 71, 73, 81, 89–90, 100–2, 104, 120, 127, 137, 143, 148–50, 163–6
Moorjani, Angela 55
multimedia 3, 4, 11, 12, 15, 34, 76
  See also intermediality
Murphy, Peter 32
music 33, 45, 63, 142, 163
music-hall *see* vaudeville

Nacht und Träume 19, 97, 99–100, 103, 104–6, 107
Naito, Jonathan Tadashi 38–9, 42
Nancy, Jean-Luc 167
naturalism 9, 10, 41, 48, 51, 56, 59, 83, 84, 85, 158, 166, 170 n.21
Nauman, Bruce 3, 4, 26, 167, 169 n.4
negation 8, 14, 21, 43, 53, 77, 109, 113, 116–17
'negative athleticism' 52, 57–8, 61, 70, 71, 166
negativity 14, 16, 19, 77, 117, 175 n.13
  See also negation
Neither (Beckett fragment) 161–2, 165, 166, 168, 189 n.40
Neither (Morton Feldman score) 163, 166, 189 n.40
Neither (Peter Brook adaptation) see *Fragments*
Nietzsche, Friedrich 98, 99
Nixon, Mark 27
non-naturalistic dramaturgy 58, 88
Not I 18, 34, 49–52, 54, 125, 144
  Auditor character 56, 143, 186–7 n.32
  hypnotic elements 130, 136–8, 140
  Mouth role 49, 51–2, 55, 57, 59–62, 67, 136–8, 142–3
  narrative 55–6, 59–60, 136–8
  performance 20, 50, 52, 59–62, 70–1, 141–3, 185 n.4
  rehearsal 49–50, 57–8, 59–62
  scenography 56–7, 58, 61–2, 141–2, 143–4
  See also Dwan, Lisa; immersive dramaturgy; 'negative athleticism'; sensory deprivation; spectatorship; Whitelaw, Billie

Oh les beaux jours see *Happy Days*
Ohio Impromptu 1, 39, 77, 86, 101, 104, 180–1 n.62
  Manichean elements 87–9, 90, 91

post-symbolist style 77
ontology 8, 14, 23, 24, 25, 32–3, 60, 68, 93, 97, 98, 99, 103, 109, 133, 147, 150, 162, 179 n.22
  See also paraontological space
Oppenheim, Lois 150

Page, Anthony 52, 57, 62, 141
painting *see* aesthetics
Pan Pan Theatre Company 33, 167, 172–3 n.30, 191 n.54
pantomime, 14, 18, 23–48, 51, 56, 83, 101, 104, 105, 126, 135, 156–66, 167, 168
  See also Mallarmé, Stephane, concept of mime
paraontological space 119–20, 122
parody 16, 25, 42–6, 74, 119, 120, 177 n.1
Paterson, Eddie 102, 120
performativity 2, 3, 4, 27, 33, 37, 53, 59, 78, 153, 162, 166
Phelan, Peggy 54, 62
phenomenology 35, 52–3, 56, 58–9, 69, 97, 155, 156
Phillips, Siân 51
physicality 4, 28, 33, 34, 35, 37, 41–2, 46, 48, 59, 61, 63, 70, 71, 81, 136, 161, 164, 165–6, 179 n.22
physical theatre 18, 19, 23, 25, 26, 27, 34–6, 37, 42, 44, 74, 156–8, 160–1
  See also pantomime
Piette, Adam 141
Pirandello, Luigi 74, 75
Piranesi, Giovanni Battista 86
Play 1, 50, 61, 142, 152
  Billie Whitelaw and 50, 71
  lighting 55, 137
  political spectacle 19, 111–14, 123
  the skull 106
  torture 55, 67
  as visual theatre 55
postdramatic theatre 56–7

postmodernism 12, 13, 56, 176 n.14
potentiality 16, 79, 111, 123, 168
Pountney, Rosemary 36
'private theatre' 127, 130, 140, 142
Pronko, Leonard Cabell 76
Proust 128–9
Proust, Marcel 128–9, 140, 141
psychological realism *see* realism
psychophysical acting 35
Puchner, Martin 43, 44, 47, 73–4, 77, 78–9, 82, 157–8, 178 n.3
pure image (Deleuzian concept) 40, 138

Quad 3, 23, 26, 27, 28, 31, 32–4, 55, 64, 65, 159, 165, 167, 172 n.30, 190 n.47
Quad II 32, 34
quincunx 32, 34

radio 25, 63, 101, 103, 149
Rae, Paul 145
Rancière, Jacques 12
realism 28, 51, 62, 74, 79. 83, 84, 85, 166
Rembrandt van Rijn 89–90
remediation *see* multimedia
Renaud, Madeleine 39, 187 n.32
repetition 6, 24–5, 32, 35, 46, 52, 57, 59, 64, 69, 88, 89, 93, 133, 153, 162, 167, 169 n.4
repetitive behaviour *see* repetition
Rimbaud, Arthur 85, 119, 184 n.29
Rough for Theatre I 35, 158, 166
Royal Court Theatre 42, 59, 60, 141, 162, 185 n.4
ritual 33, 157
Rockaby 1, 18, 20, 50, 58, 67–71, 101, 125, 130, 133–4, 140, 141, 142, 143, 144, 158, 160, 166, 185 n.4
  See also Dwan, Lisa; Whitelaw, Billie
Romanticism 11, 15, 74, 85, 91–2, 179 n.22, 191 n.57

Rosset, Barney 42, 149
routine (performance) 24, 35, 38, 46, 161, 173 n.44
San Francisco Actor's Workshop *see* Herbert Blau
Scaife, Sarah Jane 34, 35, 36, 173 n.36
Schechner, Richard 166
Scheer, Edward 165
Schiller-Theater Werkstatt 17, 162
Schneider, Alan 45, 50, 67, 163, 177 n.41, 180–1 n.62
scholar figure (visual culture) 80, 86–90
  See also aesthetics
Schopenhauer, Arthur 88, 135
screen (film and television) 3–4, 19, 27, 28, 30, 31–2, 34, 35, 40, 41, 44–5, 46, 50–1, 67, 70, 97, 101, 104–5, 107, 142, 152, 164, 165, 177 n. 41
self-effacement 39–40, 42
  See also negation
self-experimentation 5, 6, 13, 166
self-negation *see under* self-effacement
sensorium 5, 18, 20, 50, 51, 52, 53, 56, 58, 61, 65, 69, 70, 133, 141, 165
sensory deprivation 18, 49–71, 125, 126, 131, 142, 151, 156
Shakespeare, William 62, 74, 120, 164
simulated applause 9, 10, 118
simulation 1, 2, 10, 19, 20, 31, 38, 41, 48, 59, 64, 65, 66, 67, 77, 94, 102, 112, 113, 119, 120, 127, 128, 129, 131, 133, 141, 142, 145, 176 n.14
  See also simulated applause
site-specific performance 34, 35
slapstick (comedy) 44, 46, 135, 160
sleep 19, 67, 97–107, 125, 126, 131, 133, 186 n.23
sleeplessness 19, 98–100, 102–5
  See also *Happy Days*, sleeplessness in
Slow Angle Walk (Beckett Walk) 3–4, 167, 169 n.4

sound 15, 32, 35, 50, 56–7, 63, 65–6, 68, 70, 90, 101, 113, 126, 129, 136, 137, 138, 143, 144, 148, 153–4, 160
soundscape *see* sound
spectatorial gaze *see* spectatorship
spectatorship 1, 2, 5, 6, 9, 18, 20, 41, 42, 45, 50, 51, 53–4, 62, 66, 68, 69, 71, 78, 90, 95, 102–3, 104, 115, 118–23, 125–45, 148, 150, 154, 155, 161, 165, 167
spectrality 1, 5, 66, 86, 125, 131, 177 n.45
spectre of dissent 19, 110–12, 118, 122
Spiel see *Play*
stage politics *see* political spectacle
States, Bert O. 8–10, 53, 112
Stein, Gertrude 74, 89
Stengers, Isabelle 127, 129, 145
Stinson, Emmett 12, 16
Strindberg, August 75
subjectivity 1, 8, 58, 69, 84, 101, 102, 105, 110, 117, 122, 129–30, 133, 136, 137–41, 142–5, 148, 150, 151, 154, 155
Süddeutscher Rundfunk 31, 32, 33, 183 n.25
Sultan 6–8
surrealism 85
  aesthetics 27, 74, 76
  Surrealists 76
  theatre 75, 76
suspended animation 40
symbolism 19, 46, 48, 52, 73–95
  See also Mallarmé, Stephane, symbolism

Tandy, Jessica 50, 57
Taylor, Paul 142
Taymor, Julie 164
technology 41, 58, 131, 135
That Time 19, 97, 99–102, 103, 106
Théâtre de Babylone 76, 94
theatre of the real 10–11
  See also expropriation

theatricality 3, 8, 15, 41, 42–3, 47–8, 52, 69, 73–4, 78, 80, 82, 88, 93, 94–5, 102, 122, 136, 149, 153, 159, 165, 166
   Peter Brook's (anti-) theatricality 156–8
   theatricality in the clinic 129–31, 138–40
   See also metatheatricality
Tubridy, Derval 4
Tzara, Tristan 75

Uhlmann, Anthony 68, 134

Van Hulle, Dirk 91, 191 n.57
van Velde, Bram 82
van Velde, Geer 82
van Velde, Jacoba (Tony Clerx) 27, 178 n.14
variety theatre *see* vaudeville
vaudeville 44–6, 74, 78, 159
   See also pantomime
verbatim theatre *see* theatre of the real
Verdonck, Kris 165
Vermeer, Johannes 89
Victor, ou, Les enfants au pouvoir see Vitrac, Roger
video art 3, 4, 34
virtual field *see* simulation
virtuosity 4, 25, 37
Vitrac, Roger 76
von Kleist, Heinrich 78–9, 81, 151, 179 n.22

Waiting for Godot 1, 19, 25, 27, 32, 73, 75, 81, 84–5, 145, 160
   Lucky 44–6, 81
   post-symbolism 77, 80–1, 90–3, 95
   prison 93–4
   Roger Blin and 39, 75, 178 n.11
   See also adaptation, *Godot* for television; avant-gardism, *Godot* and

Warrilow, David 148, 150, 152, 161, 163, 181 n.62
Weber, Samuel 17, 48, 77–8, 153, 170 n.34, 175 n.77, 179 n.19
Weil, Simone 16, 48, 93, 167, 170 n.32, 175 n.76, 191 n.56
Weller, Shane 98–9, 130
Welston, Martin 167
What Where 1, 99, 114
Whitelaw, Billie 18, 49, 51, 52, 53–5, 57–64, 66–71, 126, 131, 141–3, 162, 177 n.41, 185 n.4, 189 n.37
Willie (*Happy Days* character) 39–42, 48, 103–4, 180 n.38
Wilson, Robert 56–7
Winnie (*Happy Days* character) 39–42, 51, 102, 103–4, 106
Wittgenstein, Ludwig 8, 23, 119
Wittman, Blanche 129, 137, 139, 140, 144
Woolgar, Steve 7, 9, 18
Wooster Group 13–14
Worth, Katherine 77, 80, 83–4, 85, 86, 87, 91–2
Worthen, W. B. 26, 27, 33, 52, 57, 61, 126, 159, 166, 172 n.27

Yeats, Jack 133
Yeats, William Butler 74, 88
   At the Hawk's Well 83
   Edward Gordon Craig and 81, 85–6, 88
   The Hour-Glass 86–9, 90
   Purgatory 91–2
   theatre 79, 80, 81, 85–6, 86–9, 90, 91, 92
Young, Jordan R. 164

Zarrilli, Phillip 35–7
Zola, Émile 9, 10, 74

www.ingramcontent.com/pod-product-compliance
Lightning Source LLC
Chambersburg PA
CBHW062224300426
44115CB00012BA/2210